Globalization and Transnational Capitalism:

Crises, Opportunities and Alternatives

Edited by:

Li Xing

Li Jizhen & Gorm Winther

Aalborg University Press

Globalization and Transnational Capitalism: Crises, Opportunities and Alternatives
Li Xing, Li Jizhen & Gorm Winther (Eds.)

© Aalborg University Press 2009

Cover: Særpræg ApS
Layout: Lars Pedersen / Anblik Grafisk
Printed by Narayana Press 2009
ISBN: 978-87-7307-956-0

Distribution:
Aalborg University Press
Niels Jernes Vej 6B
DK - 9220 Aalborg
Denmark
Phone: (+45) 99 40 71 40, Fax: (+45) 96 35 00 76
E-mail: aauf@forlag.aau.dk
www.forlag.aau.dk

Supported by Project 70873070 of NSFC and Research Center for
Technological Innovation, Tsinghua University, China

GLOBALIZATION AND
TRANSNATIONAL CAPITALISM:

Crises, Opportunities and Alternatives

TABLE OF CONTENT

Part II: Searching and Debating Alternatives

INTRODUCTION

Conceptualizing Capitalism in the Era of Globalization

Li Xing, Gorm Winther & Michael Kuur Sørensen

The year 2008 marked two important events. One generated shock waves across the world while the other passed unnoticed. The first was the global financial crisis which has since spread around the world and has caused a considerable economic slowdown in most developed countries. Now the crisis is affecting the financial markets and growth prospects in developing countries as well. This crisis has clearly demonstrated the fact that globalization has reshaped the terrain and parameters of social, economic and political relations both at the national and the global levels and has exerted pressure on the dynamism of the capitalist system. It once again raises the fundamental question on whether capitalism is intrinsically flawed and crises are inevitable especially in the current era of transnational capitalism when the legitimacy of capitalism's hegemony and its resilient capacities are becoming less sustainable (Li and Hersh, 2006).

Interestingly and somewhat ironically, the second was directly or indirectly linked to the first. It was the 160th anniversary of Marx and Engels' political program for the League of Communists – *The Communist Manifesto*. It is one of the most concise and intelligible political statements of Marx's materialist view of history and social development. The prophetic analysis by the *Manifesto* was one of the first works in which the logics of capitalism and the driving forces behind the capitalist expansive and profit-driven development as well as the inherently crisis-ridden nature of the capitalist system were elucidated.

However, the immanent collapse of capitalism predicted by Marx never occurred; capitalism turned out to be a resilient and enduring economic system capable of adapting to numerous social, economic and political challenges. During the last 160 years, capitalism has transformed from national to international development into the latest as transnational capitalism, also known as the economic process or market forces of "globalization." In these phases of capitalist development, the antagonism between capital and labour was compromised through various political interventions into the capitalist economy. For example, the 19th century Poor Law was for the small incremental developments of various forms of welfare states, in order to institutionalize labour unions and employers unions through the taxation of wealth for redistribution and the creation of universal healthcare. Common to all of these modifications is that the initiatives were created during the period when the capitalist system was created, organized and even expanded around the nation-state framework.

This is not so any more. Today, globalization has made it possible for transnational companies to control and manipulate global supply and production chains to by-pass the controlling and intervening sphere of the nation-state. Below and through some chapters in the book, we outline and explain these "market mechanisms" that make up the base line for globalization today.

QUESTIONS GENERATED BY TRANSNATIONAL CAPITALISM

In one way or another, the expansive nature of capitalism described by the *Manifesto* seems to be much truer today than in 1848 when it was written, as one distinguished scholar has noted:

> ... for the first time, capitalism has become a truly universal system. It's universal not only in the sense that it's global, not only in the sense that just about every economic actor in the world today is operating according to the logic of capitalism, and even those on the outermost periphery of the capitalist economy are, in one way or another, subject to that logic. Capitalism is universal also in the sense that its logic – the logic of accumulation, commodification, profit-maximization, competition – has penetrated just about every aspect of human life and nature itself....(Wood, 1997: 1)

The notion of "transnational capitalism" denotes a conceptual difference between *national* and *transnational* with the latter implying that "the globalization of production has entailed the fragmentation and decentralization of complex production chains and the world-wide dispersal and functional integration of the different segments in these chains" (Robinson and Harris, 2000: 18-19). Transnational capital adopts a supra-territorial mode of organization behaviour such as: transnational mergers and acquisitions, global strategic alliances, shareholder manipulation and ownership, supply and demand control and transcontinental business associations among other strategies, thus increasing the level of concentration of wealth while at the same deterritorializing capital (Scholte, 1997: 429). The new relationships brought about by transnational capitalism seriously affect a number of existing relationships in the system's constitutive rules and regulative capacities that generate new social constellations of actors and agencies.

The background motivation of this book project is derived from a number of questions concerning the present transformation of capitalism:

In the contemporary world, when capitalism become universal with every state and actor submitting to its logic, the issue is, will it be possible to diffuse the social problems of capitalism when civil society no longer has a state to turn to in order to watch over and regulate capital for the public good?

With productive forces becoming globalized, whereby production relations are still locally based, will Gramsci's "passive revolution" (Gramsci,
1971) be able to play the traditional role of neutralizing the inherent
contradictions between them?

Can the resiliency of global capitalism survive when fundamental
changes that are taking place in the international political economy in
the relations of capital-labour, capital-capital, and capital-state in which
domestic politics and policies are intertwined with nation-states who are
finding it difficult or unwilling to respond to these challenges in the name
of the "national interest"?

When the transformations of international political economy reduce
the maneuvering space for Polanyi's "double movement", will the endless capital and market expansion eventually bring the capitalist system
into crises not only of economic origin, but also in political and cultural
conflicts?

Can state intervention, regulations, economic policies, and political
corporate structures be revitalized as the necessary prerequisite for making markets work?

In terms of emerging modes of production relations such as ESOPs,
worker-ownership, co-op's, social enterprises and local community enterprises, where do we find the cases and what are the pro's and con's of
these alternative structures?

The heart of the issue we are facing is the fact the consensus-oriented
and welfare-based model of nation-state capitalism has to give way to
the market-oriented global capitalism because deregulation, technological
change, and the integration of global markets has largely increased the
competitive pressures on forms of national and sectoral governance. The
central paradox which the book intends to underline is that the conditions, under which the resilient features of capitalism have been sustained,
can no longer be taken for granted under the present conditions of transnational capitalism. This is to say that the institutionalization of various
interventions into the economy are no longer viable when the mobility of

capital is becoming transnational and where the role of both civil societies and the state in intervening, controlling, and directing the economy is substantially marginalized, if not totally lost.

Therefore, one of the theoretical questions the book intends to address is whether Gramsci's conceptual and analytical apparatus (e.g. hegemony, civil society and historical bloc, Gramsci, 1971) as well as the analytical thoughts of Karl Polanyi concerning the dialectics of market-society relations can still be useful in explicating the hegemony and counter-hegemony under the present stage of transnational capitalism which has displayed a number of unique characteristics (Li and Hersh, 2006: 39). Consider for example:

The disproportionate power of transnational capital is expressed as its lopsided mobility decreases the consent basis of hegemony by having a negative impact on the system's resilient capacities following the post-Cold War geopolitical changes;

The relative decline of the state's intervention capability and policy-making sovereignty, together with the lack of organic civil societies as consent-generating mechanism in balancing and neutralizing contradictions, reduces the system's "social basis of hegemony";

Transnational capitalism is awakening the forces for the second phase of the "double movement" in an effort to re-embed the economy while attempting to regulate the market partakes a potential impact on the interests of the core powers of the existing international system as well as on individual societies and people. This contradictory outcome is due to the nature of an established market system where society is already shaped and patterned in such a manner in order to make it function according to its own laws (Polanyi, 1957: 57).

Transnational capitalism, or global capitalism, signifies the fragmentation and decentralization of the global production chains, as well as the world-wide dispersal and functional integration of the different segments in these chains in which NGOs, TNCs, transnational movements other than states, are equally important actors. Apart from the economic realm, dramatic transformations taking place in the post-Cold War world order are giving rise to profound political and social changes on a global scale: the dismantling of Statism in Eastern Europe, the disintegration of the USSR, the collapse of communist-led regimes in many parts of the world, the process of restoration of capitalism in China and Vietnam, the end of planned socialism as well as the challenge to welfare capitalism in the Nordic Countries. This evolution for capitalism has nevertheless brought about a renewed ideological and political combat against Marxism and by mistaken association, socialism. Gloating over these developments, mainstream ideologists and opinion-makers have unleashed a discourse offence relegating Marxism and socialism to the dustbin of history and proclaiming capitalism as the end of human social evolution (Fukuyama, 1992). This is the fundamental debate in the USA today with President Obama being called a "socialist" (as if that is bad) by the transnational capitalists from the President Bush and Regan eras (Clark and Isherwood, 2009).

GRAMSCI AND POLANYI REVISITED

Like all other social economic systems, capitalism must require a social structure of vertical and horizontal order. The market (economic system) represents the vertical order, whereas liberal ideology (political democracy) represents the horizontal order. The fundamental function of the capitalist political order is not only to protect its own economic order through coercive means but also to facilitate and create universal consensus which consents to the market so that it can fully develop, expand and flourish without interference. In other words, the capitalist political order must serve the economic order on which the hegemony of the dominant classes is based. To lose the economic order is to lose the reproduction of the material basis on which the dominant classes will rely to sustain their hegemony.

The crisis tendencies within the capitalist system to create inequality and social disruption, as Marx ruthlessly uncovered, have historically been regulated and circumvented through the intervention of market dominated by politically controlled civil societies and the state system. In modern times, capitalism underwent constant reforms and transformations from laissez-faire capitalism to a more regulated system based on controlled and rationalized production back to a deregulated, privatized or liberalized system. Although the Marxist analysis of the contradictions of capitalism's "modus operandi" was vindicated by the evolution of the 20th century, capitalism has so far been able to pull out of its recurrent crises through a number of adaptive strategies, such as subsidies, incentives and "bail outs" as well as focus on tax credits and stimuli packages. This is especially true seen from the perspective of the historical experiences of the developed West where capitalism survived severe economic crises. Capitalism worldwide underwent a series of transformations from laissez-faire capitalism to a more regulated system based on controlled and rationalized production, such as Fordism, Keynesianism, and the New Deal. What is interesting in each of these economic crises, however, is that the government was needed to save capitalism. The markets could not do it themselves. The pattern is repeating itself today globally, thus giving new meaning to transnational globalization.

These far-reaching adjustments in the socio-political and socio-economic structures were promoted and supported by the economic ruling classes in order to contain social contradictions and counteract social upheavals. These "conciliations" demonstrate a certain degree of genuine realization of economic self-imposed consensus or consent through which the fundamental features of capitalist order are maintained. Politically, in Western capitalist societies social consent has come to be regarded as the system of democratic institutions and liberal ideology through which an exchange of ideas between the population and the state seems to be functional to the stability and maintenance of the existing societal structure. The problem is that that exchange is controlled by financially supported "lobbyists" representing certain economic special interest groups and companies.

The above indicates the resilient adaptability of the economic ruling classes, who are able to go beyond their narrow corporative interests, to exert a moral and intellectual leadership, and to make compromises (within certain limits) with a variety of allies and blocs of social forces, which Gramsci called the *historical bloc* (Gramsci, 1971). The hegemony of the ruling classes is established on the basis of convergence of interests with those of all subordinate classes. In this way, the social order, which the ruling classes have created and recreated in a web of institutions, social relations and ideas, represents a basis of consent (Bottomore, 1983: 201). The recurrent process of a hegemony establishment and its re-establishment is termed as a "passive revolution" by Gramsci (1971). By making necessary compromises and modifications as well as social reorganizations, the ruling classes can re-establish their hegemony.

The concessions from the ruling classes aim at promoting a general consensus or consent through which social control can be maintained. Politically, social consent is believed to have its root in the system of democratic institutions and liberal ideology through which an exchange of ideas between the population and the state aims at maintaining social and political stability. In this way, the social order, which the capitalist ruling classes have created and recreated in a web of institutions, social relations and ideas, represents a basis of "popular public consent" (Bottomore, 1983: 201). Herein lies the contradiction to which the crucial question today is: Will it be possible or even necessary for the ruling classes to follow the path of continuous passive revolution in the era of transnational capitalism? If not, what will this mean for the resiliency of the capitalist system?

While Gramsci examined the resilient features of the bourgeoisie classes accepting socio-political and economic reforms to the modalities of its rule, Karl Polanyi looked at the disfunctioning of the interdependency between society and market as the reason for the unleashing of tensions latent in the relationship. In the Polanyian interpretation of the history of industrial capitalism, two movements are discerned: one is the liberation of the market from political and social control, i.e., the "disembedding" of the economy; the other being the second phase of the "double movement" with the reimposition of political supervision and control of the market in order to safeguard the interests of society (Polanyi. 1957). The constant attempt by the capitalist classes to escape from the control of the state and society encapsulated in the endeavor to shift the balance of power in their favor by imposing a "self-regulating market" led to a popular political reaction in order to protect society from the ruthless "rule by capital." This double-movement process entails a simultaneous dual process in which the creation process of numerous new structures went hand-in-hand with the destructive consequences on the existing arrangements.

COUNTER-HEGEMONIC ALTERNATIVES
IN THE ERA OF TRANSNATIONAL CAPITALISM

In light of the above conceptualization, transnational capitalism is seen as reducing the resilient capacity of capitalism since it is creating un-balanced relationships between state, market and civil society. It is an undeniable fact that such unbalanced relationships have produced the marginalization of consent/consensus-generating elements which are the institutions, practices, and social relations that constantly exist as alter-natives or balances of power. Consequently, without a consent-building mechanism and capacity, transnational capitalism entails a movement towards potential crisis, unless a successful global "double movement" is generated by powerful social, political and economic forces in an attempt to push capitalism to accept new rounds of passive revolution process. At the present time, it is still difficult to foresee the possibilities of an effective global counter-hegemonic project which is able to generate the possibili-ties of embedding global capitals and markets in shared social values and responsibilities. The conundrum that needs to be understood is the nature of the totalizing force of capitalism vis-à-vis counter-movements in a nexus of hegemony and contradictions (Li and Hersh, 2006).

However, confronting the enforced preference in favor of "turbo-capitalism" and the negative socio-economic impacts taking place both in the developed centers and in the underdeveloped peripheries, we must not neglect successful counter-hegemonic examples. In Eastern Central

Europe and the former Soviet Union the experiences of the transition towards a capitalist system has been disappointing in many respects for many years. In the 1990s, all these countries had to go through a recession which resulted in inequality, poverty, mortality and organized crime have been rising in many parts. Countries such as Russia and Ukraine had to wait until 1998 before their GDP started to grow again.

China, by contrast, stands among the transition countries as a case of a remarkable success of continuous growth. China's transition to a market economy along with the fundamental institutional transformations characterizes a distinctive style of Chinese capitalism in which the marketization of the command economy, the active role of the central and local governments, the variety of forms of property and business ownership, the traditional culture of clientele-based social relations, the institutional legacies of socialism, and the emergence of market-based institutions, all provide a rich empirical context to theorize the "embeddedness" of the socio-institutional hegemony in post-Mao China. None the less, there has been a cost. China now holds the distinction, surpassing the USA, as being the #1 global polluting nation with the highest income inequality.

Even more apparent is the need to analyze how the people affected by capitalism in its global stage are still struggling to search for and create alternatives, and how these alternatives fare in the context of the globalization process. Even Francis Fukuyama himself, who proclaimed the victory of liberal capitalism as the "end of history" (1992) in the aftermath of the end of the Cold War acknowledged that the new traditional economy of fundamentalist Islam in the Middle East and Central Asia does not mean an "end to History." In the era of transnational capitalism we can observe various forms of counter-hegemonic alternative efforts, such as democratic employee, worker's ownership, consumer and supplier ownership, participatory decision-making, self-government, profit-sharing, governed markets, macroeconomic regulation, etc. Some of these alternative attempts at various local levels are aimed at neutralizing the ill effectives brought by globalization, such as environmental degradation, poverty and hunger.

At the micro level of the firm and at the meso level of networks of firms, we see alternative forms of ownership and organization constituting participation in finance and decision-making (employee stock ownership, worker-ownership) and democratic ownership and organization (co-operatives and social enterprises, local community enterprises). At the macro-economic levels, the role of state, economic policy and planning, the size of government, the interaction between state and capital, the variety of forms of property and business ownership, traditional culture of clientele-based social relations, still represent "managed capitalism", something very different from laissez faire capitalism

THE OBJECTIVES OF THE BOOK

The objectives of this book are twofold. First, it aims at providing a framework for understanding globalization and analyzing transnational capitalism in a critical light. The expansion of capitalism and liberalization of the economies as a political projection to accomplish (Li and Hersh, 2004) is leading to a radical rearrangement of social relations on a world scale. With the strengthening of capital/market and the weakening of state and civil societies, the neoliberal forces have reshaped the terrain and parameters of class struggle by shifting the balance of forces in favour of transnational capitalism. The book proposes an examination of how the relations of domination and subordination are reproduced in new forms beyond national boarders and continuously undergoing transformations and how the "hegemony of transnational capitalism" can be possibly realized by taking into consideration all these changing relations.

Second, it intends to explore the impact of globalization on alternative economic systems and modes of production. On the one hand, transnational capitalism has no challenging rivals today, but it cannot avoid creating serious worldwide economic crises as seen in the global depression today. On the other hand, these crises are also unleashing potential forces for creating alternatives, including alternative economic systems, and alternative understandings and measurements of human well-being. When transnational companies have global supply and production chains, what type of interventions can the ruling classes facilitate so as to create a passive revolution? And what are the means that the civil society have to influence, regulate and control the market forces of capitalism when the traditional democratic means by which to do so no longer exist or controlled by economic political elites? In what ways are the present social reformers trying to cope with this condition?

THE CONTRIBUTIONS IN THE BOOK

The book has received valuable contributions from scholars with different interdisciplinary backgrounds.

In Chapter 1 of the book, Li Xing and Li Jizhen attempt to provide a framework for understanding the way globalization has reshaped the terrain and parameters of social, economic and political relations both at the national and the global levels through the exerted pressure on the resiliency capacities of capitalism. It examines the ways social relations of domination and subordination are produced, reproduced and maintained while continuously undergoing transformations. Through conceptualizing the evolution of the capitalist world order in a historical perspective and by exploring the changes of relations brought about by the intensification of globalization since the 1990s, the intention is to generate a perspective for understanding such a process based on the application of Gramscian and Polanyian theoretical and analytical categories. The objective is to comprehend that the process is contingent on structures as well as agencies. Globalization also tends to undermine capitalism's own foundations by reducing the legitimacy of its hegemony and especially limiting its resilient capacities.

In Chapter 2 Christian Ydesen takes its starting point in the predominant role of neoliberal globalisation today. From this perspective, the chapter seeks to raise a discussion of human conditions of life in general and of multiculturalism in particular. It is argued that neoliberal globalisation induces a number of negative consequences for human conditions of life and the prospect of multiculturalism. However, it is concluded that there is reason for a certain degree of optimism as neoliberal globalisation actually creates better opportunities for doing away with the hegemony of the capitalist system.

In Chapter 3 Li Xing and Woodrow Clark discuss the ideological triumph of the free market and liberal democracy from the developed nations after the end of the Cold War and its impact upon developing nations. They utilize an integrated historical-economic-political approach to study the concepts and inherent logic, primarily from the USA and UK as they steer international finance organizations toward their particular definition of globalization and the "Next Economy." Globalization is the current manifestation of the "free market" as companies contract and form "Next Firms" in developing countries for goods and services from less expensive work-forces, limited regulations and restrictions including environment, taxation, corporate governance and political influence, The chapter reveals that this particular paradigm is an ideologically rooted one that cannot serve as a universal political-economic model.

In Chapter 4 David Ellerman supplies a perspective on the current debate about globalization. Often that debate is posed in simplistic terms of whether or not a country should be "open" to globalization. According to Ellerman, this seems to be the wrong question. Of course, a country needs to be open to whatever is compatible with and will augment its independent development. He argues for a synthesis quoting a metaphor by Gandhi for an openness that is compatible with one's autonomy. "I do not want my house to be walled in on all sides and my windows to be stuffed. I want the cultures of all lands to be blown about my house as freely as possible. But I refuse to be blown off my feet." By building on enough transformation of the old into the new, local decision-makers could remain "on their feet" and have the self-confidence to seek out, assimilate, adapt, and own the external knowledge, experience, and relationships that are available to them in a globalized world.

In Chapter 5 Michael Kuur Sørensen argues that capitalism has brought with it a number of problems such as environmental degradation, inequality and poverty. In this chapter two cases that seek to counter these problems in a somewhat radical way are presented. The first is Community Supported Agriculture, which is a local organic alternative to the traditional capitalist production of food. It seeks to create direct bonds between producer and consumer and thereby to create normative ties between the otherwise abstract producer and consumer in traditional capitalist production. The second is the Ithaca-HOURs, which is a local credit-system that is based on the idea that hours of working time can be exchanged equally. The HOUR system thus seeks to circumvent the tendency to create inequality and poverty in the capitalist system.

In Chapter 6 Gorm Winther and Michael Kuur Sørensen present the earlier performance records of the Mondragon co-operatives in the Basque region of Spain (Euzkadi). The records in the early years from the late fifties to the early eighties are impressive. In these times, the co-operative network adopted a unique co-operative and democratic structure based on both individual and collective savings. The co-operatives were then mainly worker-owned and –operated. Comparative studies suggested that the co-operatives did better on comparable data at sector levels and regional levels. These structures as well as newer comparative data suggest that the Mondragon Co-operative Corporation the latest years does not fare as well as before the network of co-operatives adopted a corporate structure and went global. It seems that global capitalist institutions are not geared for the dissemination of co-operative principles.

In Chapter 7 Steen Fryba Christensen analyzes Bolivia's and Brazil's current development strategies in order to assess if they have departed from the neo-liberal model of the 1990s. He argues that the government of Evo Morales and MAS in Bolivia and the government of Luiz Inácio Lula da Silva and the PT in Brazil, both have embarked on development strategies that represent a shift. He discusses the differences of the two state strategies and seeks to explain what accounts for these differences on the basis of historical, ideological and structural arguments.

In Chapter 8 Li Xing and Mammo Muchie seek how Amartyr Sen's contribution on the conceptualization of development is to be taken forward. Sen has brought an appropriate starting point for further research with his broad alternative development thinking. This chapter can be seen as part of the on-going endeavours by many scholars in an attempt to contribute to the discussion of social well-being. The overall objective is to formulate conceptual framework and a fresh approach for ranking the different countries in the world not merely on the number of individually reckoned well-being attainments, but on the determination of the structural social capacity for sustaining and making such attainments irreversible.

In Chapter 9 Johan Galtung argues that globalization should be studied along four power dimensions; economic, political, cultural and military, without giving primacy to one of them. Therefore, it follows that all four dimensions must be addressed to render globalization more democratic. Global democracy, through a reformed UN, with no veto power for superpowers, and democratic control over transnational companies for the political and economic dimensions, along with respect for cultural diversity, and conflict transformation capabilities for the military dimension, would direct the present state of globalization into a more peaceful world with respect for basic human needs.

REFERENCES

Bottomore, Tom et al. (eds.) (1983) *A Dictionary of Marxist Thought*. Oxford: Basil Blackwell Publisher limited.

Clark, Woodrow W. and Isherwood, William (2009) "Leapfrogging Energy Infrastructure Mistakes for Inner Mongolia", *Utility Policy Journal*, Special Issue (forthcoming).

Fukuyama, Francis (1992) *The End of History and the Last Man*. London: Hamish Hamilton.

Gramsci, Antonio (1971) *Selections from the Prison Notebooks*. Quintin Hoare and Geoffrey Nowell Smith (eds.), London: Lawrence & Wishart.

Li, Xing and Hersh, Jacques (2006) "Understanding Global Capitalism: Passive Revolution and Double Movement in the Era of Globalization." *American Review of Political Economy* 4(1/2): 36-55.

Li, Xing and Hersh, Jacques (2004) "The Genesis of Capitalism: The Nexus between 'Politics in Command' and Social Engineering." *American Review of Political Economy*, 2(2): 100-144.

Polanyi, Karl (1957) [1944] *The Great Transformation*. New York: Farrar and Rinehart.

Robinson, William I. and Harris, Jerry (2000) "Towards a Global Ruling Class? Globalization and the Transnational Capitalist Class." *Science & Society*, 64(1): 11-54.

Scholte, Jan Aart (1997) "Global Capitalism and the State." *International Affairs*, 73(3): 427-452.

Wood, Ellen (1997) "Back to Marx." *Monthly Review*, 49(2): 1-9.

Wood, Ellen (1999) "Unhappy Families: Global Capitalism in a World of Nation-States." *Monthly Review*, 51(3): 2-12

Part I

Conceptualizing Globalization
and Transnational Capitalism

Chapter One

The Dual Crisis of Hegemony and Counter-hegemony in the Era of Transnational Capitalism

Li Xing & Li Jizhen

Introduction: Hegemony and Counter-hegemony Revisited

The concept of hegemony was sophisticatedly applied by Gramsci (1971), who referred it to a situation in which a dominant class exercises power over subordinate classes by means of a combination of coercion and consent. The Gramscian theory of hegemony attempts to explain why Marxist assertion – the doom of capitalism – was not realized by looking at: "a powerful mechanism of consolidation exists within the social and political superstructure which helps to stabilize the ascendancy of a class at the limiting point of production compatible with its continuity" (Scruton, 1996: 219). The theory tries to widen the analytical perspective and stress the necessity and importance of studying social and political aspects other than the economic sphere. The resilient phenomena of advanced capitalist societies, in which the regeneration of hegemony of capitalism is made possible and elite economic classes are able to adapt to modifications or changes without altering the system's fundamental features of organization, is the mode of functioning that has been an important area of research for political and social sciences, as well as for socio-political movements.

The notion of hegemony emphasizes "social consent" as a component of the system of democratic institutions and liberal ideology whereby the general interests of population are to a larger extent taken into consideration by the leading class. Seen from this perspective, liberal or conservative ideology must not be simply reduced to a matter of "false consciousness" or "manipulation". Historically the dominant ideology of capitalism has received a certain degree of active consent, not passive submission, from the subordinate classes. Nor is it imposed, but rather, "it is 'negotiated' by unequal forces in a complex process through which the subordination and the resistance of the workers are created and recreated" (Simon, 1982: 64). Simultaneously, non-state or semi-state institutions such as education, media and the church exerted a significant impact on people's consciousness in influencing their ways of living, thus contributing to the maintenance of the position and legitimacy of the rule of capital.

This pattern of social control assisted with ideological penetration, which was part of a truce in the ongoing "war of position" in the post-World War II arrangements, revealed the potency embedded in bourgeois political hegemony. Its skilful competence in winning the "rule of legitimation" through successful nurturing of "false consciousness"[1] (Gramsci, 1971) resulted in the general acceptance of the perception of the capitalist political and economic system and social structures as inherently rational and natural. In other words, the ruling elites have been able to depoliticize social conflicts or issues of contention with "a 'prepolitical' process that constructs the public agenda and thus predisposes 'politics' to a narrowed set of choices" (Ross & Trachte, 1990: 9). What must not be ignored, however, is that the success of this political evolution was preconditioned in a *welfare* economy characterized by a certain degree of employment and social security.

While Gramsci ascribed the passive-revolution resiliency of bourgeoisie class to its active adaptation of socio-political and economic development to the modalities of its rule, Karl Polanyi looked at the malfunctioning of the interdependency between society and the market as the reason for the unleashing of tensions latent in the relationship. The continuous endeavor by capitalist classes to escape from the control of the state and society, which encapsulated in the effort to shift the balance of the "war of position" in its favor by imposing the force of the "self-regulating market", generates constant socio-political reactions in order to protect society from the ravages of capital. Thus, in the Polanyian interpretation of the history of industrial capitalism, two movements are discerned: one is the liberation of the market forces from political and social control, i.e., the "disembedding" tendency of the market (economy); another is the second phase of the "double movement" with the struggles of re-imposing political supervision and control of the market, i.e. "reembedding" move-ment, in order to safeguard the interests of society (Polanyi [1944]1957). This "reembedding" of the economy (re-humanization of the market) is society's spontaneous responses to protect itself against the advent of the logic of the markets.

Not abandoning the structural level of analysis, the attempt of this paper is made in the thrust of these two approaches to surmount the dichotomy between *structure* and *agency* and emphasize the role of politics in the evolution of capitalism. The combination of both insights is useful to the analysis of the turmoil's of the 20th century with the alternation between revolution and counterrevolution, reform and contra-reform, as well as war and peace. Following the Great Depression, capitalism world-wide underwent a transformation based on the rejection of laissez-faire capitalism for a more regulated macro-economic system of controlled and rationalized production. This process can be identified as a "passive revolution", such as the reorganization of capitalism in the United States and Europe in the 1930s and in the post-war era through the adoption of the "New Deal", Keynesianism and Fordism.

While some countries reacted to the crises and potential revolutions in the first half of the 20th century through socio-economic measures pre-serving parliamentary democracy, the political elites of catching-up coun-tries such as Germany, Italy and Japan resorted to Nazism and Fascism characterized by ultra-nationalism, militarism and contra-imperialism. Nonetheless, the common denominator for the reaction of all industrial-ized countries to the worldwide crisis of capitalism can be grasped in

Polanyi's "double movement" – hegemony and counter-hegemony, the attempt to shield societies from the ravages of the world market and pre-empt the consummation of the "war of movement" into revolutions and class wars, through a retrenchment from the international economy by the implementation of protectionism and self-centered economic policies.

As a continuation to the author's previous research on the dialectical understanding of the evolution of capitalism (Li and Hersh, 2002, 2004), the placement of the discussion of this paper is derived from reflections over a number of challenging questions arising from the evolution of the capitalist system into the stage of transnational capitalism:

- How to conceptualize the notion of hegemony under transnational capitalism given its transformative differences from the nation-state and inter-state system?

- Is the resiliency of capitalist classes able to transcend to retain its "passive revolution" capacities under the conditions of trans-national capitalism when the balancing force of an *organic* trans-national civil society is not yet in shape, i.e. an *organic* counter-hegemonic historical bloc?

- If conventional boundaries of nation-states are becoming vague, how will classes and groups be integrated into organic social forces? And how will a transnational "common sense" and "col-lective will" (Gramsci, 1971) be generated?

- Where is the transnational "passive revolution" mechanism that plays the traditional role of neutralizing the inherent contradic-tions between productive forces, which are becoming tranasnation-alized and production relations that are still more or less nationally based?

- Can the "disembeddment" of transnational economy from societal constraints succeed in transforming the socio-economic pattern into a transnational market society, or will it release a new "second movement" (Polanyi, 1957)?

- Will transnational capitalism eventually develop the capacity of "trasformismo"[2] (Gramsci, 1971) whereby reformism, civil societies and subordinate groups are incorporated into the dominant project of transnational capitalism so as to prevent the legitimation crisis and the rise of counter-hegemonic forces?

Methodological considerations

The modes of many modern social science theories are constructed within a nation-state framework and under additive processes: 1) subdividing areas of a collective unit, for example, dividing the state into separate spheres, such as politics, economics, civil society, etc; 2) conceptualizing and theorizing these domains with their own distinct prototypes, logics and rationalities so as to distinguish them from each other, such as political science, sociology and business economics, etc; 3) then adding them to form a whole. For instance, within the framework of the nation-state, social theories tend to treat and analyze the "public" and the "private" separately and finally to regroup them into an entity, namely the "society".

However, if we go beyond the nation-state level and move to the global level in order to understand globalization and transnational capitalism, then we are facing a problem: there is not a collective entity to separate, and in other words, there is no a "global society" to be subdivided and added together as it can be done with nation-state. The current international order consists of multiple "unequal" states. This is to say, theories derived from a nation-state entity cannot be fully applied in the global context, rather, they become good reference tools to reflect the contradictions brought about by globalization and transnational capitalism, which in return, are affecting the relationships among the subdivided domains within each nation-state that are conceptualized and theorized by social theorists.

In this paper, an issue of debate is whether a political theory with its basic notions and concepts rooted in a nation-state's historicity, such as the Gramscian political theory, can be applied to the analysis of globalization in the contemporary era. An affirmative position stresses the criteria of whether Gramsci's political ideas are able to discern "long-term organic tendencies" and differentiate them from "immediate, contingent and short-term" effect so as to determine "what indeed is historically original and novel in social reality and what is the reproduction of the 'old', in different forms, that is, to understand the intersections of elements of continuity and change" (Sassoon, 2001: 6). Gramsci's innovative conceptual framework of hegemony rejects the reduction of politics as a predetermined social topography; rather, it constructs politics as constitutive of the social itself. Thus, hegemony, from the Gramscian perspective, is more than economic dominance and is an art of politics that treats society not as a self-regulating totality but as a complex plurality of contradictions and antagonisms.

The critical position on extending Gramsci's conceptual relevance to the global level challenges the ontological and epistemological foundation of the neo-Gramscian school in bringing the historically specific notions and concepts of Gramsci's political sociology into the IR and IPE realms, i.e. the socio-historical origin of Gramsci's concepts and theories cannot be directly reflected in their contemporary language, such as "transnational state" and "transnational civil society". In this connection, a similar point can also be leveled at the applicability of Polanyi's "double movement" – that is the transposition of the dialectics of civil society's organically organized counter-movement within the nation-state to the global level.

The paper finds its heuristic value in the application of the extended Gramsci's conceptual and analytical apparatus (hegemony, civil society and historical bloc) in combination with the analytical thoughts of Karl Polanyi concerning the dialectics of market-society relations to explicate our thesis on the crisis of hegemony and counter-hegemony under transnational capitalism (see another relevant publication, Li and Hersh, 2006):

a) The disproportionate power of transnational capital expressed in its lopsided mobility decreases the "consent basis of hegemony" by having a negative impact on the system's resilient capacities shown in connection with the post-Cold War geopolitical changes;

b) The relative decline of the state's intervention capability and policy-making sovereignty, together with the lack of organic civil societies as consent-generating mechanisms in balancing and neutralizing contradictions reduces the system's "social basis of hegemony";

c) Transnational capitalism is awakening the forces for the second phase of the "double movement" in an effort to re-embed the economy while the attempts at regulating the market partakes a potential impact on the interests of the core powers of the existing international system, as well as on individual societies and peoples. This contradictory outcome is due to the nature of an established market system where society is already shaped and patterned in such a manner in order to make it function according to its own laws (Polanyi, 1957: 57).

Propositions

The main analytical framework, on which the paper is based, proposes an analysis of present-day contradictions in globalization and transnational capitalism as related to the questions of legitimacy, hegemony, counter-hegemony and the embeddedness of the economy:

I. Globalization and transnational capitalism is challenging the foundations of hegemony of nation-state capitalism, while creating a truly global market. Meanwhile, it is problematic to discern at the global level a similar scale of integration of state (political society with the key concerns on domestic politics) and civil society ("common sense" in connection with culture and religion). In other words, transnational capitalism does not really constitute *in organic substance* a "transnational state" vis-à-vis a necessary counterparts in the form of a "global civil society" which could represent the social basis of hegemony (Germain and Kenny, 1998: 15-16).

II. Economic globalization through increased functional integration of markets is promoting a tangible historic bloc of global elite capital classes but less-organically founded global civil societies making it difficult to envisage a genuine Polanyian "double movement", i.e. civil societies responding to the alienation and repression of the market. Transnational elite classes (hegemonic forces), despite their formal nationalities, have much more in common than transnational working classes, which are supposed to be the core counter-hegemonic forces.

III. States are collectively becoming a tool promoting economic globalization whereas transnational civil societies in their diversified forms are being currently pulled apart in various directions. The contradiction facing the state is that, on the one hand, states are becoming committed to the transnationalization of economic activities (production, finance and service), while on the other hand, they are organically tied to national structures through a wide range of functions and provisions, not least welfare.

IV. Many "resistance movements" found in the self-proclaimed transnational civil societies are not more than *conjunctural responses* to the immediate effects of "maldevelopments" (poverty, environment, terrorism, etc,) or to general principles of common concern (democracy and human rights, etc) without any *organic foundation* in having concrete influence in both state politics and market mechanisms.

V. Transnational capitalism serves the interest of capital in the short run but not of the capitalist system in the long run, the reason being that capital is given excessive power in creating a one-directional relationship in which hegemony is ever more defined by the transnational capital class on its own terms and then imposed on the rest of the system. As a consequence, capitalism is bound to loose its resilient capacities and unleash tendencies leading to self-destructive dislocation and disintegration. This notwithstanding, any successful "double movement" against the ravages of neoliberalism remains embryonic due to the contradictory relationship between *market economy* and *market society* in which the market pattern and logic remains at the heart of the social organization; this means the returning to our original question regarding the realizable possibility of "passive revolution" in the age of global capitalism.

RECONCEPTUALIZING HEGEMONY IN THE ERA OF TRANSNATIONAL CAPITALISM

The question regarding how to conceptualize the hegemony of transnational capitalism is still an issue of debate. One way to conceptualize the new form of hegemony is to see it as *transnational liberalism* (Agnew and Corbridge, 1995) in which the ideological base of the hegemony is *the market, or market capitalism* (marketization and market-access) and the power base of the hegemony that has transformed from hegemonic order/stability (*balance of power* under nation-state and inter-state structures) to hegemonic liberalism and market fundamentalism (*imbalance of power* under transnational structure) (Agnew and Corbridge, 1995). The hegemonic objective of transnational capitalism is to structure a global economic system with a dominant mode of production that is meant to be solely legitimate and universal, The best way to realize this objective is to set up new types of transnational institutions with laws and rules that not only preserve the traditional hierarchy but also generate interests for the expansion of transnational capital in new ways while setting up constrains for others.

For example, the conceptualization of the contemporary American hegemony under transnational capitalism is quite different from that during the Cold War when the essence of hegemony was primarily defined in terms of conventional Realism. Among critical theorists of international political economy, there has been disagreement regarding the extent of US dominance of the world system. While some people adhere to the position of seeing American hegemony being in a process of declining, others call for a dialectical understanding of American power and the notion of "American decline" through the lens of a proto-Gramscian perspective (Cox, M. 2001: 324-327). According to the latter, American hegemony in the era of globalization should not be conceptualized in a conventional manner, i.e. its structural shaping power to impose international order among nation-states and its imposition of the rules of the game in the global economic system. Rather, this hegemony today is less based on the state power but more reliant upon "a complex of international social relationships that connect the social classes of the different countries" (Cox, R. 1993: 62) as seen most explicitly in the formation of a transnational capitalist class (Sklair, 1998, 2000)[3].

This type of hegemony of intertwining capital and state poses both advantages and disadvantages to the transnational capital class on the one hand because "The TNS does not yet (and may never!) constitute a centralised global state and *formal* political authority remains to a considerable extent fragmented, and fragmented unevenly, among weaker and stronger national states." But on the other hand, "This peculiar institutional structure, an historic contradiction of the global capitalist system, presents transnational elites with the possibility, and the need, to influence a multitude of national states" (Robinson, 2005: 9).

As emphasized before, the Gramscian concept of social formation is less an economic mode of production but more a complex interaction of economic, political, cultural and ideological practices. Accordingly, people (classes and groups) who share the fundamental interests within the interaction are referred to as the "historical bloc" or the "social forces". The inter-relationship between state, market and society is mutually determining and organically interdependent. Here, "organic" refers to the elements of linkages between the three, and when the "organic" interdependent linkage is decomposed or weakened, the moment of the "hegemony crisis" begins to take place.

Cox has succinct descriptions of Gramsci's notion of a "crisis of hegemony":

> What he identified by these terms was a disarticulation between social groups and
> their putative political leaders, in sum a crisis in representation. In such as situa-
> tion, old and new social forces coexisted, but the old ones had become detached
> from the political organizations that had formerly represented them, and the new

ones had no produced organizations or "organic" intellectuals who could lead them effectively and bring them into coalescence with existing social forces to form a new hegemonic bloc. Two outcomes are possible in an organic crisis: either the constitution of a new hegemony or caesarism, .i.e., the freezing of unresolved contradictions. (Cox, 1986: 273)

The crisis of transnational capitalism can be analyzed from two important perspectives according to Robinson (2005: 12): A) a structural crisis of over-accumulation and social polarization (crisis of social reproduction, inequalities, and economic crises, the limit of expansion); B) a crisis of legitimacy and authority (the lack of consensual integration and mechanism of legitimation). In order to substantially verify these analytical propositions it is necessary to look at new developments against the backdrop of the societal and geopolitical adjustments caused by the globalization process, which is bringing about transformative modifications to existing social, economic and political structures both nationally and internationally.

TRANSNATIONAL CAPITALISM AND ITS "DE-CONSTRUCTIONS"

Transformation under transnational capitalism denotes a conceptual difference between *internationalization* and *transnationalization* (globalization). The former refers to "the extension of trade and financial flows across national borders", whereas the latter implies that "the globalization of production has entailed the fragmentation and decentralization of complex production chains and the world-wide dispersal and functional integration of the different segments in these chains" (Robinson and Harris, 2000: 18-19). Transnational capital adopts a supra-territorial mode of organization: transnational mergers and acquisitions, global strategic alliances, and trans-world business associations, thus increasing the level of concentration while at the same deterritorializing capital (Scholte, 1997: 429). These transformations in the capitalist world system seriously affect the system's constitutive rules and regulative capacities which are in the process of and transforming and restructuring. This process can be analyzed by looking at a number of changing relationships:

Labour: organic relations decomposed

The situation and status of the working class has, since the industrial revolution, been related to the position of the individual country on the international scene. From its genesis, capitalism developed unevenly in different parts of the world creating a system of dominating and domi- nated nations. When conditions of capital mobility are geographically limited within the nation-state boundary, it is possible for organized labor to compel capital into allowing it a certain participation in societal rear- rangements, and not necessarily remain in a state of passive submission. In Gramscian terms, this path of passive revolution "is 'negotiated' by unequal forces in a complex process through which the subordination and the resistance of the workers are created and recreated" (Simon, 1982: 64).

In the context of the war of position, the exploitation of working classes in developed countries historically went hand-in-hand with the economic surplus pumped out of the peripheral nations, which led to the improvement of workers' well-being in rich nations. Internationally, this contributed to weakening global working class solidarity in such a way that "labour organizations in all of the advanced capitalist countries have not only supported their own multinationals in the brutal exploitation of the economies and workers of the poor nations, they have even sup- ported wars in which the workers of one rich nation fought against those of another" (Yates, 2000: 49). This has been empirically demonstrated in the case of the American hegemonic position. Modern history of the labor movement in the United States reveals that trade unions have been not only exclusionary in form but also pragmatic and selective in action. The objective of the American organized labor solidarity movement was aimed not at conducting class struggle but at sharing benefits with business by supporting US corporations abroad and strengthening the country's foreign policy regardless of the social costs on workers in other countries (Fletcher, 2003). As a consequence, this imperialist patriotism contributed to the distortion of US trade unions' perception of globalization's impact on the deterioration of their own job opportunities, welfare and social contract, as well as on their understanding of the post-9/11 anti-terrorism policies.

In the present phase of transnational capitalism, the transnationalization of production and finance permits the use, or threatened use, of capital mobility and relocation of parts or phases of production to countries and regions where low wages and politically-repressed working conditions provide a greater degree of surplus extraction and exploitation. Domestically, the mobility power of financial and productive capital as a historical bloc has thus *decomposed* the traditional organic interdependent relationships between the market, productive forces and production relations, thus weakening the bargaining power of trade unions and the counter-hegemonic civil societies both in developed and developing countries.

It is common that each nation-state's working class and civil societies has its own historical heritage, its unique class formation, tradition and practices. However, as a result of the changing structure of traditional nation-based industrial production to one that is being restructured on a transnational scale, the global fragmentation and supra-territorial mode of accumulation means that class formation also appears to be less rigidly tied to territory and jurisdiction of nation-states, in contrast to the traditional societal structure largely based on the dynamic interaction between national capital, the state, civil societies and workers. According to one line of argument, globalization is reorganizing relations to production by which "the proletariat worldwide is also in the process of transnational class formation" (Robinson and Harris, 2000: 18-19).

Nevertheless, despite the increasing common awareness over the negative impact on jobs and working conditions in the industrialized nations, it is still questionable whether a bourgeoning transnational working class is able to transcend the limit of a "class-*in*-itself" to become an organic "class-*for*-itself"[4] because it has not realized the fact that:

> The corporations operate only in their own interests. Sometimes these interests will coincide with those of a disadvantaged group, but only by disadvantaging another. For centuries, we have permitted ourselves to ignore the extent to which our welfare is dependent on the denial of other people's. We begin to understand the implications of the system we have created only when it turns against ourselves. (Monbiot, 2003)

An organic global working class-*for*-itself can be realized when working classes, especially in developed countries, are able to grasp the initiative in the war of position, whereby workers together create a counter-hegemonic alliance in the hope of challenging the continued dominance of capital. Under the present conditions, the formation of an organic transnational working class resistance to transnational capitalism under a collective and shared identity of interests has still a long way to go. To further extend this point, an analysis of the counter-hegemonic limit of global civil society is presented in the second section of this paper.

Capital: organic relations strengthened but embedded with crisis potentials

Historically, the capitalist world order developed from the *Pax Britannica* historical bloc marked by realistic common understanding of balance of power, harmony of interest and political multipolarity to the *Pax Americana* historical bloc marked by US unipolar leadership, formal international institutions, security alliance under a general framework of a Fordist-Keynesian social structure of accumulation with "moderate organized labour and big capital" (Gill, 2003: 58). Now the shift is moving towards a transnational historical bloc "an American-centred and –led *transnational historic bloc*, where organized labour has been virtually marginalized" (Gill, 2003: 59).

The condition of globalization is imposing changes that affect the political constellations between the ruled and the ruling elites. This can be seen in the evolution of historical blocs, which are in close connection with social movements to deal with specific historical conjunctures or solve concrete problems that have to be confronted by different social groups. According to Gill and Cox,

> An historical bloc refers to an historical congruence between material forces, institutions and ideologies, or broadly, an alliance of different forces politically organized around a set of hegemonic ideas that gave strategic direction and coherence to its constituent elements. Moreover, for a new historic bloc to emerge, its leaders must engage in 'conscious planned struggle. (Gill, 2003, p.58)

In the struggle for hegemony, historical blocs form, dissolve and reform. For instance, in the current context of increasing awareness of the consequences of industrial capitalism on nature and ecology, big businesses attempted to mobilize a historical bloc around the themes of "sustainable development" and "corporate social responsibility" against what it saw as a threatening movement organized around the powerful idea of the capitalist specificity of the ecological crisis.

In the context of capitalism, competitive capitalist interests may, at least for a time, coalesce into a relatively unified hegemonic bloc. Seen from today's transnational capitalism, the situation is perhaps more true than in Kausky's time. The breaking-down of physical barriers promoting the convergence of international capital means that transnational companies are not only global in what they produce and sell in many parts of the world, but become conglomerates united under similar interests. Former national companies have been merging with those of other countries maintaining a relation of hierarchical dependency to the larger ones. Thus, in the view of some scholars, the transnational capitalist class (TCC) is no longer "Western" but is "global" (Sklair, 2000).

According to this interpretation, the TCC is becoming the ruling class that controls global decision-making and shapes the development agenda;

in other words, a transnational capitalist *historical bloc* has been created. Such a coalition encompasses the North-South dichotomy and consists of various economic and political actors including national elites (parties, media, technocracies and policy-makers), transnational corporations, global financial institutions, and international organizations (Robinson and Harris, 2000). In the new era of corporative capitalism, local and national markets are linked together into forming a global market while national capitals have fused into transnational capital. This bloc is striving to withdraw most of the concessions previously made as a response to labour pressures, as well as to socialist and other anti-systemic movements. Its hegemony is said to be so decisive that whether or not its position and ideology is agreed upon by the society as a whole becomes less important. However, what deserves particular attention with the rise of neoliberal globalization is the emergence of financial capital as an engine of capitalist accumulation.

With an estimated worth of $360 trillion (larger than the value of the entire global economy), world financial capitalism is ushering an age of complexities and instabilities (Gilpin, 2001: 6-7). The basic principles of finance, and related branches such as insurance, property market, stock market and public finance are not only increasingly integrating national economies into the capitalist world economy but also fundamentally changing the way economic activities are organized and operated. Contrary to conventional economic theory, financial capital, unlike productive capital, does not lead to relatively stable price formation based on a rational assessment over a number of criteria, such as management, products, marketing, or record of profitability. Rather, financial capital is highly speculative by nature and is inherently inclined to avoid the logic of equilibrium in favour of the momentum of self-fulfilling expectations. Since the 1990s, the East Asian financial crisis, the Mexican crisis, the Russian crisis, and the American financial crisis were all indications of the grave consequences created by financial speculations that appear to be beyond anyone's capacity to control.

State: organic relations weakened and changed

When mentioning the state, it is stamped largely by the logic of coercion and power. Historically, it is not uncommon to establish an evolutionary connection between the mergence of capitalism and the rise of the nation-state because this connection is theorized from the prism of "modernity" and "rationalization" especially in the European context (Wood, 1999).

What is witnessed today is a situation in which transnational corporations, financial institutions and powerful individual investors have the capacity to move production to countries or regions where a state's policies may be more compliant to their interests. They are thus in a position to influence states' foreign politics and development policies. In this general context, the social concerns of nation-states are being hollowed out by the promotion of neoliberal policies leading to a "race to the bottom". In order to accommodate the transborder processes of accumulation, states have become more and more instrumental to global economic forces penetrating local borders and markets. They behave as organs of capital, destined to create favourable conditions for its maximal expansion. In Europe, the transition from the *welfare state* to the *competition state* has become a reality.

In contrast to this interpretation, some scholars argue that states and globalization are "mutually reflexive and are embedded in, or are co-constitutive of, each other", which implies that globalization generates both constraints and opportunities for states (Hobson and Ramesh, 2002: 8). This line of thinking emphasizes the "dual aspects" of the state in which neither the structuralist approach (conforming to globalization) nor the agent-centric approach (resisting extra-territorial influences) can adequately capture the relationship between the state and globalization.

This notwithstanding, there is a general consensus today on the basis of overwhelming facts and data that globalization has largely weakened the state, as well as national and global civil societies in which the power and dominance of capital resides. French diplomat and political scientist, Jean-Marie Guehenno, argues that the idea of the nation-state as a political form spread from Europe over the rest of the world, but with the on-going weakening of the Western nation-states it is evident that capital, on the basis of new forms of technological modernization does not need the nation-state anymore (Guehenno in Grunenberg, 1998: 414). Nor does capital feel pressured by labour or anti-systemic forces. Other scholars, on the contrary, take an opposite position in claiming that the nation-state remains the primordial actor in both domestic and international economic affairs (Gilpin, 2001). In-between scholars recognize the interplays of continuity and change regarding the relationship between globalization and the state with a keen awareness of the notable changes in the character of the state in terms of capacities, constituencies, policy-making processes and contents, etc (Scholte, 1997). As Gindin puts it:

> Neoliberal globalization also tends to undermine, or at least weaken the capacities of states to legitimate capitalism itself; the earlier promises of steady material security and growing equality have given way to the demands of competitive insecurity: that of growing control over our lives has been trumped by the requirements of expanded accumulation; free trade agreements expose the centrality of constitutionalizing and guaranteeing property rights over other rights. (Gindin, 2003: 121)

Economic globalization, especially financial and capital market liberalization, has systematically increased the process of the transnationalization of state autonomy in favour of global capital over national welfare social policies. Consequently, neoliberal globalization not only intensifies the global process of the "disembedded economy" – disembedding the market from society (Polanyi, 1944), but also further integrates and assimilates non-capitalist elements, as well as non-market societies in its realm.

Despite the different views on the relationship between the state and globalizatioin, the general agreement is that the nation-state does not have a free hand in decision-making but rather is dependent on decisions made by transnational actors. The state is no longer the indispensable organizing principle of capitalism and the legitimate mediator between contending forces as it is indicated by the breakdown of social order and the collapse of state authority in many parts of the world. However, the relative success of the Chinese development model and the lessons drawn from the financial crises in 2008 prove the fact that the guiding role of the state is still crucial without which the market can run rampant causing serious sufferings.

The notion of social contract as citizen-state interactions has undergone dramatic transformations whereby the consent and consensus involving obligations of both citizens and government and accountability-control mechanisms are increasingly being marketized. Consequently, the "social" part of the contract is becoming less universal but more selective, while political participation is becoming less inclusive but more exclusive. This implies the fundamental transformation of the essence of the social contract that – in its original meaning – emphasizes social and political rights. The concept of citizenship as a means of political rights and participation is changed into one of economic empowerment, defined in terms of consumers and customers. Under the economy-dominated social contract, the market is ideologically perceived not only as a neutral place (institution) for the exchange of goods, resources and services, but also as the most efficient mechanism to regulate society and human relations.

In the context of developing countries, the global market contributes to transforming civil society into becoming a kind of "social cushion" as well as objective ally to neoliberalism, i.e. grass-root organizations across the world with an anti-statist ideology step in among conflictual social forces and function as mediators between local organizations, the free-market state, foreign donors and transnational companies (Petras, 1997: 10).

The consequence of social order break-down

Globalization is usually conceptualized in economic terms. However, it is equally a political process that has societal and cultural consequences. To the extent that the object of passive revolution is to maintain the hegemony of capital, the question that arises is: where are the counter-hegemonic forces that need to be defused through passive revolution? Is capital more threatened by the non-existence of contending political forces than by their existence? Who and where are the opponents in a world of capital dominance?

Most of the world has been unprepared for the new cleavages that have emerged in the contemporary world and which fall out of the traditional analysis. A surprising development after the West's victory over state socialism, interpreted triumphantly as the "end of history", has been the resurgence of religious and ethnic ideologies under violent forms and diverse expressions. This is considered to be the new challenge to the international order. Based on their own historical evolution, many in the West tend to assume that development following social, cultural, and economic modernization would ultimately lead to the marginalization of religion. In contra-point to this view, Huntington has argued that the hegemonic dominance of democratic liberalism encompassed in the notion of "the end of history" would pave the way for religious and cultural counter-hegemonic forces. In this perspective, global boundaries will no longer be defined by states but by cultural identities and the confrontation between cultural and religious ideologies will replace the conflict between political systems (Huntington, 1993).

The 9/11 attacks on the United States appeared to confirm the prophecy of the "clash of civilizations" by positing that the collision between West and Islam is the source of terrorism. However, the alleged conflict should not be one-sidedly conceptualized and theorized in terms of cultural essentialism. Rather, political Islamism can be analyzed as a counter-hegemonic project representing an outlet for action and a force for change. Conflicts between the West and Islam can be understood as a struggle between two rising historical blocs: market dogmatism and Islamic revivalism (Li, 2002). Modernization and market fundamentalism cause severe disruptions in traditional ties of identity, authority and community paving the way for the resurgence of radical counter-hegemonic socio-political forces. This intrusion and the way it has been pushed forward can be identified as the source of religious resurgence, as well as the rise of Islamic fundamentalism.

Contrary to the dominant discourse of modernization that tends to place the blame on traditional ideologies and societies for the "backwardness" of Muslim countries, there is a need to put the problematique in the context of international political economy (Hersh, 2000). Religion was in fact used during the Cold War era as a bulwark by the United States in the Islamic world against the nationalist forces of secularism and socialist modernization. As Ahmad put it: "The defeat and/or decline of the democratic, secular, anti-colonial nationalism has given rise, in a host of countries, from India to Egypt to Algeria, to hysterical, irrational forms of cultural nationalism and atavistic hysteria" (Ahmad, 2004: 57).

Since the objective of passive revolution is to consolidate the position of capital through adjustments in state-market-civil society relations, can it play a similar role in mediating the more fundamental clashes of deep-seated values and norms between market essentialism and religious fundamentalism? Where are the civil societies or other mechanisms, in this context, which can fulfill the role of mediating between global capitalist forces and cultural and religious anti-systemic movements (Islamic terrorism)?

THE CRISIS OF COUNTER-HEGEMONY IN THE ERA OF TRANSNATIONAL CAPITALISM

Historically, the expansion and legitimization of the capitalist system is materialized through not only the productive and technological driving forces but also the political and military imposition of capitalism on extra-European areas as during colonialism. The post-war capitalist world order has been primarily maintained under the US "hegemonic stability" (*coercion* based on geopolitical and material necessity) in combination with a Cold-War ideological "historical bloc" (*consent* on the basis of anti-communism commonality). The end of the Cold War between state socialism and market capitalism, following the rise of US unilateralism and militarism, symbolizes the strengthening of coercive realism and the weakening of consent-based hegemony.

The paradigm of nation-state governance around the notions of "the end of history", "democratic peace" and "new world order" after the end of the post-Cold War was soon replaced by beliefs and discourses of "the clashes of civilization", "illiberal democracy" and "global chaos". This transformation was followed by such an advocacy that since the nation-state had become incompetent and the international institutions had been ineffectual, civil society should perhaps be given a greater role in order to create a peaceful and equitable world. Coincidently, civil society as an emancipatory term was enthusiastically embraced by Western powers giving the rise to numerous NGOS. Thus, transnational civil societies together with its social movements are an outcome of the wide-ranging social transformations in tune with liberalization, marketization and privatization promoted by the Washington Consensus..

The analyses of the previous section propose that globalization and transnational capitalism is NOT expanding the European type of nation-state capitalist hegemonic project around the centrality of modernity and rationality, rather, it is a "class project without a national strategy" (Robinson, 2005: 11). As Deak argues, capitalism "is moving towards a non-hegemonic world structure. The emerging conflicting power centres, or more precisely, the counter-hegemonic movements, are a direct result of the non-hegemonic moment" (Deak, 2005: 50). Gill also maintains, "any attempt to construct a hegemonic system of rule will tend to gener-ate, dialectically, a set of counter-hegemonic forces, which may or may not be progressive" (Gill, 2003: 37).

One of the key questions this paper is addressing is whether hegemony and counter-hegemony embedded in the conventional state-centric system of national capitalism and inter-state order is able to transcend to become "transnational hegemony" and "transnational counter-hegemony" under the domination of capital. To paraphrase it more precisely, the questions are: 1) whether the resilient passive revolution capacity of capitalism is able to transcend: 2) whether the organic counter-hegemonic social forces are able to transcend. These two aspects are two sides of the same coin.

Wither transnational civil society?

It is a less disputable fact that since the 1990s transnational civil societies (also termed "global civil society") grew both in number, size and scope. Seen from Keane's point of view, this previously unfamiliar notion was "a neologism of the 1990s" and the "revival of the old language of civil society" of the 1980s and became increasingly popular not only in the domestic socio-political domains but also in international and regional economic and financial institutions such as the IMF, the World Bank and the WTO (Keane, 2003: 1-2). Rieff also argues that the rise of transnational civil society is more in tune with the post-Cold War dominant ideology of liberal market capitalism representing "a projection of our desires" rather than with the ideal roles of civil society in fostering democracy and good government (Rieff, 1999: 11-12).

Furthermore, the rise and struggles of global civil society, in the view of a scholar, should be conceptualized through analyzing global civil society – movements, organizations, groups, and individuals – as an outcome and effect of global complexity:

> These plateaux are shaped by a number of ideological inputs, including: liberal constitutionalism (human rights, anti-corporatism, fair trade, democratic represen-tation); socialism (trade unions, welfarism, internationalism); anarchism (participa-tion, direct democracy, direct action); and, ecologism (environment, sustainability, nature) – each of which interacts with the others exchanging, assimilating, and adapting concepts, slogans, symbols and other cognitive, emotive, and affective resources. (Chesters, 2004: 14)

In line with this thinking, it has been a continuous debate regarding the paradoxes of transnational civil societies as counter-hegemonic social forces. A variety of social movements, under the banner of opposing the polarizing inequalities, declining social and environmental conditions, economic liberalization and unaccountable corporate power, etc, are coalescing into transnational networks in the process of shaping transnational civil societies. They protest against injustice, advocate radical democracy and promote the global public sphere. They embrace participatory democracy but without a logocentric narrative or grand ideology such as liberalism and socialism (Esteva and Prakash, 1998). They believe in cosmopolitan or transnational citizenship and have great faith in global governance. But the question is: whether these cross-border interest groups, cultural groups and social networks are able to create transnational organic social forces that are capable of reshaping the political structure of the global order and bringing about democratic and redistributive justice for the world system?

One concrete example of the conceptual problems regarding trans-national civil society is the issue of "transnational citizenship". A lexical interpretation of transnational citizenship refers to the extension of rights and political and social justice beyond nation-state boundaries. However, it makes big differences whether the criteria of "citizenship" is based on *rights* (citizenship rights in a nation-state framework), or whether it is based on *community/society* (membership rights within and across borders) since the former is enforceable and the latter is not (Fox, 2005: 175) It is often used in connection with transnational social movements as "globaliza-tion from below" in the sense that transnational pressure is mobilized to discipline domestic politics. Nevertheless, it is fundamentally different between citizenship rights defined within an institutional framework and those are defined by collective action and shared identity (Fox, 2005: 174). The challenge of applying such a concept is whether the objectives and expectations, which the notion implies, can be realized.

State-market- civil society: relationship contested

There are fundamental differences between the notions and functions of transnational civil society conceptualized at two levels – from above (the capital class) and from below (the working class and subordinate groups). For the former, civil society can be utilized to politically *reduce* statism and authoritarianism so as to protect its economic position and class interest; whereas for the latter, civil society seeks to *break* the monopoly of the economic classes. However, the contradiction is that civil society from below still needs nation-states to make necessary social, political and economic policies so as to protect and improve its socio-economic well-being; and by undermining the state civil society from the below destabilizes "the only remaining power able to oppose the privatization of the world" (Rieff, 1999: 12). Not reducing transnational civil society to the logic of the global political order and the mode of functioning of the global market, the critical question to be addressed, as Chandhoke argues, is "should our normative expectations of civil society blind us to the nature of *real* civil societies whether national or global?" (Chandhoke, 2002: 37).

As early mentioned, the subdivision of "society" by socio-political theories into state, market, civil society has also bestowed these sub-domains with their special logics: the state always associated with power and *coercion*, the market with *competition* and exploitation and civil society with alternatives to both the state and the market where re-humanization and alternatives can be generated to amend the defects of both the state and the market. Civil society in classical political theory is seen as a space where political agency and selfhood are realized (Chandhoke, ibid.: 37). However, is such a realization achievable within a nation-state framework? Can it also be achieved at the transnational level? The Gramscian notion of civil society as an independent political force denotes its consensual power and legitimization authority without which the "political society" (state) would not be able to survive. Again, the question is whether the legitimacy of the state-centric world system needs the confirmation of civil society.

The conventional organic composition and embeddedness of the state-market-civil society relations under a nation-state context can be quickly decomposed and disembedded when the market becomes transnaitonalized leaving the state and civil society still nation-based. Although the mobility of transnational capital necessitates the coalition between the state and society to enforce the task of regulating the market and securing the well-being of the people, dialectically it is the exact mobility of capital that delegitimizes the state and civil society and rolls them back from their role as a counter-hegemonic force to the market.

Wither "passive revolution"?

The notion of "passive revolution" implies a transformation process – "revolution without revolution" (Adamson, 1980: 186) – i.e. crisis in hegemonic consensus and changes in production relations are contained within existing social and institutional structures but without funda-mentally challenging the established political order. The role of passive revolution includes the use of "trasformismo" strategies to rein in popular support for the elite-engineered "revolution" – an elite project of change (Sassoon, 1987: 210).

The analyses from different perspectives on the impact of transnational capitalism from the previous section reveal areas of potential problems and conflicts in applying the concept of passive revolution. It can be argued that passive revolution has lost a great deal of significance after decades of transformations; and the instrumentality of this notion in the context of nation-state capitalism cannot be automatically applied to the understanding of reformism and resilience of transnational capitalism at a time when these mechanisms are urgently needed to deal with a number of vital backlashes created by globalization[5]. Transnational capitalism to-day does not possess the same kind of hegemonic resilience in which state, market and civil society respond to each other's legitimacy. Furthermore, the analytical categories within global capitalism's political order have not yet been fully developed, which makes it difficult to act either on the basis of state's coercive power or on civil society's consensual power.

In the past, capitalism survived from recurrent crises, assisted by both the trench system of civil society and the coercive apparatus of the state helping to maintain a particular social order with "a necessary combination of consent and coercion" (Cox, 1983: 127). The regime change that is currently taking place in many parts of the world with the transition from "embedded liberalism" under a hegemonic structure to the dis-embeddedness of the economy under non-hegemony is threatening the former societal arrangement. The current world is seen as in a state of "non-hegemony" with resistance more related to the system's legitimate crisis than to the contradictions of the system's mode of production:

> If hegemony is based on consent and effective inclusion of subaltern groups, then counter-hegemony would emerge from the contradictions of a non-hegemonic period. When consent or legitimacy of an ethical hegemony is lost, then subaltern groups become discontented. The conditions would be ripe for a legitimate and popular challenge the social order that had marginalized them. (Deak, 2005: 50)

In essence, this evolution means entering uncharted territory with the world having to cope with transnational and financial globalization as dictated by the hegemony and strategies of neoliberalism. In this context however, the question that arises is whether and how capitalism is able to transgress the historical limits of its *modus operandi* that permits and reinforces capital accumulation without generating counter-hegemonic blocs and anti-systemic movements?

In political terms, the second phase of the "double movement" brought about through the implementation of Keynesian macroeconomics and the welfare state, could be understood as a "passive revolution" of the bour-geoisie, i.e. reforms in socio-economic conditions. In contrast, the present offensive of market neoliberalism can be conceptualised as the "active counter-revolution" of transnational corporate capitalism. While social-democratic reformism aim ostensibly at the formation of a permanent alliance between labor, capital and the state, market neoliberalism aims at the deconstruction of this structure and the utilization of the state in returning labor to a subaltern political position. While the agency of the state had partially protected society from the market forces at the global level, the post-welfare state, in contrast, has become the transmission belt of globalization. That is articulated in the adjustment of domestic societies to the requirements of global capitalism and the redistribution of the economic surplus in favor of the transnational capitalist classes worldwide.

The stability and resilience of social power in modern capitalism has rested not just on the coercive apparatus of the state as traditionally understood, but also on eliciting consent through hegemony in consciousness and non-coercive sphere of "civil society" into forming the "extended state". However, we are currently at a historical moment in which the "disembedded economy" at both the national and international levels is substantially raising the coercive potentiality of capital. The uncontested power of capital is at the same time reducing the consensual capacity of the elite class and is creating the fertile soil for a "double movement" in the form of worldwide anti-capitalism and anti-globalization movements joining forces in de-legitimizing the on-going coercion of market capitalism. As expressed by Mittelman, there might be a similarity with the period around the Great Depression:

> Perhaps similar to the global economy of the 1930s, contemporary globalization appears to be approaching a conjuncture in which renewed liberal-economic structures will generate large-scale political, social, and economic disruptions, as well as sustainable pressure for self-protection. (2000: 8)

Wither "double movement"?

While the Gramscian political analytical framework guides us to look into the dynamics of social relations and the dialectical roles of different social forces on which capitalism's resilience, sustainability and hegemony is built, Polanyi (1957) draws our attention to the market-society relations encapsulated in the "double movement": on the one hand, the market (fictitious commodities) continuously extends its sphere by marketizing non-economic aspects of human life in the way that human relations are constantly converted into impersonal ones or into acquiring a thing-like character, whose result is the disintegration of the social bond which is an essential constituent of humanity; but on the other hand, as humans are not guided solely by economic motivations, they consciously or unconsciously resist marketization by reclaiming their humanity, i.e. sociality, dignity, freedom and sense of security, as well as by reactivating the essential role of the state as the institution that can be used to discipline the market. Thus double movements are embedded in the state-civil society relations as well.

The contemporary debate over the interpretation of the notion of "double movement" in re-embedding the economy lies in whether this concept should denote "societal protectionism" and "political intervention" to control or regulate the market's mode of functioning, or whether it should imply that re-embedding in a given market society can only be achieved through "a complete subjugation of the market" rather than any attempt to control it (Lacher, 1999a: 315). The complexity of the "double movement" in market society as a given structure is spelt out by Polanyi himself:

> Our thesis is that the idea of a self-adjusting market implied a stark utopia. Such an institution could not exist for any length of time without annihilating the human and natural substance of society; it would have physically destroyed man and transformed his surroundings into a wilderness. *Inevitably, society took measures to protect itself, but whatever measures it took impaired the self-regulation of the market, disorganized industrial life, and thus endangered society in yet another way.* (1957: 3, italic added)

The dialectic dilemma, as Polanyi explains, is that when "society" is pegged to the "market", it becomes complicated in the sense that the divisions in society between those who do and do not benefit from the market and "the economy", including the institutions of market society, are always shaped by political struggles.

Based on the above understanding of capitalism, the common simplification of Polanyi's market critique within IPE is challenged on the basis of the historical evolution of the industrial revolution, meaning that capitalism's unique character as a form of economic organization has institutionalized the embeddedness of economic rationality and principles in social relations. This implies that counter-movement is not without problematic consequences and the social democratic model was only a partial de-commodification of the economy because of its non-eradication of labor as a commodity. In a contribution aiming to dispel the confusion surrounding the question of the transition from the welfare state to the neoliberal competition state, Lacher puts it in the follow manner, "Precisely because the postwar economy had not been re-embedded, it was possible for the welfare state to succumb so rapidly to the revival of laissez-faire ideology" (Lacher 1999b: 350).

CONCLUSION

The contemporary coercive expansion of capitalism and the post-Cold War withdrawal of the United States as the only stabilizer of global hegemony together with its unpopular foreign policies after the 9/11 crisis have brought about the crisis of hegemony of the capitalist system, as well as the marginalization of consensus-generating elements, i.e. the institutions, practices, and social relations that constantly exist as alternatives or balances of power. Consequently, without consent-building mechanisms, transnational capitalism entails a *self-denial potential* towards dissolution and disintegration, unless a powerful transnational social force is successful in generating a transnational "double movement" to push capitalism to negotiate a substantial process of passive revolution. At the present time, it is still difficult to foresee the possibilities of an effective global counter-hegemonic project able to generate the possibilities of embedding global capitals and markets in shared social values and responsibilities. The key issue (conundrum) that needs to be understood is the nature of the totalizing force of capitalism vis-à-vis counter-movement in a nexus of hegemony and contradictions.

The difficulties of forming a counter-hegemonic historical bloc compelling capitalism to engage a genuine process of "passive revolution", as analyzed earlier, partake the complexities of the "double movement" in regulating the market. Both Gramsci and Polanyi independently converged on a similar critique and transcendence of mechanical Marxism aiming to grasp the dialectics behind state-market-society relations with the dynamism and complexity of society as a key to understanding the durability of capitalism in a global order. As Burawoy pinpoints:

> We can stretch Gramsci and Polanyi to generate new insights into the idea of the transnational society. From a Polanyian perspective, we can think of the way transnational society is forged in response to commodification generally but in particular to the commodification of land, labor, and money. But we must be very careful not to romanticize this transnational society. It, too, is a very uneven political terrain, populated by hierarchies of power, sloping down from center to periphery, and having its own fissures and ravines. From a Gramscian perspective, we can think of transnational society in its relation to supranational state-like agencies, but that connection contains struggles against capitalism as often as it provides grounds for its transcendence. (Burawoy, 2003)

This complements well this paper's proposed contradictions of transnational capitalism as a dialectical and dynamic unity embedded in the interaction of reciprocal and paradoxical relations, which, on the one hand, opens the door for progressive transformations, while on the other hand, sets the limit of counter-hegemonic protectionism within market society. The paper has come to the conclusion that a return to the reformism of the double movement and passive revolution does not have favorable conditions for implementation under the current situation.

NOTES

1   Classical Marxism and Leninism regard capitalist ideologies, such as democracy and freedom as "false consciousness", "indoctrination" and "manipulation". However, Gramsci attempts to look at the capacity of bourgeoisie class to materialize these false ideologies and turn them into common sense.

2   "Trasformismo" used by Gramsci refers to a strategy of elite politics aiming at accom-

modating opposing forces that may disrupt the status quo and threaten the hegemony of the elite. It concludes the creation of a flexible, centrist coalition of government to isolate the extremes of the left and the right and the incorporation of extended cultural, social, economic, and political networks.

3   The transitional capitalist class encompasses four main interlocking groups: 1) TNC executives and their local affiliates, 2) globalizing bureaucrats, 3) globalizing politicians and professionals, and 4) consumerist elites.

4   "Class-in-itself" refers to the general common characteristics of being a worker in relation to the conventional classification based on production relations. "Class-for-itself" refers to the category of self-activity and self-representation, i.e. collective political identity and common struggle. The difference between them is political, i.e. while everyone works for a living, not everyone struggles against injustices embedded in work and fights for a common cause. See Lewis A. Coser, *Masters of Sociological Thought: Ideas in Historical and Social Context, 2nd Ed.*, Fort Worth: Harcourt Brace Jovanovich, Inc, 1977.

5   John Gerard Ruggie (6 June 2002), in a lecture given by to the London School of Economics, described three key globalization backlashes: 1) Globalization distributes benefits highly unequally; 2) There is a growing imbalance in global rule making; 3) Globalization is generating greater vulnerability to unfamiliar and unpredictable forces leading to economic instability and social dislocation. See the lecture transcript *Taking Embedded Liberalism Global: The Corporate Connection* available at: http://www.lse.ac.uk/collections/globalDimensions/globalisation/takingEmbeddedLiberalism/transcript.htm

REFERENCES

Adamson, Walter L. (1980) *Hegemony and Revolution: A Study of Antonio Gramsci's Political and Cultural Theory*. Berkely: University of California Press.

Agnew, John and Stuart Corbridge (1995) *Mastering Space: Hegemony, Territory and International Political Economy*. London: Routledge.

Ahmad, Aijaz (2004) "Imperialism of Our Time", in Leo Panitch & Colin Leys (eds) *The New Imperial Challenge; Socialist Register*. London: the Merlin Press Ltd.

Bergsten, C. Fred (2001) "America's Two-Front Economic Conflict." *Foreign Affairs*, 80(2): 16-27.

Burawoy, Michael (2003) "For a Sociological Marxism: The Complementary Convergence of Antonio Gramsci and Karl Polanyi." *Politics & Society*, 31(2): 193-261.

Chandhoke, Neera (2002) "The Limits of Global Civil Society", in Glasius, Marlies, Mary Kaldor and Helmut Anheier (eds.) *Global Civil Society 2002*. London: Centre for the Study of Global Governance.

Chesters, Graeme (2004) "Global Complexity and Global Civil Society", a working paper, Working Papers Volume IV Toronto Conference *Contesting Citizenship and Civil Society in a Divided World*, 2004.

Cox, Robert W. (1983) "Gramsci, Hegemony and International Relations." *Millennium: Journal of International Studies*, (12)2: 162-75.

Cox, Robert W. (1993) "Gramsci, Hegemony and International Relations: An Essay in Method", in Stephen Gill (ed.) *Gramsci, Historical Materialism and International Relations*. Cambridge: Cambridge University Press.

Cox, Michael (2001) "Whatever Happened to American Decline? International Relations and the New United States Hegemony." *New Political Economy*, 6(3): 311-340.

Deak, Andrew (2005) "The Condition of Hegemony and the Possibility of Resistance." *Undercurrent*, 2(3): 46-56.

Esteva, Gustavo and Madhu Suri Prakash (1998) *Grassroots Post-Modernism: Remaking the Soil of Cultures*. London: Zed Books.

Fletcher, William Jr. (2003) "Can U.S. workers embrace anti-imperialism?" *Monthly Review*, 55(3): 93-108.

Fox, Jonathan (2005) "Unpacking Transnational Citizenship." *Annual Review of Political Science*, 8: 171-201.

Germain, Randall D. and Michael Kenny (1998) "Engaging Gramsci: international relations theory and the new Gramscians." *Review of International Studies*, 24(1): 3-21.

Gill, Stephen (2003) *Power and Resistance in the New World Order*. London: Palgrave.

Gilpin, Robert (2001) *Global Political Economy: Understanding the International Economic Order.* Princeton: Princeton University Press.

Gindin, Sam (2003) "Prospects for Anti-Imperialism." *Monthly Review*, 55(3): 117-124.

Grunenberg, Antonia (1998) "Public Spirit and Civil Society: How to Conceptualize Politics in a Globalizing World." *International Review of Sociology*, 8(3): 413-424.

Hersh, Jacques (2000) "Civilizational Conflicts: A Critique", in Johannes D. Schmidt and Jacques Hersh, *Globalization and Social Change*. London: Routledge.

Hersh, Jacques (1993) *The USA and the Rise of East Asia Since 1945*. London: Macmillan.

Hoare, Quintin and Geoffrey Nowell Smith (1971) *Selections from the Prison Notebooks of Antonio Gramsci*. London: Lawrence & Wishart.

Hosbon, John M. and Ramsech M (2002) "Globalisation Makes of States What States Make of It: Between Agency and Structure in the State/Globalisation Debate." *New Political Economy*, 7(1): 5-22.

Huntington, Samuel (1993) "The Clash of Civilizations?" *Foreign Affairs*, 72(3): 22-49.

Keane, John (2003) *Global Civil Society?* Cambridge: Cambridge University Press.

Klare, Michael (2001) *Resource Wars: The New Landscape of Global Conflict*. New York: Henry Holt/Metropolitan.

Lacher, Hannes (1999a) "The Politics of the Market: Re-reading Karl Polanyi." *Global Society: Journal of Interdisciplinary International Relations*, 13(3): 313-326.

Lacher, Hannes (1999b) "Embedded Liberalism, Disembedded Markets: Reconceptualising the Pax Americana." *New Political Economy*, 4(3): 343-360.

Li, Xing (2002) "Dichotomies and Paradoxes: the West and Islam." *Global Society: Journal of Interdisciplinary International Relations*, 16(4): 401-418.

Li, Xing and Hersh, Jacques (2006) "Understanding Global Capitalism: Passive Revolution and Double Movement in the Era of Globalization." *American Review of Political Economy* 4(1/2): 36-55.

Li, Xing and Hersh, Jacques (2004) "The Genesis of Capitalism: The Nexus between 'Politics in Command' and Social Engineering." *American Review of Political Economy*, 2(2): 101-144.

Li, Xing and Hersh, Jacques (2002) "Understanding Capitalism: Crises and Passive Revolutions." *Competition & Change: the Journal of Global Business and Political Economy*, 6(2): 193-212.

Mills, David G. (2004) "It's the Corporate State, Stupid," *Dissident* Voice, online article at http://www.dissidentvoice.org/Nov2004/Mills1110.htm

Mittelman, James H (2000) *The Globalization Syndrome, Transformation and Resistance*. Princeton: Princeton University Press.

Monbiot, George (2003) "The flight to India." *The Guardian*, October 21, available at http://www.guardian.co.uk/comment/story/0,3604,1067344,00.html

Petras, James (1997) "Imperialism and NGOs in Latin America." *Monthly Review*, 49(7): 10-27.

Polanyi, Karl (1957) *The Great Transformation*. New York: Rinehart.

Rieff, David (1999) "Civil Society and the Future of the Nation-State: Two Views." *The Nation*, 268(7): 11-16.

Robinson, William I. and Jerry Harris (2000) "Towards A Global Ruling Class? Globalization and the Transnational Capitalist Class." *Science & Society*, 64(1): 11-54.

Robinson, William I. (2005) "Gramsci and Globalisation: From Nation-State to Transnational Hegemony." *Critical Review of International Social and Political Philosophy*, 8(4): 1–16.

Ross Rober J. & Trachte, Kent C. (1990) *Global Capitalism: the New Leviathan*. New York: State University of New York.

Ruggie, John (1982) "International Regimes, Transaction and Change: Embedded Liberalism in the Postwar Economic Order." *International Organization*, 36(2): 379-415.

Sassoon, Anne Showstack (2001) "Globalisation, Hegemony, and Passive Revolution." *New Political Economy*, 6(1): 5-17.

Sassoon, Anne Showstack (1987) *Gramsci's Politics*. London: An Imprint of Century Hutchinson Ltd.

Scholte, Jan Aart (1997) "Global Capitalism and the State." *International Affairs*, 73(3): 427-452.

Scruton, Roger (1996) *A Dictionary of Political Thought*. London: The Macmillan Press.

Simon, Roger (1982) *Gramsci's Political Thought*. London: Lawrence and Wishart.

Sklair, Leslie (2000) *The Transnational Capitalist Class*. London: Blackwell Publisher.

Wood, Ellen. (1999) "Unhappy Families: Global Capitalism in a World of Nation-States." *Monthly Review*, 51(3): 1-12.

Yates, Michael (2000) "'Workers of all Countries, Unite:' Will This Include the U.S. Labour Movement?" *Monthly Review*, 52(3): 46-59.

CHAPTER TWO

Fundamental Aspects of Human Conditions of Life and Multiculturalism under the Reign of Neoliberalism

Christian Ydesen

INTRODUCTION

In line with manifestations of social change, like globalization and migration, it is increasingly necessary to develop adequate theoretical understandings in order to address new practical problems. The necessity is accentuated by the contemporary multicultural and multireligious reality of most states in the world. As the forces of neoliberal globalization today occupy an increasingly predominant role in policies on both local and global levels it is appropriate to raise a discussion about fundamental aspects of the human condition in general, and of whether a diversified multicultural and multireligious reality in particular is possible, within the framework of neoliberalism.

Initially, it is appropriate to dwell on the term neoliberalism as it is certainly a contested concept among researchers; the differences are particularly important in relation to the role of the state: Does neoliberalism necessarily imply a gradual abolition of state control or does it merely imply a different way of control and regulation empowered by the state? A common denominator in this discussion seems to be that the state has become more and more instrumental to global economic forces (Li & Hersh, 2006: 48). Moreover, there seems to be some kind of scholarly consensus to recognize "…. the interplays of continuity and change regarding the relationship between globalization and the state with a keen awareness of the notable changes in the character of the state in terms of capacities, constituencies, policy-making processes and contents, etc" (Scholte, 1997). Thus, in order to treat neoliberalism in relation to different societal phenomena it is fruitful to focus on the different functionalities of the state. As the focus of this article is on fundamental aspects of the human condition in general and on multiculturalism in particular, I find it adequate merely to describe neoliberalism as a rearticulation of the boundaries between state and market combined with the expansion of certain values and types of behavior rooted in an expansive market capitalistic logic.

In accordance with the expansion of neoliberal globalization, market domination and expansion as a means of coordination and regulation in the world are often perceived as being applicable on all areas in society. In this article I will argue that this development induces a number of consequences for the fundamental aspects of the human condition. One of the most important is the societal structure of recognition which, under the reign of neoliberalism, first and foremost is bound to the ideal of the successful, productive and innovative entrepreneur and secondly to the ability to constantly create economic value and growth. This is the yardstick against which humanity is to be measured and this gives rise to a thesis of a societal uniformity process in the world: Dissenters must firmly be directed back to a "virtuous" and "correct" way of life. This neoliberal structure of recognition is of utmost importance for society's recognition of work and it thus impacts on human social status, self-esteem and identity (the self-told story about who we are) – in other words it is of utmost importance for comprehending the fundamental aspects of the human condition under the reign of neoliberalism.

Another significant consequence of neoliberal market capitalistic logic is that relations between employer and employee are predominantly individualized. This is among other things reflected in contract formation as well as individualized and result oriented wages. A problem in this connection is that these tendencies undermine trust, loyalty and mutual commitment between people. For instance the introduction of result oriented wages is tantamount to an increased competition between employees and hence the individual employee is inclined to merely look after himself and fine-tune his positional competences. Under the reign of neoliberalism other people naturally become competitors. Therefore, it can be very difficult to experience trust and love, whereas mistrust, skepticism and competitive sets of mind thrive, because colleagues and other human beings in general basically are perceived as having conflicting interests. This again has an inevitable impact on fundamental aspects of the human condition as it threatens to amputate crucial dimensions in human existence.

Of course these consequences are more developed in some areas of the world than others but in line with the expansive logic of neoliberalism it seems appropriate to raise a general discussion of these tendencies of neoliberal market capitalistic logic.

In order to pinpoint the overriding problem of this logic in relation to human existence from a philosophical point of view it can be said that the dynamic capital is working as some kind of metaphysical force in the lives of human beings. It is metaphysical because economic growth is an independent goal – dislodged from the human being – and therefore the human being succumbs to the dynamics of an apparently uncontrollable force. By the promotion of external purposes such as growth and competition to a primary status through cultural and value dictates, the human being is being governed, suppressed and impoverished by his or her own mental creation because they accept, worship and subject themselves to such a construction.

Moreover, these market capitalistic developments can be highly problematic in relation to the conditions of a diversified multiculturalism; there are implications for general minority rights in a neoliberal society since only the members of society who can display an ability to generate economic growth are able to gain explicit societal recognition.

Thus, a number of forward-looking questions must be addressed: How can the fundamental aspects of the human condition in a neoliberal society be characterized and how do these aspects correspond with a multicultural reality? Which role can be ascribed to "the other" in the future of neoliberalism and its functionality? Will the reaction be inclusion or exclusion or perhaps something else? Is it possible to establish a "both/ and" logic which has the potentiality of transcending neoliberalism as we know it? I will attempt to treat these questions both from an empirical and a philosophical point of view. However, the consistent focus of the article is the fundamental logic of neoliberalism (market capitalism). Thus, the inclusions of empirical examples – some taken from a predominantly western context – are merely seen as manifestations of that logic with a purpose of raising a general discussion of neoliberal market capitalistic logic in relation to fundamental aspects of the human condition and multiculturalism.

Let us begin the journey by attempting a diagnosis of one of the key structures in neoliberal society: The relation between human beings and the labor market.

THE CHANGES OF WORK IN OUR TIME
– THE FORMATION OF NEW CONTROL MECHANISMS

In recent years work has changed fundamentally all over the world. In poor parts of the world comprehensive industry and time-consuming assembly line work in sweatshops owned by transnational corporations have spread like wildfire. In the rich part of the world we are witnessing ideas, knowledge and service form the focal points in human work life while the division between working hours and spare time has broken down: An idea is not only spawned in the office but also in the bath tub or in a dream (Hardt & Negri, 2004: 109ff).

There are however some underlying laws and logics which have not changed notably. Among other things, capitalism is still characterized by a structural imperative to exploit work. At the same time economic growth constitutes the foundation of the societal assessment of all work – work has to create value in an economic sense. Thus, in a capitalist system the objective is no longer just to provide the possibilities of a materially adequate life, which is a pivotal difference in comparison with pre-capitalistic societies.

Among other things, this perpetual and ubiquitous dictate for economic growth entails that acceleration becomes an intrinsic value in capitalist society: It is quite simply natural to perform things increasingly rapidly, more effectively and productively, which has an unmistakable spill-over effect on the whole of societal values (Rosa, 2005). Hence, the intrinsic dynamics of capitalism becomes significant – and to a certain degree pri-mary – for social and cultural values in society. The market is ideologically perceived as the most efficient mechanism to regulate society and human relations (Li & Hersh, 2006: 48). The mode of production is in other words structuring social relations, culture, possibilities of recognition and at the same time it exercises great influence on the human horizon of experience and expectation and thus on the entire way we view our life, our dreams, our hopes and aspirations. Consequently, it seems reasonable to say that work in contemporary neoliberal societies constitutes a central focal point in the human forming of identity through its inevitable impact upon our views on challenges, responsibility, sociality and recognition. Thus, work becomes a very significant source of self-respect. It is no longer considered legitimate to view work as a mere means to achieve other life goals as was the case in earlier phases of capitalism. In other words we live for the sake of work. This development can be characterized as lifelong learning in the service of work and at the same time we want to do this because we subscribe to the concept of personal development via work.

This integration of the values of capitalist work in human life forms the foundation of the introduction of new means of control characteristic of neoliberalism. More specifically these means of control can be summed up as attempts to control the way people administer their freedom. An ex-ample of such a means of control is teamwork where the leader delegates a job to a team in the company. The team is hereafter responsible for seeing the job done and thus room for a certain work ethic is encouraged through the establishment of self-policing within the team – a good team player does not whine and "evaders" are excluded from the fellowship because they are unable to live up to team expectations and demands. At the same time the team is in perpetual competition with other teams who stand ready in the wings to take over the job in case the first team should fail. This means of control is specifically explicit if the boss is just a team player along with the rest of the team. In other words the worker is no longer a notable counter power but rather the junior partner of the company. This development is among other places widespread in the area of marketing and commercials, where work often take place in innovative teams (Sennet, 1998).

Moreover, the worker is ultimately perceived as being responsible for his/her own position in the labor market, which is in perfect alignment with the liberal tradition of political thinking. This perception of the worker as free and responsible entails that he/she can be judged, punished and pronounced guilty: Any act is thought of as being rooted in the rational conscience and sovereign will of the employee. There lies a foundation for the control mechanisms of modern working life.

An example of such a control mechanism is closely knitted with the problem of the human forming of identity via work which again is knitted with societal structures of recognition. As a rule the human being can only gain recognition by conforming to the values of society which are saturated with capitalist work. Therefore, human striving for recognition from peers and superiors can be activated as a basis for disciplining. In order to illustrate the problem one might ask what work really is: Is it speculation on the stock market, volunteer work in a youth club, lobbying work for the chemical industry or welding in a shipyard? More closely the issue is what concept of work is prevalent in a society and if this concept can be characterized as inclusive or exclusive? The answer to these questions is of immense importance for society's recognition of work and thus for human social status, self esteem and identity – among other things because the human being itself, as mentioned, is perceived as being responsible for its own position.

A third control mechanism which can be viewed in continuation of the above mentioned can be identified under the term "LEAN", which more closely implies a detailed control of time consumption and work processes among employees. All waste of time is eliminated and the workers even often bring their problems home from work. The inner commitment of the employee is controlled and seemingly checked by an external commitment dictated by the employer and the norms and values of the surrounding society. Undoubtedly, this has a negative impact on the value of work for the employee. Many workers find it hard to find time and strength to do what they care about, both at work and at home. This is a valid explanation for the widespread problems of stress in many contemporary societies.

In relation to multiculturalism these control mechanisms can best be described as highly problematic. The reason is that the immanent logic of neoliberalism does not correspond with the cosmovision of other cultures. This stems from the insight that it is impossible to express the richness and fullness of existence through the notions of only a single culture. But when the western discourse speaks of developed and developing countries it shows that we are in a monocultural world: Only one culture sets the rule of the game (Panikkar, 1996). The hegemonic status of western culture proposing neoliberalism all over the world is manifest in the severe problems of democracy prominent in the world today. These problems centre on complaints of representation, complaints of poverty and the resistance to warmongering (Hardt & Negri, 2004).

One fundamental problem in relation to multiculturalism is that abstract concepts like e.g. "competition" and "balance of payments" might be incomprehensible in other cultures because meaning and sense simply are dissolved as the full implications and connotations of the concepts erode in another framework of understanding. Thus, it is potentially harder for people with a different cultural background to understand the processes and the logic of the new culture in general and of neoliberalism in particular. This often puts people from a different cultural background in a disadvantageous position – a point boosted by that fact that people from so-called developing countries often have to justify their presence in a given country, which makes the above mentioned control mechanisms particularly active in relation to this group of people.

Michael Hardt and Antonio Negri describe this problem of the ever-expanding values of neoliberalism through their concept of empire which can be described as a certain kind of logic striving to standardize the world. One of Hardt and Negris points in this relation is that the differences between national territories increasingly are differences of degree rather than differences of character. This means that the world no longer is able to display the same level of diversity and pluralism as it once was: McDonald's, falafel and standard TV-concepts have spread all over the world and concurrently everyone has to live up to the unquenchable demands for economic growth, success and productivity of the empire (Hardt and Negri, 2003: 361).

Let us move on by taking a more in-depth look at the conditions of human existence under the reign of neoliberalism.

THE CONDITIONS OF HUMAN EXISTENCE UNDER THE REIGN OF NEOLIBERALISM

A quick glance at job advertisements reveals a staggering frequency in the occurrence of a number of buzz words: productive, responsible, service minded, team player, flexibility, enthusiasm, proactive, challenges.

These tendencies are in perfect harmony with the above mentioned reflections on self responsibility for lifelong learning with an eye to constant productivity. There is a more or less explicit demand for perpetual growth on all areas – not only professionally but also as a human being. From a philosophical perspective it seems plausible to emphasize the difficulty in being really present in the now generated by this demand for perpetual growth. The reason is that we are always on our way to something else and whatever we are doing now is never adequate. To bring matters to a head one might say that the contemporary human being is condemned to self development.

This development spawns an explicit focus on the near future in the work life and at the same time it is responsible for the clear and unambiguous spreading of temporary jobs, loose employment and contract hiring. In fact one might compare the modern employee with pre-modern day laborers: One is hired to do a certain job or to join a certain team or project organization for a limited time span (Sennet, 1998).

As already mentioned in the introduction, this development sparks a tendency of undermining trust, loyalty and mutual commitment between people. Under the reign of neoliberalism other people naturally become competitors.

This causes complications regarding the establishment and development of an identity due to the fragmented experience of life caused by the inevitable values of capital dictating acceleration and productivity: Who am I? Many people undoubtedly have an idea of who they are but they so rarely experience having the time to be that person. Obviously, this might trigger existential crises aggravated by the competition with colleagues and the fellow human beings along with the many loose employments and projects creating an uncertainty: Will I be needed in the long run? Do I really know who I am and will it be possible for me to be that person?

On a more general level this uncertainty is boosted by a new role played by the state under the reign of neoliberalism. It can be argued that the primary task of the state under the reign of globalization is to interpret international tendencies regarding market development and conditions of investment in order to secure national competitiveness. This role causes a sense of uncertainty in society because of exposure to uncontrollable international market variations aggravated by the irresolute nature of state initiatives.

Moreover, the work conditioned problems in relation to the forming of identity are accelerated by some of the trends of the working life such as value based management and human resource management. These phenomena can namely be described as frontal assaults on human professional integrity because strategic demands must be taken into consideration constantly and at the same time the employee is responsible that these demands are met. A strategic demand could be a general cut down in the entire company dictating the employee to deliver only 80 per cent solutions in a given period. Thus, the professional pride of the employee is subdued because mediocrity for a while is given pride of place. This makes it hard to claim a cohesive identity in work, as for instance a nurse or a librarian. Of course, this does not mean that it is impossible to form a human identity under the reign of neoliberalism, but it means that the array of possibilities of forming human identity is diminished and amputated. Thus, people may feel alienated as they find it hard to recognize themselves in the offered set of opportunities under the reign of neoliberalism.

The described problems regarding difficulties in the forming of human identity in the work life is among other things conditioned by the explicit focus on effect and profit of capitalism rather than substance. Thus, the idea of forming human identity and culture as well as creating a good citizen via education and enlightenment is leading a rather difficult life in a majority of contemporary societies. Knowledge and virtues as intrinsic values have become problematic because knowledge and education have become factors of production and hence commodities on the market. We are thus witnessing a collision between perceptions of knowledge and education as use value and as intrinsic value: In other words, do knowledge and education have a value of their own or is their value merely determined by what is useful economically?

However, this fragmentation of life is not necessarily a uniform phenomenon for all employees in modern society. Some employees experience to be spun into work in the same company over a considerable number of years. Although the work forms centered on projects, teams and result orientation also seem to be valid in this connection. These are the key employees representing a special value for the company.

It is characteristic for this group of employees that they experience and act out an obligation towards their job. This obligation may very well be founded materially in a significant number of fringe benefits – a spreading phenomenon in our time. Because of the fringe benefits the employee is retained along with his/her commitment, loyalty and devotion because there are no real alternatives on the labor market. At the same time the fringe benefits cause the employer to be reluctant to hire more employees because they will also want fringe benefits. Instead the employer draws heavily on the sense of duty with the key employees in relation to tasks and jobs that only seldom are limited to a "normal" work week. This point is supported by American research which shows a clear connection between fringe benefits and overtime work (Schor, 1991).

A common denominator for human work life under the reign of neo-liberalism is its impact on human attitudes which is often reflected in cases of voluntary workaholism. In general it can be deduced that working life and the neoliberal logic seek to dictate:

- The standards which human beings must meet
- Competition between employees and divisions/teams within companies
- Elasticity and flexibility in ever-increasing working hours
- The treadmill of productivity and the individual responsibility of each employee
- The connection between work and consumption

At the same time capitalism offers consumer goods as a bribe for this institutionalization of work as a psychological contract.

THE CANONIZATION OF THE SUCCESSFUL ENTREPRENEUR – TENDENCIES OF A SOCIETAL UNIFORMITY PROCESS

Today it can hardly be doubted that the private initiative, the individual executive and the efficient and productive private individual are perceived as the very backbone of the economic system that is "the national cor-poration" locked in competition for market shares on the international market.

Evidently, private property as well as the innovative and productive entrepreneur has been canonized as the yardstick against which we all are to be measured. Moreover, the state constantly seeks to adjust and fine-tune different areas of society in order to meet the supposed demands of the unpredictable international market. Hence, a marked increase in state interference; often expressed through intensive evaluation demands, is increasingly manifest (Dahler-Larsen, 2006: 80). In other words, states are trying to find out what their competitors are up to and then they hurry to implement the same kind of measures that other states are doing.

In this process the OECD plays a pivotal role as key-adviser for states in the rich parts of the world. One example would be the OECD Programme for International Student Assessment (PISA), which is an internationally standardized assessment of school children based on statistical models. The PISA has been used as a lever for political reforms in many participating school system – reforms that are not in any way recommended by the PISA reports (Pedersen, 2006: 54). This interpretation is supported by linguistics Professor Tim McNamara, who sees a clear increase in political interventionism in several countries:

> ... they [policymakers and system managers] are increasingly interventionist in the interests of policy objectives such as efficiency, reform, modernization, globalization and the like. This intervention often takes the form of demands for greater accountability and more accurate reporting of outcomes of effort. (McNamara, 2001: 10)

In relation to the logic of neoliberalism it seems fair to say that this quantification tendency – so characteristic of accountability and evaluation (Mouritsen, 1997: 151ff) – is boosted by the fact that market control is dependent on quantitative competitive parameters in order to generate transparency and a standard of reference for the market actors.

Moreover, in a knowledge economy only talents and competences of what can be termed "symbol analysis" are appreciated. This means that manual skills – no matter how skilful they are employed – are deprived of status and value. Concurrently, it is evident that a large minority of the population do not own the kind of resources necessary for qualification on the labor market of a knowledge economy. There seems to be an elimination race where only certain skills, values and abilities grant access to the elite (Bourdieu, 2005).

This gives rise to a thesis of a societal uniformity process as mentioned in the introduction. At the same time our so-called free choices have already been structured by the decision-makers of capital and we are only allowed to choose from within a predetermined palette of choices. A valid example mentioned previously would be standardized TV-concepts spreading all over the world. Other examples are cellular wallpapers and ringtones which have the purpose of enabling the owner of the cell phone to put his/her individual touch on the cell phone. But at the same time it is only possible to choose from a selection decided by the providers and producers. It can be argued that human freedom under neoliberalism is a structured freedom.

From a philosophical point of view this worship of the golden calf is nothing less than an existential absurdity given that not everyone can be private entrepreneurs and successful producers – if everyone is the same no one would know who they are. Therefore, global capitalism is tainting society with a very questionable yardstick which, for the majority of people, results in alienation because the societal structures of recognition are bound to this "productive private individual". The problems concerning multiculturalism are evident. At the same time the idolization of private interest may result in a loss of meaning in life since private interest most often is actualized at the expense of common interests. In other words there is no common good or interest to generate meaning and security in life.

Therefore notions of a meaningful life can be hard to obtain since capitalism does not present any other meaning or value than consumption (in order to satisfy the intrinsic ideology of growth) and at the same time people only seem to act according to their own interest, which fundamentally creates insecurity as it can only lead to skepticism and uncertainty in relation to your fellows and your horizon of expectation.

Moreover, the canonization of the successful entrepreneur entails that the value of the single human being is determined by an external yardstick dictated by society; namely to what extent the single human being is able to be productive and to create economic value. Thus, the political starting point of liberalism is undermined; namely the intrinsic value of each human being. As the Danish theologian and philosopher K.E. Løgstrup has pointed out: "If we let the value of a human life depend on its contribution to society, then contempt for the weak will guide the organization of our society, if even it stays at that" (Løgstrup, 1993: 18 – my translation).

HUMAN RELATIONS UNDER THE REIGN OF GLOBAL CAPITALISM

Basically it is reasonable to say that capitalist consumption, which also is capitalism's only offer for meaning and value in life, creates a mimetic desire of structured choices – "I want what they want". Thus, individuality is threatened and concurrently the competition between people is strengthened. In other words we are brought up to think like others do and to desire the same goods as others do, which is in perfect alignment with the above mentioned points about a societal uniformity process, which, as we have seen, is also boosted by the canonization of the productive entrepreneur. These tendencies of uniformity are furthermore intertwined with the problems surrounding the human forming of identity because the supply of otherness (that which is different) is lessened. This connection is anchored in a philosophical reflection that the human being cannot know beforehand what it means to be a self if it does not have an otherness (i.e. a different human being) as a mirror image.

As mentioned in the introduction people naturally tend to become competitors under the practice of neoliberalism. As a consequence it can be difficult to experience trust and love, whereas mistrust, skepticism and competitive sets of mind thrive, because colleagues and other human beings in general basically are perceived as having conflicting interests.

This point is somewhat supported by the buyer/seller logic of capitalism, which more specifically threatens to generate a hawker mentality where trust is in short supply because how can you feel trust in an impersonal relationship between supplier and customer when their interests are conflicting? The logic of the economic sphere and the demands of work thus heavily restrain human existence – among other things by promoting certain values – and constantly threatening to amputate essential dimensions in human life. For instance one might say that love and solidarity cannot be reduced to deficiency needs since these phenomena contain numerous dimensions which are incomprehensible on that basis. Just imagine the myriads of descriptions of the overwhelming feelings of incomprehensibility and magnificence connected with fellowship and love in world literature. Love and solidarity are tantamount with spontaneity, self-forgetfulness, surprise, potentiality and an unfinishedness which does not merely correspond with an intrinsic process in the individual human being. As the philosopher Martin Buber writes:

> Feelings dwell in man; but man dwells in his love. That is no metaphor, but the actual truth. Love does not cling to the I in such a way as to have the Thou only for its 'content', its object; but love is between I and Thou. The man who does not know this, with his very being know this, does not know love; even though he ascribes to it the feelings he lives through, experiences, enjoys, and expresses. Love ranges in its effect through the whole world. In the eyes of him who takes his stand in love, and gazes out of it, men are cut from their entanglement in bustling activity. Good people and evil, wise and foolish, beautiful and ugly, become successively real to him; that is, set free they step forth in their singleness, and confront him as Thou. In a wonderful way, from time to time, exclusiveness arises – and so he can be effective, helping, healing, educating, raising up, saving. Love is responsibility of an I for a Thou. In this lies the likeness .... of all who love .... (Buber, 2004: 19f.)

By reducing the anchorage of valuable lasting identity on which society is founded global capitalism creates a societal destabilization. Among other things large numbers of people fail to see the meaning of life just like the faith in society with loyal citizens is undermined. Instead fear of falling into the group of people who cannot handle the pressure and therefore are excluded increasingly becomes a motivating factor. Capital cannot create a good life as its goal is fundamentally different.

After this discussion of the human condition under the reign of neoliberalism it is fruitful to turn to the question of which role can be ascribed to "the others" in the future of neoliberalism and its functionality?

THE ROLE OF THE OTHER UNDER THE REIGN OF NEOLIBERALISM

As the discussions above clearly indicate the conditions of alterity are under severe pressure in a neoliberal society – both because of the described uniformity process as well as the mentioned neoliberal control mechanisms. In philosophical terms one might say that the otherness is being alienated in the totality of neoliberalism.

One of the problems is that people from another cultural background simply do not know the unwritten rules on the labor market, as they do not understand the culture and the norms of society. Consequently they often find it hard to cope and it is difficult for them to become socially accepted. Another consequence is that they miss job opportunities and in worst case they even get fired. A symptom of these conditions is a book by political scientist Mehmet Yüksekkaya who seeks to describe the unwritten rules of the Danish labor market in order to address these problems (Yüksekkaya, 2007). The need for information on these issues is clearly there.

However, the philosophical points about the human forming of identity in relation to that which is different may give multiculturalism back the edge, as people from different cultures are able to supply society with that very otherness needed as a mirror image. This could be a room for introducing and realizing a multicultural reality that has not succumbed to a primary logic; namely that of neoliberalism.

The essential aspect in this connection is how we meet the other – do we choose a dictatorial or a dialogical angle? By claiming and defining the world the opportunity of dialogue is irrevocably lost.

The Spanish theologian and philosopher Raimon Panikkar (1918-) is a leading scholar and proponent of multiculturalism and its conditions. He states that the great challenge of intercultural dialogue is the relativization of all apriori (Panikkar, 1996: 5). Panikkar writes: "There are no cultural universals. But there are, for sure, human invariants. Every man eats, sleeps, walks, speaks, establishes relationships, thinks... But the way according to which each one of the human invariants is lived and experienced in each culture is distinct and distinctive in each case" (Panikkar, 1996: 7).

In understanding this process Panikkar's concepts of "diatopic places" and "homeomorphic equivalents" can advantageously be involved as they respectively are founded in a dynamic perspective as well as in an assumption where concepts are not necessarily compatible because each culture entails a cosmovision of reality. This is especially relevant in relation to interreligious dialogue. What is important to understand in relation to intercultural and interreligious problems is the necessity to focus not on conceptual equivalents but on functional equivalents. As Panikkar writes: "One does not seek the same function but the function that is equivalent to that exercised by the original notion in the corresponding cosmovision" (Panikkar, 1996: 3). This is a recipe for dialogue in a multicultural context.

The big question now is whether this is possible under the reign of neoliberalism. As we have seen the contemporary conditions do not leave much hope. However, it might be fruitful to direct the attention towards the constructed ontology of civilizations and cultures. On one hand they are essentially constructions but on the other hand they are realities for human beings – realities that might exert great influence on people's horizon of actions. In order to use the terminology of Samuel P. Huntington one might speak of a clash of notions rather than a clash of civilizations. This provides us with a dynamic room for action since a notion is moldable whereas an essence like a civilization is not.

Concurrently, this means that the logic of neoliberalism is manmade and its authoritative status generated by political and administrative elites must be questioned. The main reason for this is the fact that neoliberalism excludes a large number of political options. Neoliberalism presents itself as the only realistic approach and consequently all alternatives are either utopian or deeply irresponsible. If one needs further justification of putting the logic of neoliberalism into question than has already been mentioned in this article, one could point to at lack of legitimacy because of the number of wars and conflicts all over the world. Neoliberalism has not been able to create peace, which is a solid reason for acting in other directions.

One way of starting or helping this budding process is to change or emphasize a different way of perceiving the human being. Instead of perceiving the human being as a monad the process of constituting the self should be given pride of place. This does not merely imply personal development through work but an awareness of the vegetative significance of the other for developing the self (cf. the above points about otherness as a necessity for human self being).

Undoubtedly, such a quantum leap will be most problematic to perform, but here the thinking of the Norwegian philosopher Thomas Mathiesen could prove to be useful. Mathiesen has described the processes of inclusion and exclusion that take place in the practice of a hegemonic discourse. Either new currents are placed inside the "system" to show that they really are identical with the hegemonic discourse or they are placed outside the "system" to proclaim them as dangerous and the expressions of utopia (Mathiesen 1982). The point is that a hegemonic discourse – in this case neoliberalism – can work with two different processes of neutralization. One erases the characteristics of the new current by including it and the other makes the new current insignificant by repelling and condemning it. Thus, the processes are characterized by a binary "either/or" logic.

If new currents are to be able to establish a counter power they must avoid being caught up in this "either/or" logic and replace it with a "both/and" logic.

In continuation of these rather theoretical reflections it is fertile to examine how we can practice interaction with the other, who – just like us – is interested in establishing a balance between existential meaning, and safe, free social interaction.

FUTURE PERSPECTIVES FOR HUMAN BEINGS AND MULTICULTURALISM UNDER THE REIGN OF NEOLIBERALISM

The capitalistic market logic of neoliberalism and its ensuing problems for human beings in general and for multiculturalism in particular have now been diagnosed on several levels. Therefore it is appropriate to make some concluding remarks to assess the future perspectives for multicultural human beings under the reign of global capitalism – in particular in relation to overcoming the problems described.

In order to identify solutions the attention can advantageously be directed towards the many changes imposed by neoliberalism. There lie a number of potentialities which point to a constructive future.

One of the characteristics of contemporary neoliberalism is the transition to immaterial work (i.e. ideas, slogans, texts, services, feelings, knowledge and experiences). This transition contains the possibility to abolish the logic of scarcity. This means that the principle of "bellum omnium contra omnes" rooted in the logic of scarcity no longer (if ever) is adequate to describe the economic system. Immaterial work is infinitely reproducible and someone's use of something does not negate another person's use of that same something (Hardt & Negri, 2004: 310f). Because of this new characteristic neoliberal forces are struggling to update the concept of private property so vital for its survival in order to be able to once again enclose the commons. However, it could seem that this is a losing battle as immaterial work is extremely hard to control, among other things because time and space are no longer controllable factors.

At the same time human behavior as an economic asset also contains a possible way out of the power and control mechanisms of neoliberalism. The reason is that human behavior is irreversible in every situation; therefore, the economic profitability of neoliberalism is dependent on its ability to school and control people. The question is whether this effort will be successful or if the human existence will continue to generate and spark resistance and evasion because the existence contains so many dimensions that cannot be incorporated in the logic of neoliberalism.

In other words it is highly doubtful if neoliberalism can contain humanity in all its diversity – multiculturalism included – and thus room for other paths is opened. One might say that something is left out in the process of adapting humanity to neoliberalism. Moreover, the introduction of a new notion of the human being can contribute to enhance the possibilities of overcoming neoliberalism as well as minimize shrill nationalism and religious fundamentalism which are both causing insecurity and instability in the world – not least because of the built-in "either/or" logic in such notions.

In order to promote this development the existence and development of critical thinking must be advanced. It is often counted as one of the fundamental principles of democracy that people are free to think and say whatever they want. As a matter of fact this right is consolidated in the constitution of most democratic states. In spite of this there is reason to alert since the uniformity of the media, the attempts of reactionary forces to gain hegemony on moral issues, the re-calvinisation of work and dubious references to national security as legitimization of more control constantly threatens this source of diversity. In this connection the attention might very well be directed towards the hallowed principle of justice of ancient Rome termed "Qui Bono?" (who benefits?). This is an important tool in the effort to unveil camouflaged attempts to realize special interests at the expense of common interests.

It has been argued in this article that neoliberalism is guilty of creating several societal pathologies; some of them founded in internal contradictions – i.e. the contradistinction between the liberal anchorage in the intrinsic value of the individual and the capitalist dictate to make the value of the single human being dependant on its ability to be productive. Thus, there is cause for a certain degree of optimism as neoliberalism does not present us with a consistent and united front. Of course the adaptation capacity of modern capitalism should not be underestimated. Neoliberalism will not disappear if people do not engage in making another world possible. But it can be argued that neoliberal globalization in fact creates better opportunities for doing away with the hegemony of the capitalist system. The reason is that

> ... the relative decline of states' intervention capability and policy-making sover-
> eignty in balancing and neutralizing contradictions reduces the capitalist system's
> "social basis of hegemony". The system's passive revolution capacity is substantially
> weakened due to the lack of an organic global civil society as a consent-generating
> mechanism. (Li & Hersh, 2006: 39)

And with the sociologist Richard Sennett one might say: "... a regime which provides human beings no deep reasons to care about one another cannot long preserve its legitimacy" (Sennet, 1998: 148).

References

Beder, Sharon (2004) *Arbejdsmoral til salg*. Aarhus: Klim.

Bourdieu, Pierre (1991) *Language and Symbolic Power*. Cambridge: Polity Press.

Buber, Martin (2004) *I and Thou*. London: Continuum International Publishing Group Ltd.

Hardt, Michael & Negri, Antonio (2003) *Imperiet*. Copenhagen: Informations forlag.

Hardt, Michael & Negri, Antonio (2004) *Multitude – war and democracy in the age of Empire*. New York: The Penguin Press.

Løgstrup, Knud Ejler (1993) *Solidaritet og kærlighed*. Copenhagen: Gyldendal.

Mathiesen, Thomas (1982) *Makt og Motmakt*. Oslo: Pax.

McNamara, Tim (2001) "Language Assesment as social practice: challenges for research." *Language Testing*, 18(4): 333-349.

Mouritsen, Jan (1997) *Tællelighedens regime*. Copenhagen: Jurist- og Økonomforbundet.

Panikkar, Raimon (1996) *Religion, Philosophy and Culture*. http://them.polylog.org/1/fpr-en. htm

Pedersen, Ole (2006) *Kampen om skolen*. Århus: KVAN.

Rosa, Hartmut (2005) *Beschleunigung – Die Veränderung der Zeitstrukturen in der Moderne*. Frankfurt am Main: Suhrkamp.

Scholte, Jan Aart (1997) "Global Capitalism and the State." *International Affairs*, 73(3): 427-452.

Schor, Juliet B. (1991) *The overworked American: the unexpected decline of leisure*. New York: BasicBooks.

Sennett, Richard (1998) *The Corrosion of Character: The Personal Consequences of Work in the New Capitalism*. New York: W.W. Norton.

Li, Xing & Hersh, Jacques (2006) "Understanding Global Capitalism: Passive Revolution and Double Movement in the Era of Globalization." *American Review of Political Economy*, 4(1/2): 36-55.

Yüksekkaya, Mehmet (2007) *Uskrevne regler på det danske arbejdsmarked*. Copenhagen: People's press.

Chapter Three

Globalization and the Next Economy:
A Theoretical and Critical Review

Li Xing & Woodrow W. Clark

Introduction

The end of the Cold War and the collapse of the socialist bloc, along with the crisis of the Nordic welfare state model[1], allowed two fundamental Western ideological values to triumph as the dominant paradigm for economic development throughout the world: free market economy and liberal democracy. The contemporary combination of these two values has become the prerequisite for interactions between nations expecting political "acceptance" by the international community or seeking economic aid from international financial institutions. This position can be seen repeatedly in a number of international multi-lateral organizations such as the UN, World Bank, WTO and others throughout the early and mid-1990s.

Beside dramatic transformations in political ideologies taking place in the post-Cold War era, even the so-called "market economy" has also undergone qualitative and quantitative changes. Today, it is termed the *Next Economy*, which refers to a computer technology- and internet-based economy not bound by the same physical constraints as the "old economy" (Baker, 2000: 14). Clark and Feinberg (2003) studied The Next Economy in an analysis of the California economy as it began to emerge in the 21st Century (Clark and Feinberg, 2003). This Next California Economy has impacts globally. It implies new ways of doing business where the keys to employment creation, economic growth and higher standards of living are ideas, knowledge, innovations and technologies embedded in services and manufactured products. The rules of the game of The Next California Economy are simple and clear: risk, uncertainty, temptation, challenging, gambling, and constant adaptation (ibid., 2003). However, by the beginning of the new millennium, serious questions were raised about the feasibility and viability of such economic models beyond only a few developed nations (Clark, 2002a). No less than the mass media champion of the free market, *The Economist* (Sept. 13, 1997 and July 24, 1999 in particular and then repeated since then) has questioned some basic tenants in the established manner in which developed nations conduct business: are these nations "internationalized" as in "globalization" so that they produce cheap goods and services? And how do they lead in high technologies and emerging markets?

This questioning even within the establishment of these political or theoretical propositions has lead to some serious theoretical reflections and the need for in-depth critical thinking. The end of the Cold War means that history, in the sense of ideological conflict, has come to an end with the final triumph of the Western ideological value system (Fukuyama, 1992). Recently, the free market and liberal democracy are being promoted by an even more grand vision called "globalization." Some authors, like Thomas Friedman, claim that "The World is Flat" because everything and everyone is dependent on one another. Now however, in the 21st Century a new twist has occurred to once more challenge even these assumptions. The advent of the internet, web sites, and a plethora of "dot. coms" has caused enormous international self-analysis and re-discovery (*The Economist*, July 24, 1999: 21-24 and *Business Week*, March 28, 2000 among others). Ideology is no longer confined to the school books, mass media and politicians. It literally excels over cyber space being challenged, driven and modified daily. What underlies these fundamental changes?

Globalization is one key element which can be easily conceptualized by its impact on three basic arenas of social life: the economy, the politics and culture. In other words, the notion of globalization maintains that a multiplicity of states with unique political cultures (nation-states) is being integrated by a common economic system. The possibility of such a common economic system requires at the same time a common political culture, social system, common language, and common policies. This is also the point of departure on which the arguments of Fukuyama and Huntington are based: The nation-states of the world are moving towards a common political culture of liberal democracy. Liberal democracy has come to mean a commitment to free market capitalism because it is believed that only the free market can guarantee individual freedom and rights that lead to liberal democracy. This is the discourse on which the ideology of free market and liberal democracy is conceptually grounded and the American "New World Order" is politically founded along with the Anglo-Saxon imperative drawn from neo-classical economics (Reinert, 1997 and Clark and Fast, 2008).

The triumph of neo-classical economics, despite persistent criticism, has nowadays reached an elevation as the paradigmatic framework to analyze all spheres of society and human life including international relations. However, concern over it has now become enormous to the global recession that is quickly in 2009 becoming a "depression." At the same time democracy has in recent years been elevated to the position of good government on a global scale embracing all systems and cultures (Helgesen and Li, 2000). The combination of these two is being promoted to become what Heilbroner (1996) calls "science" – the explanation system, or a way to study human beings and societies. But some of the key issues concern what are the elements of the "next economy" and what is the role of government(s) getting each nation-state there?

This chapter critically analyses this ideological paradigm by revealing that it is neither scientific nor universal. Aside from the inherent contradictions within each concept and between them, it is demonstrated that the particular Anglo-Saxon focus on neo-classical economics is extremely narrow (ideological at best) and biased toward only one way of viewing economics, business policies and programs. In this chapter, the focus is primarily placed upon the ideological economic issues which confront all nations including the political dimensions as well as internationalization. For developing, transitional and emerging economies, the reliance on Anglo-Saxon economic ideologies is both disastrous to their national economy, but also an inhibitor to any movement for the creation of a stable liberal democratic society (Reinert, 1998). The current (2009) world economic crisis is proof of that argument.

Understanding "economics"

The economic order of market capitalism is philosophically and ideologically based upon a set of assumptions that focus on the *individual*. As Casson argues, "economists have been too narrow-minded in the way that they have sought to apply their analytical principles. Economists have become prematurely attached to a very materialistic view of human motivation" (1996: 1152). The results , following the neo-classical paradigm of Adam Smith, are a view of the world whereby individuals need to accumulate wealth, much as nations need to do as well. Reinert (1998) noted, however, that this particular approach was unique to Anglo-Saxon philosophical traditions and was not common among other European or developed countries, let alone, developing or emerging economics.

The conventional market economic ideology argues that economics should be: 1) the dominant institution in modern society; 2) a sustained economic growth is necessary to provide jobs and to provide the resources to clean up the environment; 3) the steady increase in productivity is necessary for continued gains in standards of living; 4) all technological advances and competition are essential for progress; and 5) a "free" and unregulated markets generally result in the most efficient and socially optimal allocation of resources. All in all, it assumes that all human behaviors are aimed at involving actors who have strong motivation and desire to maximize their utility and profit from the markets. And this assumption is argued to be applicable to all human behaviors including different types of human beings and different cultures (Buckley and Chapman, 1996).

In essence, the system of market capitalism is conceptualized by Marxism and other scholars to be a unique mode of production. Consider the argument that most conventional market economists advocate. The dominant paradigm in economics argues from a deterministic view or theoretical perspective rooted in the Aristotelian philosophical tradition. As outlined by Hume and Locke this paradigm was "scientific" and came to influence contemporary social science to the present day (McNeill and Freiberger, 1993). The dominant social science and economic neo-classical paradigm (e.g. market capitalism) in particular have been under this theoretical perspective for centuries. Economics is "modeled upon the great successes of the natural sciences: they are in this sense, 'positivist'" (Buckley and Chapman, 1996). It is this argument over what is "science" that is the heart of the modernist and post-modernism debate. In a recent book, Clark and Fast (2008) present an opposing case whereby linguistics makes a far better case for a model of economics (see Chomsky, 1988 and 1997).

However, one critical point needs to be made. Few, if any of the scholars, who debate the issue of "scientism", actually get into the details of what is science. The economists simply use terms like mathematics and models and the social scientists back off. Casson (1996) documented this struggle, for example, between the fields of economics and social anthropology. Rarely does either the economists or the social scientist consult or study the natural sciences of today, not as the philosophers pondered on them centuries ago. When doing so, the economists would learn that science is mathematics as a tool and that formalism does not mean rigid formulas run on computers (Lakoff, 1988). Clark and Fast (2008) explore this basic issue in great detail in their new book, "Qualitative Economics: toward a science of economics" which explores the philosophical and practical aspects of economics in such a way as to make it into a more scientific discipline. Linguistics, as a proven science for language over the last 50 years, provides a perfect model for creating a science of economics.

In essence, the social scientist research argument for being scientific traditionally points to statistical and quantitative theories and methods.

Either a new definition must be given to science or another term use to describe the work of social scientists. Science, for one thing, is far more than the gathering of statistics. Science means that an activity, phenomena or event can be "described", "explained", and "predicted" (see various works listed below by Chomsky in linguistics; and Lakoff, 1988). While chemists and physicists will use control and experimental groups (the favorite methodology of social scientists), they will do so to check theories, results and provide predictable or verifiable numerical data. The primary mode of hypothesis generation is through observation and recording every day data. In economics, data can be quantified, described and explained, but rarely predicted. In fact, when the social science fields are confronted with that fact, they will use probabilities and percentage of outcomes rather than have any degree of certainty. Besides that, a fact, from social science perspective, can be interpreted in different ways.

So what then is economics? The author and philosopher C.P. Snow raised this question many times several decades ago when he noted that science is really an "art." This observation is certainly true of the social sciences. Snow extended that observation to all scientific fields, including medicine. In the end, the issue is that "unlike physics, economics yields no natural laws or universal constants. That is what makes decisive falsification in economics so difficult. And that is why, with or without experiments, economics is not and never can be a proper science." (*The Economist*, May 8, 1999: 84) However, consider other academic fields that do meet scientific criteria of description, understanding, explanation, and predication.

Within the social sciences over the past few decades, the only field that qualifies as a science is "linguistics." As Chomsky notes, "The beginnings of science is the recognition that the simplest phenomena of ordinary life raise quite serious problems" (1988: 43). If economics is to get beyond the ideological tautology that it now finds itself, it must adhere to being scientific rather than biased to one paradigm or another. There are other newer approaches to logic and mathematics which could assist economics, as McNeill and Freiberger point out:

> In economics the mathematical and linguistic realms stand quite apart. Since economics is money and money is numerical, math brings powerful tools to the field. Yet the precision of math leads to overly crisp estimates and idealized models that seem to describe a society of robots. Hence, economics also employs verbal concepts like recession. Language handles real-life questions better and treats details more subtly, but it also narrows the scope of models and shortens chains of reasoning. (1993: 96)

In other words, modern linguistics, with the seminal work Chomsky, is the exception in the social sciences. It may hold some significant keys to a new paradigm and a different approach to economics. Elsewhere (Clark and Sorensen, 1994; and Clark, 1997) has explored how Chomsky's transformational linguistic theories (generative grammar)[2] might be applied to business economics. At this point, the issue is to create a scientific field of economics that is devoid of ideology, biases, and hyperbole. Economics can be a dynamic and changing field and that is basically the study of human and group interaction. Within the field of sociology, an interactionist paradigm has been explored thoroughly by Mead and Blumer as "symbolic interactionism" (Mead, 1962; and Blumer, 1968, respectively).

THE MYTH OF THE FREE MARKET

The free market is the pillar of the capitalist economic order. Buckley and Chapman (1996) provide a short but cogent outline of the economic theory as it centers primarily around the neo-classical or conventional economic paradigm today. While most economists would not argue that the free market is an ideology, it is clear that its focus on the individual, materialism, and wealth are "culturally biased" if not narrow views of economics. Indeed, the free market has roots shaped by particular cultural and religious norms with values that in return promote particular forms of human interactions and social relations; and the outcome of free market interactions is always the empowerment and inclusion of some, while the marginalization and exclusion of others creating political and social contradictions and inequalities Current discussions in international trade over the importance and role of "intellectual property rights" is a very pronounced and demonstrable indicator of this ideological bias.

Following the dominant neo-classical paradigm, the free market is the central category and the core of capitalist economics. Blaug claims that, "The history of economic thought ... is nothing but the history of our efforts to understand the workings of an economy based on market trans-actions" (1985: 6). However, the free market is concerned exclusively with capitalism both as a mechanism of exchange and allocation as a regulator of human and social relations. The history of market economics is not a neutral and value-free genesis. Rather, they have cultural and philosophi-cal roots that are embedded with peculiar political power relations due to historical happenstance and dominance of one paradigm over another.

Consider the neo-classical paradigm in economics again. "Any seri-ous social science or theory of social change must be founded on some concept of human nature. A theorist of classical liberalism such as Adam Smith begins by affirming that human nature is defined by a propensity to truck and barter, to exchange goods: that assumption accords very well with the social order he defends" (Chomsky, 1988: 70). Furthermore, "If you accept that premise (Adam Smith's which is hardly credible), it turns out that human nature conforms to an idealized early capitalist society, without monopoly, without state intervention, and without social control of production" (ibid., 70).

A pure concept of market exchange can hardly exist if it is based on the assumption that the market operates free of any political, cultural and socio-organizational constraints. Yet this is exactly the claim of con-temporary "transactional costs economists" (Williamson, 1975, 1993, and 1996) built upon Coase's earlier observations about the firm (Coase, 1937). Otherwise, the market exchange as an abstract concept could only make sense if a transaction took place between many actors who are unaf-fected by any kind of established social, political and cultural relations. Neoclassical economics regards the free market as being separate from and autonomous of social, political and cultural specificity.

Theoretically, the market mechanism, where exchanges of goods and services are motivated by profit, can only operate adequately when business people follow certain behavioral norms. Among economists, there is little dispute about the logic, measurement tools and mathematical formulas of such deterministic market mechanism. However, there is a fundamental disagreement about whether the market mechanism is based upon "human nature" or "learned" behavior. Neoclassical economists believe the response to the market mechanism is an inherent part of human nature in search for profits. They fail to understand that business activities and economic accumulation processes are influenced by socio-cultural factors, which lead to various forms of capitalism, such as the East Asian "crony capitalism" in general and the "Chinese capitalism" in particular with its peculiar "Chinese characteristics." In other words, they fail to understand that the business situations and everyday life of the firm comprise the economic phenomenon worthy of comprehension.

In reality, what the free market does is not limited to its economic function in allocating resources and distributing income. To a large extent, the free market shapes certain forms of culture; cultivates or impedes forms of human interactions and social relations; and supports a defined structure of power. The free market is as much a political and cultural institution as it is economic. Economics must be expanded to include the effects of markets on both the structure of power and the process of human development. In order to do this, an entirely non-political and non-culture specific approach to economics must be taken, one that recognizes the everyday economic realities of a firm and the interactions of people within the firm as well as the general public (Clark and Fast, 2008). Some scholars have advocated a Marxist or socialist approach. However, each of these frameworks bring with them political and ideological trappings that involve idiosyncratic and ethnocentric biases. Instead, we must turn to different basic philosophical approaches to economics other than those traditions of neo-classical and free market ideologies (Clark and Li, 2003).

To say the free market is a cultural institution is to suggest that the way people interact in the market exchange process (i.e. regulating and coordinating their economic behaviors) shapes what kind of people they become because, the Economy with its markets, workplaces and other sites, is a gigantic school. Its rewards encourage the development of particular skills and attitudes while other potentials lay fallow or atrophy. We learn to function in these environments, and in so doing become someone we might not have become in a different setting. In other words, firms and people within them conduct everyday business activities which are constantly changing and forming "new relationships." Business interactions across different socio-cultural and socio-political backgrounds cannot be fully understood and explained by the free market, nor can they be directed by the market's "invisible hand." What the neo-classical text book notions of the free market do is limited to allocation or distribution because the parties to the exchange – their culture, preference, values – are exogenously determined and not influenced by the exchange process itself. The "next relationships" phenomenon in the era of globalization with embedded and constant features of innovation is challenging the fundamental discourses of neoclassical and neo-liberal economic paradigms.

The contemporary free market economy implies not only an exchange institution for production of goods and services, but also an updating or upgrading process from tradition to modernization in which the creation of an ideological conformity between population and corresponding institutions is indispensable. In this sense, what is necessary to create a modern industrial society has less to do with cultural, social and political factors, but more to do with market mechanisms and economic forces? This approach to economics strives to justify itself as being "objectivist" (or "positivist") and not culturally biased through the use of statistics and mathematical models. Accordingly, an economic development approach to economics which is rooted in the everyday business life presupposes a revolutionary transformation in ideology, philosophy, cultural traditions, psychological attitude as well as way of life. Those very elements that possibly cause sufferings and dislocations are turned into the inevitable prerequisite for creating a modern, rational, and industrial society. The grave policy failure of the "Washington Consensus" prescriptions in connection with economic stagnation in Lain America, financial crisis in East Asia, political and economic collapse in the post-socialist transition economies, and continuous underdevelopment in Africa is a perfect example (Li, 2007)! And is evidenced today (2009) in the world wide economic depression.

Contrary to the neo-classical conceptualization of the free market where each individual (or state) is able to act upon his/her own goals, values and objectives without subordination or subjection to any other individual or collective, the realities of the actual market is a political institution that eventually empowers some and marginalizes others. The free market rules out the free exercise of collectives, other groups or individual initiatives: an individual is free to do anything as long as it is through the market exchange. This is one of the reasons that neo-classical economics has a difficult time understanding and explaining entrepreneurship. It simply does not fit the free market ideology despite various attempts to do so.

At the current stage of global capitalism, the market is redefining the concept of "national economy" within the framework of the nation-state. The relative decline of state autonomy is a manifestation of the power of capital – the mobility of transnational firms, financial institutions and powerful individual investors to transfer production to countries or regions where state policies may be more preferential to capital. Into the 21st Century, the market defines the limits of state politics and economists exert unprecedented influence on policy-makers. States no longer have the capacity to act as buffers between domestic and international economic actors. Rather, they have to adjust domestic policies or priorities to respond to the world economy. Consequently, states become "transmission belts" (Cox, 1993) of global economic forces penetrating local borders and markets. The domestic political and institutional spheres face an inherent contradiction. On the one hand, states are the custodians of society that have obligations to fulfill the role of providing social welfare and security and protecting national interests; on the other hand, the indisputable power of capital mobility reduces their capacity to do so. Yet in the end, governments have a "social contract" with their public.

The state must play a role in economic activities, since the consequences impact every citizen (Clark,and Demirag, 2003 and 2005). More about this appears below.

GLOBALIZATION AND "THE NEXT ECONOMY"

The Anglo-Saxon neo-classical paradigm approach to economics fosters and promotes globalization as a key component to business development. For all countries the necessity for integration into the global market system in order to trade, prosper, and grow entails structural differentiation and functional specialization. Trade, for example, as a means of exchange of goods and services is dependent upon laws (Porter, 1990 and Williamson, 1996). This is precisely why developed nations, lead primarily by the USA, insist upon the creation of intellectual property laws, their enforcement, and recrimination (Casson, 1996: 1168). Reinert (1998) criticizes this neo-classic approach to trade and free market because in reality the raw materials producing countries are not embarked upon free trade but act simply as colonial suppliers of goods and services to the developed nations.

In most cases, the globalization process entails that the national labor forces be divided into contract and temporary workers with members of each group receiving differentiated salaries and welfare benefits. Since economic mobility in the hierarchy of the world economy requires higher levels of production and technology, the ruling economic and political leaders in most countries are pushing forward greater vertical linkages to the capitalist market and deepen their internal accumulations through exploitation of surplus labor (Clark and Demirag, 2002). The economic and business leaders therefore hope that the globalization of local economies to the world market could reinforce their own position and promote internal economic expansion. Rapid industrialization with in the country, in their view, hence attracts foreign direct investment by providing "favorable" labor conditions to multinational companies and by reducing welfare costs, as well as providing tax free zones, and mitigating environmental regulations.

Consequently, the credibility of any government has come to rest on its economic performance and its relations with the international capital markets. Some scholars have argued that it is exactly this problematic relationship which lay at the heart of the Southeast Asian economic crisis in the late 1990s. Others are now arguing that it lays as the root cause today (2009) of the economic collapse in the USA and now globally. The tendency toward globalized economic systems in developing nations makes them politically vulnerable to the setbacks of in their own domestic economy and predicates the further breakdown of the international financial markets. Many government officials thus realize that the only way to stay in power is to promote global economic growth and expansion by all means, even by political authoritarianism through harsh labor exploitation. In other words, the neo-classical globalized market is closely connected with political legitimacy and internal power struggles.

Now in the new Millennium, the free market is seen as responding far more rapidly to subtle changes in both people's choices and social values than ever before. The latest economic concept heralded as "The New Economy" (*The Economist*, July 24, 1999 among other sources) is not fully understood. In fact, Clark (2003 and Clark and Feinberg, 2003) notes that the best approach is to label the phenomenon, "The Next Economy" because it challenges most of the basic economic assumptions that underlie neo-classical economics (Clark and Jensen, 2001). Arguments are purported that undermine, for example, Europe's so-called "social or welfare" states, especially in Scandinavia, as not being competitive in The New Economy (The Economist, Aug. 23, 1997: 37-39). The problem, according to many editors and some politicians is that governments are "encouraging people to work less (which) is a bad way to create growth" (*Newsweek*, Dec. 27, 1999: 116). The basic economics question is "who says so?" In fact, a strong argument could be made that what has encouraged The Next Economy in America is exactly that free time for workers who in turn spend money but more importantly develop new business ventures. To suggest the opposite is not supported by facts. Yet this is exactly what was done by the Republican Party in the USA, before the

American election of Obama, a Democrat to be President, and continues with the current debate on stimulus packages and incentives to reverse the Republican caused depression.

The Anglo-Saxon logic of organizing economic activities supposes to be entirely based on competition and "market forces", as Porter (1980 and 1990) has clearly demonstrated in his pervasive influence on political and economic leaders during the Regan and Bush eras in the USA. However, in retrospect both the English and American historical examples showed the opposite, since protected trade and competition demonstrate. As List sharply observed:

> Had they (England) sanctioned the free importation into England of India cotton and silk goods, the English cotton and silk manufactories must of necessity soon come to a stand. India had not only the advantage of cheaper labour and raw material, but also the experience, the skill, and the practice of centuries. These effect of these advantages could not fail to tell under a system of free competition.... Accordingly, England prohibited the import of the goods dealt in by her own factories, the Indian cotton and silk fabrics. (1885: 42-43)

There lacks no evidence[3] that it was protectionism rather than the free market that made the United States the richest and most powerful country in the world:

> In Latin America, Egypt, South Asia, and elsewhere, development was to be "complementary," not "competitive." ... Marshall Plan aid was tied to purchase of U.S. agricultural products, part of the reason why the U.S. share in world trade in grains increased from less than 10 percent before the war to more than half by 1950, ... U.S. Food for Peace aid was also used both to subsidize U.S. agribusiness and shipping and to undercut foreign producers, among other measures to prevent independent development. (Chomsky, 1997b)

Theoretically and logically, the owners of the means of production and their financial capital have to compete with each other in the market in order to get a larger share of the overall profits produced. When competition is driven for profits, it does not necessarily mean that actors in the market like to behave in that way. Nor are the same actors addicted to an endless process of wealth accumulation, as the neo-classical economists argue. Rather, what is seen in reality is that when competition becomes systematic, "the interaction of class and competitiveness create not just an economic system but a social system: what happens in the kind of economy tends to dominate every aspect of our lives" (Hargrove, 1995: 2).

The paradox facing most nations and states, especially developing countries, is that on the one hand, they are under pressure to cut spending for the sake of competition, while on the other hand, they have to provide the necessary ingredients for competitiveness, such as infrastructure, education, job training research and development policies. The classical economic assumptions of comparative or competitive advantage, mutual benefit and equilibrium are becoming increasingly outdated. Casson (1996) makes an interesting series of arguments in outlining the need for economist to have equilibrium. As he puts it, "The (economics profession) initial position is therefore of no consequence for the final position that is attained. History, therefore, does not matter under these assumptions: today's equilibrium is explained entirely by today's circumstances, and the state of the system yesterday is quite irrelevant" (Casson, 1996: 1159). To do otherwise forces the economic analysis of business "recursive" or a nightmare for any economist since the amount of data is never-ending (ibid., 1159). Hence the logic and nature of market competition eventually leads to limited information flow by the privileged and inevitably create a monopoly to the exclusion of new enterprises not sanctioned or controlled.

The globalization of capitalism in the name of The New Economy is maintained not only through competition but also through the constant reproduction of new commodities and through innovations and revolutions in modern technology controlled by those same nations and corporations. Those exceptionally skilled in advanced engineering and computer technologies are supposed to be rewarded with higher levels of income than those less skilled. As Greenspan claims, "So long as material well being holds a high priority in a nation's value system, the persistence of technological advance should foster this process" (1998: 421).

Rooted in the material process of market competition, the neo-classical ideology of globalized competitiveness has been taken for granted as a fact of life to which the general public acquiesces. The free market been seen as a natural law, a natural force that is beyond questioning and resisting. As J. Rinehart observes, "Historically, the concept of competitiveness has been used to justify business opposition to unions, reduced hours of work, wage increases, paid vacations, health and safety regulations, anti-pollution laws, and so on" (1995: 14). Nowadays, competitiveness is used to transform democracy and remove from the agenda of government tasks which are defined as barriers to business competitiveness, such as income and wealth distribution, business restrictions, laws on taxation and protection of union activities.

THE NEXT ECONOMY AND THE OLD "SOCIAL CONTRACT"?

Contrary to the neo-classical argument that the free market system is the most effective means of reducing poverty, it is actually the globalization of this system that is pushing forward technological revolution, financial and trade liberalization, environmental pollution and degradation, welfare downsizing, corporation restructuring, production relocation, free movement of cheap labor and other consequences. Any sub-set of these economic conditions rests as the roots to permanently impairing and hurting economies in Eastern Europe, East Asia and Latin America, not to mention Africa,

The collapse of the financial markets in East Asia 1997 and globally in 2008-2009, has caused dramatic decline of living standards of millions. For example, mis-directed privatization policies and forced bankruptcy of hundreds of state enterprises in China, caused millions of workers to be laid off in the 1990s and now again in 2009. At the same time, the Chinese state is distancing itself from spending in welfare and social programs. It is unofficially confirmed that the rich-poor gap in China has already surpassed that of the United States (Clark, 2006). Now, the current 2008-2009 global financial crisis is pushing the Chinese government to restructure China's traditional export-based economy by boosting its domestic market demand and by investing on social welfare and human security.

Even so, the free market is viewed by political and economic leaders as the most efficient way to regulate society. It is increasingly becoming the societal ideology, and at the same time economic growth is growing to become a standard way of viewing social development. As a result, the three market elements – supply, demand and price – become not just exchange utilities, but are embedded with political and socio-cultural implications. In other words, market relations and social relations are implicitly becoming the two sides of one coin. Accordingly, social relations have to be transformed or adjusted to aim at creating new ways of thinking in conformity with the rules and values of the market.

Seen from the above perspectives, the current globalization of the free market system can also be described as a new age of "imperialism" (Wood, 1999). When developing countries have to integrate their economies with global capitalism based on free market parameters: free prices, the removal of subsidies, the opening up of developing, transitional and emerging economies to international trade, freely convertible currencies, privatization of the state-owned companies, absorbing foreign investment, closing inefficient enterprises and laying off redundant workers, these countries are actually playing the market rules set up by the dominant neo-classical paradigm. In other words, they are entering a trap as only a rule-player not rule-settler, where they will always feel powerless. Without a clear comprehension of the production and understanding of actual everyday business life in developed nations, they will be permanently handicapped.

Understanding neo-classical economics as it actually works and what the alternatives are requires a through understanding of the economic, political, social structure of vertical and horizontal orders. The market represents the vertical order, whereas democracy represents the horizontal order. The fundamental task of the neo-classical political order must not only protect its economic order through laws and regulations but also facilitate all mechanisms in which the market can fully develop, expand and flourish. In other words, the neo-classical political order must assist the economic order on which the continued hegemony of the dominant class is based. To lose the economic order is to lose the reproduction of the material basis on which the dominant class will rely to sustain its hegemony.

Often advanced as part of the Anglo-Saxon neo-classical economic paradigm, liberal democracy encompasses the notion of the "social contract", i.e. a contract between the state and its citizens that binds the two sides together in a collective society. The basic concept of the social contract developed by Locke and Hume centuries ago connotes an agreement that defines authority and obligations. Legitimate authority is created when individuals give consent for the initiation of the agreement. As Lundvall (1992) notes, this is particularly true today when knowledge and learning are considered an important part of national innovation programs and systems.

There is a clear problem in the dawn of the 21st Century with the parallel between the firm and the state, since in both cases there is an absence of a theory of the firm in modern economic theory and an absence of the theory of the State. "Both firms and states are institutions which are brought to life by the kind of systemic synergies (e.g. Next form of social contract) which are excluded in neo-classical theory through the assumptions of full divisibility of resources, of perfect information, perfect competition, and of the absence of increasing returns" (Rienert, 1997: 14).

In other words, citizens concede certain individual freedoms and accept certain obligations in exchange for the provision of certain goods and services provided to them by the state that they would have difficulty attaining as individuals and through other mechanisms, especially infrastructures that serve everyone in a community or region or nation (Clark, 2003). Examples are highways, education, public health and welfare systems, waste treatment, and throughout most of the 20th Century, certain industries dedicated to the public good such as power, electricity and water. Extensions of the social contract have been applied to areas that needed to be regulated since much of the financial support and contracts were government driven, such as telecommunications, airlines, and defense (military weapons).

In the current era of market-dominated economics, the notion of social contract as citizen-state interactions has undergone enormous challenges and tremendous transformations, namely that the consent and consensus involving obligations of both citizens and government and accountability-control mechanisms are increasingly being marketized. In other words, the agreements embodied in the social contract is being maintained and relegated through market-based mechanisms. This change can be seen in the state policies of "privatization" or "de-regulation" of certain formerly owned and monitored state monopolies such as energy (Clark, 2003).

Although the market mechanism as an alternative regulative method has long existed, it has a strong tendency to break contract forcing governments to "contract-out" their obligations in order to respond to competition, productivity and efficiency because, the market notoriously tends to universalize itself. It does not easily coexist with institutions that operate according to principles antithetical to itself: schools and universities, newspapers and magazines, charities, families. Sooner or later the market, under these state "reforms" or policies, is expected to absorb them all. It puts an almost irresistible pressure on every activity to justify itself in the only terms the neo-classical economist recognizes: to become business-like.

For example, in some nations and states like Denmark, Sweden and California, the governments are beginning to award private firms business contracts to manage welfare or public services which used to belong to the responsibilities of the governments, and universities are beginning to be governed by a management board where the majorities of members are from the business sectors (Clark, 2003 and 2006). In the United Kingdom, higher education has all but turned over to being "business-like." Drastically reduced funding from government has turned British education from one "seeking knowledge" to one "seeking money" in order to support itself.

As a result of the marketization of the social contract, the "social" part of the contract is becoming less universal but selective. Hence political participation is becoming less inclusive but more exclusive. Thus, the concept of citizenship as a means of political empowerment is changed to one of economic empowerment. This implies the fundamental transformation of the social contract which emphasizes social and political rights.

Furthermore, the neo-classical economic discourse that regards citizens as both consumers and customers threatens to transform the traditional conceptualization of the social contract into a social subcontract and, thus fundamentally changing the relationship between citizens and state and the political foundation of government. In fact, in many states today, documents and programs are described as such. The citizen is referred to as "customer." And the results of government are seen as being either profitable or not. As a result, democracy in the form of accountability mechanisms regulating citizen-government relationship has been permanently altered. Under the non-market-centered social contract people could use direct political mechanisms to hold the government apparatus accountable. But under the market-dominated social contract, the market is ideologically defined not only as a neutral place (institution) for allocation of goods, resources and services, but also as the most efficient mechanism to regulate society and human relations. As we have seen this is questionable and dangerous to any economy and its people.

CONCLUSION

The neo-classical economic paradigm of the free market tends to make people forget the real social aspects of human activities: share common needs (not individual preference), cooperation between divisions, and establish relationships between the owner and the owned. When neo-classical economics addresses liberal democracy, it means the capitalist free market system only. Free is mainly freedom for business and corpora-tion to operate as they chose. Individual and social rights are narrowly defined within the framework of politics. The crucial question is whether liberal democracy can really democratize the key elements within the neo-classical economic system, such as capital, means of production, wealth distribution, etc (Li, 2001).

George Soros, one of the world's biggest financial capitalists, openly acknowledges that the origin of the recent world financial crisis is to be found in the global capitalist system itself, namely in the mechanism that defines the essence of a globalized capitalist system: the free, competitive capital markets (Soros, 1998 and 2000). Furthermore, he contends as well that the ideology of global capitalism as manifested by The Next Economy faces a historical challenge that could produce a strong backlash against market capitalism, particularly in the developing world. And he should know as his own heavy financial involvement in Hungary and Russia, among other countries, has clearly demonstrated that neo-classical eco-nomics does not work universally, if at all.

Furthermore, since market power has strong tendencies to define po-litical power, liberal democracy can hardly become a governing principle in international institutions and inter-state relations. Not only Western bureaucracies themselves are organized on the basis of strict hierarchies, but also international multi-lateral organizations like IMF and the World Bank. The United Nations, especially, was established and maintained based on oligarchic structures where important decisions are made by major economic powers, since they alone hold veto power in the UN Security Council. The democratic principle of "one citizen – one vote" can barely be implemented when the interests of the state economic titans are challenged. Nor can "one state – one vote" be realized when the "na-tional interests" of developed countries' economic interests and powers are threatened.

If the global economic system and policies are not changed, the results for developing, transitional and emerging nations will be catastrophic. Neo-classical economics and its version of liberal democracy in the end will cost more in terms of health, lives, environment and even businesses. The entire world does not work according to the narrowly defined neo-classical economic propositions and theories. Nor should it.

NOTES

1   The neo-classical globalization has had a special impact on welfare states in general and Northern European welfare states in particular because their high level of social security taxes and public spending were seen to cause low competitiveness and high unemployment. Governments in these countries, such as Denmark and Sweden, responded to the wide-ranging pressures by distancing themselves from Keynesianism through gradual withdrawal from the responsibilities of welfare provision and by adopting neo-classical economic measures (decentralization, marketization and privatization) in order to become competitive (See Clark and Jensen, 2003).

2   Transformational Grammar argues that there are meanings attached to words and expression in any language. In order to understand (communicate) people have animate understanding of syntax (language structure) and must then understand words that linked together to provide a grammatical text. This is done through data collected at the surface structure (language usage) and the deep structure (the meanings for words in sentence). In a parallel analytical framework, everyday business life (surface structure) can be understood by getting at the meanings (deep structure) that inform and provide meaning to business situations and activities. The task of economics is to understood that transformational "rules" that provide the explanation between the deep and surface structures of business situation.

3   Chomsky (1997), among other scholars, has some concrete examples of the US protectionism: The virtual destruction of Colombia's wheat growing by such means is one of the factors in the growth of the drug industry; Kenya's textile industry collapsed in 1994 when the Clinton administration imposed a quota, barring the path to development that has been followed by every industrial country; in December 1996 Washington barred exports of tomatoes from Mexico in violation of NAFTA and WTO rules, which was at a cost to Mexican producers of close to $1 billion annually; steep tariffs on Japan supercomputers aimed at protecting US high-tech industry, etc..

REFERENCES

Baker, Dean (2000) "The New Economy." *Dollars and Sense*, March/April 2000: 14-17.

Blaug, Mark (1985) *Economic Theory in Retrospect*. Cambridge: Cambridge University Press.

Blumer, Herbert (1968) *Symbolic Interaction – perspective and method*. Englewood Cliffs, N.J.: Prentice-Hall.

Buckley, Peter J. and Chapman, Malcolm (1996) "Economics and Social Anthropology – Reconciling Differences." *Human Relations*, 49(9): 1124-1150.

Business Week (2000) The New Economy: Europe's Response, 28 March 2000. Special Section.

Casson, Mark (1996) "Economics and Anthropology -- Reluctant Partners." *Human Relations*, 49(9):1151-1180.

Chomsky, Noam (1998) *Free Market Fantasies: capitalism in the real world*. San Francisco: AK Press, CD Audio.

Chomsky, Noam (1997) "Market Democracy in a Neoliberal Order: Doctrines and Reality." *Z-Magazine* (electronic version), November.

Chomsky, Noam (1988) *Language and Problems of Knowledge*. Boston: MIT Press.

Clark, Woodrow W. and Fast, Micheal (2008) *Qualitative Economics: toward a science of Business-Economics*. UK: Coxmoor Press.

Clark, Woodrow W. (2006) "Partnerships in Creating Agile Sustainable Development Communities." *Journal of Clean Production*, (15): 294-302.

Clark, Woodrow W. (2006) "China: Social Capitalism in Renewable Energy Generations", Conference paper, Western Economic Association Conference, July.

Clark, Woodrow W. and Istemi Demirag (2006) "US Financial Regulatory Change: the case of the California Energy Crisis." Special Issue, *Journal of Banking Regulation*, 17(□): 75-93.

Clark, Woodrow W. and Istemi Demirag (2005) "Regulatory Economic Considerations of Corporate Governance." *International Journal of Banking*, Special Issue on Corporate Governance, Fall.

Clark, Woodrow W. (2003) "California Energy Challenge: solutions for the future. Energy Pulse: Insight, Analysis and Commentary on the Global Power Industry." January, available at http://www.energypulse.net

Clark, Woodrow W. and Demirag, Istemi (2002) "Enron: the failure of corporate governance." *Journal of Corporate Citizenship*, 8: 105-122.

Clark, Woodrow W. and Li, Xing (2003) "Social Capitalism: transfer of technology for developing nations." *International Journal of Technology Transfer*, 3(1): 1-11.

Clark, Woodrow W. and Feinberg, Todd (2003) "California's Next Economy, Sacramento, CA: Governor's Office of Planning and Research." Local Government Commission web site at http://www.lgc.org: 1-56.

Clark, Woodrow W. and Jenssen, J. Dan (2003) "The Role of Government in Privatization: An Economic Model for Denmark." *International Journal of Technology Management*, 21(5/6):540-555.

Clark, Woodrow W. (2002) "Innovation and Capitalisation." *International Journal of Technology Management*, 24(4): 391-418.

Coase, Ronald H. (1937) "The Nature of the Firm." *Economica*, 4: 386-405.

Cox, Robert W. (1993) "Structural issues of global governance: implications for Europe", in: Stephen Gill, (ed.) *Gramsci, Historical Materialism and International Relations*. Cambridge: Cambridge University Press.

Economics Focus (1999) "News from the Lab." *The Economist*, May 8: 96.

Fukuyama, Francis (1992) *The End of History and the Last Man*. London: Hamish Hamilton.

Greenspan, Alan (1998) "Market Capitalism", *Vital Speeches of the Day*, 64(14): 418-421.

Hargrove, Basil (1995) The Future of Capitalism: Does Capitalism Represent the Best Humanity Can Ever Hope to Achieve? *Monthly Review*, 46(8):1-10.

Hegesen, Geir and Li, Xing (2000) "Good Governance: Democracy or Minzhu: The East Asian Debate", in: Hans Antlöv and Tal-Wing Ngo (eds) *The Cultural Construction of Politics in Asia*, Richmond: Curzon Press.

Heilbroner, Robert (1996) "The Embarrassment of Economics." *Challenge*, 39(6): 46-49.

Holland, John H. (1992) *Adaptation in Natural and Artificial Systems*. Cambridge, MA: The MIT Press.

Lakoff, George (1988) *Women, Fire, and Dangerous Things: what categories reveal about the mind*. Chicago: University of Chicago Press.

Li, Xing (2007) "Paradigm Shift: From 'Washington Consensus' to 'Beijing Consensus'", in Kwesi K. Prah (ed.) *Afro-Chinese Relations, Past, Present and Future*. Cape Town: The Centre for Advanced Studies of African Society (CASAS)

Li, Xing (2001) "The Market-Democracy Conundrum." *Journal of Political Ideologies*, 6(1): 75-94

Li, Xing and Hersh, Jacques. (2004) "The Genesis of Capitalism: The Nexus between 'Politics in Command' and Social Engineering." *American Review of Political Economy*, 2(2): 100-144.

Li, Xing and Hersh, Jacques (2002) "Understanding Capitalism: Crises and Passive Revolutions." *Competition & Change: the Journal of Global Business and Political Economy*, 6(2): 193-212.

List, Friedrich (1885) *The National System of Political Economy*. London: Longmans.

Lundvall, Bengt-Åke (ed.) (1992) *National Systems of Innovation: Towards a Theory of Innovation and Interactive Learning*. London: Pinter Publishers.

Mead, George H. (1962) [1934] *Mind, Self, & Society – from the standpoint of a Social Behaviorist*. Three Volumes. Chicago: The University of Chicago Press.

McNeill, Daniel and Freiberger, Paul (1993) *Fuzzy Logic: the discovery of a revolutionary computer technology-- and how it is changing our world*. New York: Simon & Schuster.

Newsweek, Editorial (1999) "In Europe, the welfare state dies hard." December 27: 116.

Porter, Michael E. (1980) *Competitive Strategy: Techniques for Analyzing Industries and Competitors*. New York: Free Press.

Porter, Michael E. (1990) *The Competitive Advantage of Nations*. New York: Free Press.

Reinert, Erik S. (1997) *The role of the state in economic Growth*. Centre for Development and the Environment. University of Oslo, Norway.

Reinert, Erik S. (1998) "Raw materials in the History of Economic Policy", in Gary Cook (ed.) *The Economics and Politics of International Trade* in *Freedom and Trade*, II: 275-300.

Rinehart, James (1995) "The *ideology of competitiveness*." *Monthly Review*, 47(5):14-23.

Sores, George (2000) *Open Society: Reforming Global Capitalism Reconsidered*. New York: Public Affairs.

Sores, George (1998) *The Crisis of Global Capitalism: Open Society Endangered*. New York: Public Affairs.

The Economist (1999) "The New Economy: Work in progress." July 24: 21-24.

The Economist (1997) "Remodelling Scandinavia: will economic recovery make the nordic countries' famous welfare states look good; only after further reform" (Europe), August 23: 37-39.

The Economist (1997) "Assembling the New economy a new economic paradigm is sweeping America. It could have dangerous consequences" (Globalization and Technology), September 13: 71-73.

Williamson, Oliver E. (1996) *The Mechanisms of Governance*. New York: Oxford University Press.

Williamson, Oliver E. and Sidney, G. Winter (eds.) (1993) *The nature of the firm: origins, evolution, and development*. New York: Oxford University Press.

Williamson, Oliver E. (1975*) Markets and Hierarchies: Analysis and Anti-trust Implications*. New York: The Free Press.

Wood, Ellen M. (1999) "Kosovo and the New imperialism." *Monthly Review*, 51(2):1-9.

CHAPTER FOUR

Investment Climate and Globalization: What's Wrong with the Western Advice?

David Ellerman

INTRODUCTION: INVESTMENT CLIMATE FOR WHOM?

The improvement of "the" investment climate has become a major strategic focus of western advice to developing countries. I will take the World Bank's recommendations to be representative of this advice. However, we might "complicate" the discussion by recognizing that there are tradeoffs between different groups with different capabilities, interests, and assets. Making the investment climate better for one group may well be at the cost of making it worse for another group. Western advisors, e.g., from the World Bank or IMF, tend to ignore these tradeoffs and to implicitly identify with one group (usually external or foreign investors) and then to count an improvement in the investment climate for that group as being an "improvement" *per se*.

What are the other groups whose "investment climate" tends to get ignored? Private enterprise, particularly in difficult environments, is based on commitment to building the enterprise both on the part of the managers and workers. Over the course of time, they have to make a range of commitments or "investments" in people for firm-specific activities where they will not be able to reap the benefits of their sowing if they do not have some stability and longevity in the enterprise. If you don't know if who will be around tomorrow or next week, then you are not going to make the type of effort commitments or firm-specific investments of human capital that are really necessary for success; you will focus your efforts to grab what you can while you can.

INVESTMENT CLIMATE FOR WORKERS

One person's "stability" is another person's "rigidity." Let us take the workers and managers separately. The World Bank tends to see the legislated or organizational sources of employment stability for workers (e.g., limitations on at-will contracts, not to mention trade unions) as "labor market rigidities" to be reduced or eliminated. Indeed, the Bank has not even been able to conceptualize the role of labor-in-the-enterprise or "human resource management" in its sectorial roadmap, only the "labor market"[1] (which automatically directs the intelligence to the matter of "perfecting the labor market"). Thus little or no attention in actual Bank practice (in the trenches, not in the rhetoric) is given either the learnings of the academic literature of the "What do unions do?" tradition (Freeman and Medoff, 1984) or the human relations strategies of building worker commitment to the firm through commitments by the firm to the workers so that the workers put forth their best efforts, i.e., make their largely firm-specific human capital investments in the firm (e.g., Blair 1995).

For instance, Japanese economists have developed a whole theory about how the "barriers to exit" (i.e., neoclassical "rigidities") work to generate organizational commitment:

> The way in which underpayment of wages in the early years of service and the acquisition of firm-specific skills create barriers to exit is obvious. These exit barriers perform several important functions for the firm as an organizational entity. The first is the incentive function whereby the interests of the firm and the interests of the individual are linked. Unable easily to exit, people can only protect their interests by working to ensure that the firm prospers. ... The interlinking of interests means that when crisis looms, efforts are redoubled. The option of leaving the sinking ship is not freely available, either to the crew or the captain. (Kagono and Kobayashi 1994: 94)

This thinking, however, has not made much inroad into neoclassical economic thinking in the Bank. In constantly prodding client countries to improve "labor market flexibility," the Bank is in fact working *against* the investment climate for human capital investment within the firms. Hence one way in which the discussion of investment climate might be complicated is to recognize that certain policies promoting labor market flexibility in the interests of short-term efficiency tend to cut against the human capital investment climate within firms and to promote grab-what-you-can short-termism.

INVESTMENT CLIMATE FOR MANAGERS

Analogous considerations hold for hired managers, except now it is the owners who are the source of uncertainty. The Bank has an almost exclusive focus on the "investment climate" for external financial investors so, from that perspective, it is key to have ownership always "up for grabs" so that those assets are always "transparently" available to the investors with the highest effective demand. Any restriction of the ownership being up for grabs is a barrier, impediment, imperfection, rigidity, and all around negative thing. Thus the top and middle managers also tend to live "hand to mouth" rather than make long-term firm-specific human capital investments since one never knows who the boss will be tomorrow.

It is like a farmer with an at-will rental contract on the land where the land was always "on the market" so the farmer would have little incentive to make non-recoupable investments. Bank staffs are quite capable of understanding this point when reading de Soto's *The Mystery of Capital* (2000). Without stable property rights, asset users will avoid non-recoupable investments. But this point tends to be forgotten when the Bank's own Capital Market Department is trying to jump-start stock markets all over the world or when voucher privatization was recommended to the transition economies. Managers have problems making long-term commitments to firms in Siberia when they don't know what deals will be made tomorrow by stockbrokers in Moscow.

Here again, it is the Bank's own programs that are discouraging the sort of investment that requires stable mutual commitments where the value of investment is not recoupable other than by staying in the relationship. The conventional wisdom sees such commitments as rigidities and barriers that need to be eliminated to "perfect" the market for corporate ownership and control. The Bank's thinking and much standard economic advice does not recognize the conundrum in the *tradeoff* between the logic of exit and the logic of loyalty and voice (see Hirschman, 1970).

INVESTMENT CLIMATE FOR OWNERS

The same logic plays out for the owner. We can distill this wisdom from the academic scribblings of the defunct economist, John Maynard Keynes. Lord Keynes was much concerned with the adverse effects of the stock exchange on real investment. Investment in productive enterprise is largely irrevocable, and the management of enterprise requires a long term commitment and the application of "intelligence to defeat the forces of time and ignorance of the future..."[2] In short, it is based on the logic of loyalty and voice. But when investment is securitized as a marketable asset on the stock exchange, then it "is as though a farmer, having tapped his barometer after breakfast, could decide to remove his capital from the farming business between 10 and 11 in the morning and reconsider whether he should return to it later in the week" (Keynes 1936: 151). The stock exchange panders to the "fetish of liquidity" and thus continually undermines the bonds of long-term commitment that are so important to problem-solving and productive enterprise.

In addition to this continual erosive effect, the stock exchange also absorbs otherwise productive capital in the function of speculation – which Keynes defined as "the activity of forecasting the psychology of the market" (158). Keynes saw no problem when speculation was but a bubble on the stream of enterprise, but it was quite another matter "when enterprise becomes a bubble on a whirlpool of speculation. When the capital development of a country becomes a by-product of the activities of a casino, the job is likely to be ill-done" (159).

Today, Keynes' "stock exchange" must be updated to the global market for bonds, stocks, and currencies. The dangers to investment in enterprise that Keynes highlighted during his day are even greater in our own. Yet Keynes recognized that there is no simple answer in making investment illiquid as "this might seriously impede new investment...." Few will enter if the door locks behind them. "This is the dilemma" (160).

It is fine for Bank managers to "promote the investment climate," but do they really face up to this "dilemma" – the tradeoff between commitment and liquidity? Improving the investment climate for financial investors on the stock market may undermine the sort of long-term investment in productive enterprise by non-speculative owner-managers – particularly in complex and volatile environments.

Which of these investment climates is most important for economic development? The answer seems clear, and yet the Bank emphasized jump-starting stock market development with such policies as voucher privatization in the transition economies. The Czech Republic threw their companies onto the stock market with voucher privatization to maximize the opportunities for "investors" and the Bank and other aid agencies such as USAID promoted that policy all over the transition economies (e.g., Russia and the FSU as a whole).

Instead of belatedly learning something about these matters, the Bank even sponsored a voucher privatization program in the war-destroyed economy of Bosnia in the late 90s. Voucher investment funds that profited handsomely from the programs in other parts of East Europe then acted as vulture funds swooping into Bosnia to buy vouchers at about 6 cents on the dollar to then get control of Bosnian assets. After they have "tunneled" out the value and stripped the assets, there will be an even poorer investment climate in that country. Here again, the Bank operates to worsen the domestic investment climate, not to improve it – unless one speaks of the investment climate for vulture funds as "foreign investors."

INVESTMENT CLIMATE FOR DOMESTIC DIRECT INVESTMENT

There are several ways in which Bank/Fund policies have worked against domestic direct investment.

High Interest Rate Policies

One way was emphasized by Joseph Stiglitz in the way the IMF policies, particularly in crisis situations, tend to push up interest rates to attract foreign capital with the predictable effect of choking off domestic investment and increasing bankruptcies.

Over-valued Exchange Rate Policies

Another policy is the pressure for "over-valued" exchange rates. The net effect is that domestic demand is expended on foreign imports. In theory, this could create healthy competition for domestic industry, but where the gap is too large, it tends to bankrupt domestic industry first. The best thing to happen for Russian industry at the end of the 1990's (aside from high oil prices) was the collapse of the Bank's and Fund's "protect the ruble corridor" policies in the Fall of 1998 so that foreign imported products were priced out of the market. The increased domestic demand for Russian manufactured products led to a revival of Russian industry. Thus growth came from the collapse of the Bank's policy framework in favor of the non-Bank framework of *de facto* protectionism and import substitution.

Blackhole Government Bond Markets

Another way in which Bank policies tend to spoil the conditions for domestic direct investment is the promotion of government bond markets. For instance, early in the post-socialist reforms, great symbolic or totemic significance was attached to creating active securities markets in stocks and bonds. When the government's budget were not covered by tax collections (it was often cheaper to "buy" an exemption that to pay taxes), then the primary non-inflationary source of domestic finance was the market for government bonds. The high rates offered on government bonds operated as a financial black hole sucking in funds from banks, firms, individuals, and even foreign speculators. That, in turn, sky-rocketed the interest rates available for loans to SMEs so that loan market was throttled in the crib.

When the Russian market for their high-yield government bonds (GKOs) was booming, it was celebrated as a success for the reforms that included bringing "investment capital" into the country. The common criticism in retrospect is that the market developed into an overheated Ponzi scheme and eventually collapsed. But there is a more basic criticism. Even without the overheating and collapse, the GKO-type markets massively diverted funds away from productive investment, and a similar story played out in other transitional economies with government bond markets not quite as spectacular as the GKO scheme. Those analysts who celebrated the "improvement in investors' confidence" that brought in foot-loose portfolio investors to the GKO market had their eye on the wrong indicators. By diverting funds away from direct productive investment (e.g., the SME loan business), the high-return government bond markets detract from, rather than improve, the real direct investment climate. Have the parts of the World Bank Group that were cheer-leading the growth of the "vibrant Russian securities markets" learned any lessons or changed any policies after this debacle?

Open Capital Account Policies

Another Bank/Fund policy that detracts from domestic direct investment is the promotion of open capital accounts. These opportunities generate capital flight out of Russia and many other post-socialist countries. Great harm is done to domestic investment when government officials do not enforce the country's laws against illegal transfers of capital out to secure and discreet havens in the West. One of the biggest assists that the West can give to investment in these countries is to enact and/or enforce the laws to stop the illegal hemorrhaging of domestic capital from these countries. That, of course, is a second-best policy in the sense that we would all prefer to make the investment climate so attractive that the capital would remain in Russia of its own accord. But after the 90's decade of *de facto* open capital accounts and the yearly exodus in excess of $20 billion, one might consider a second-best policy.

Financial Games versus Production?

Another area where IFI policies have been detrimental to real investment is in the promotion of the financial sector schemes such as the voucher investment funds. I have written elsewhere (1998, 2005) at some length why these funds were non-starters to supply capital or restructuring to troubled companies and why they would end up siphoning or tunneling value out of the companies – as has happened. Government officials all across the map quickly saw "the possibilities" so these Bank policies had "true government ownership." Voucher privatization and its progeny, mandatory second pillar pension "reforms", were not "imposed" on Kazakhstan; the government officials *truly* wanted these "reforms."[3] When the complying government officials finally leave office in these voucherized countries, they tend not to become chemical or electrical engineers in manufacturing companies; they tend to go through the revolving door into the "financial sector" as board members, deal-makers, and the like. The same "motivation" reaches young people. Why go through all the years of study to get become an engineer when very little study and a few connections can get one into the Klondike of "financial engineering" where the real fortunes are being made.[4]

INVESTMENT CLIMATE FOR FOREIGN DIRECT INVESTMENT

I have taken some pains to emphasize that improving the "investment climate" for one group may make it worse off for some other groups. In spite of some nods in the direction of domestic investors, Bankthink (i.e., groupthink within the Bank) tends to interpret "investment climate" in terms of the foreign investors who are supposed to bring capital, technology, and management/marketing know-how. But does Bank think at least understand foreign direct investors?

Buying Shares on the Market versus Private Transactions

One common but persistent fallacy is the idea that foreign investors will want to come into the country through the stock market. This belief is one of the (non-cargo-cult) reasons for all the push in the World Bank Group for stock market development. But once a company is broadly owned on a stock market, why would a well-heeled foreign direct investor want to start buying shares off the market? Share owners would start holding out for higher prices from the deep-pocketed buyer or might even hold onto shares looking forward to large capital gains in the future. In either case, the foreign investor would find broad stock market ownership as an impediment, not a help, to obtaining 100% ownership. The investor would much prefer a clean private transaction for the whole company than the self-frustrating attempt to buy bits and pieces on the open market.

Indeed, some companies in the post-socialist world have deliberately worked with IFI support to do a public offering as a way to fight off being purchased by a foreign company. Once the stocks were scattered to the four winds on the stock market, the foreign company would be discouraged from trying to put all the pieces together again.[5] Here again, my point is not to argue that this was good or bad but to complicate the discourse by highlighting the tradeoff. When the IFIs are promoting the flotation of the better companies, they are at the same time thwarting foreign direct investment in the companies of the most interest to the multinationals.

Share Deals or Asset Deals?

Indeed, most foreign investors would think twice before doing a share deal at all. If the investor really wants 100% ownership, then an asset deal (e.g., part of a greenfield or brownfield investment) might be far cleaner with no complications of hidden liabilities or employment expectations in enterprises that will need some restructuring. For instance, when IKEA bought a furniture company in Romania as a going concern, they made it clear that one of the plants was problematic and that if it was not profitable in one year, they would have to shut it down. The Federal Government was in full agreement and the deal went through. After a year, the plant was not profitable so IKEA announced the closing (while continuing to operate other plants). The next day the local police arrived to notify the IKEA managers that they had violated local laws and would have to leave. The Federal Government said it was a local matter. IKEA ended up negotiating a new agreement and learned a hard lesson about buying a company as a going concern.

Dating Before Marriage?

Another persistent fallacy is the idea that foreign companies will come in and buy a company without having some prior trust-building getting-to-know-you relationship. This might take the form of a trade relationship, subcontracting production agreements, technology licensing agreements, or sales/service representation. And if that is one of the main paths to investment, then the investment climate work should include *the climate for trade relationships as well as production, technology, and sales/service agreements.*

There seems to be considerable implicit resistance in the IFIs to recognizing that companies can acquire export markets, technology, and know-how all without selling equity – as did the Japanese or Koreans.

Whatever the reason, this leads to the under-emphasis in the IFIs on these intermediate forms of involvement which are beneficial in their own right and which may or may not lead to foreign equity investment. A comprehensive program to promote the benefits of "foreign investment" would include the promotion of these forms of foreign involvement. Dating before marriage – involvement before investment.

Transfer Pricing vs. Dividends: Misdirected Corporate Governance Policies

Another area of misdirected "investment-climate"-related policies is in the sphere of protecting minority shareholders. There seems to be the remarkable assumption that majority or controlling shareholders who are trade-related to a company "should" take value out of the company only through dividends to be equally shared with the free-riding and passive "minority shareholders." However, it is quite normal and to be expected for controlling trade-related shareholders to take their value out in a variety of other ways such as transfer pricing and licensing agreements. It is hopeless to try to extend the scope of "corporate governance problems" to somehow control and exclude these hard to monitor or verify business practices.

The problem lies in the minority shareholders who exhibited less than brilliant judgment in investing in a company with a trade-related controlling shareholder without any other safeguards such as mandatory buy-back clauses that would be normal for a minority position in a closely-held company in the West. That would be a foolish investment, and the World Bank Group should not broaden the "corporate governance" agenda to include "protecting" foolish investors.

LOGIC OF EXIT VERSUS THE LOGIC OF VOICE, LOYALTY, AND COMMITMENT

My remarks on the theme of investment climate promotion have focused on complicating the discourse by arguing that there are often tradeoffs between different types of investment. A better investment climate for one group may create a worse one for another group. There is also a theoretical structure common to most of the comments. Neoclassical economics focuses on markets, and (arms-length) markets are driven by the logic of exit. The areas where I argued that the focus on investment climate was one-sided were those areas where the Bank tends to adopt a "Wall Street" view of business. Then "investment" is taken as investment in securities. The logic of markets in general and securities markets in particular is the logic of exit, liquidity, mobility, and flexibility.

There is another logic of voice, loyalty, and commitment that comes more into play *within organizations* that is usually neglected by economists in general and in Bank policy-making in particular. The investment climate tradeoffs come from the cases where investment goes hand in hand with commitment and is *undercut* by the logic of exit, liquidity, mobility, and flexibility.

In the face of decline, there are always two different strategies for renewal: replacement or transformation:

- After a few years when the family car starts to emit strange clunking sounds, one has the choice of replacing it or trying to fix it (transformation).
- Many years ago, there was a cigarette ad about the loyal consumers who would "rather fight than switch" – the other option being "rather switch than fight."
- Albert Hirschman, in his 1970 classic, *Exit, Voice, and Loyalty: Responses to Decline in Firms, Organizations, and States*, developed these two strategies as the logic of exit (replacement, the quintessential logic of the market) and the logic of loyalty, commitment, and voice (transformation, the quintessential logic of stable organizations).

When facing decline, a commitment-based strategy "fights" for renewal by fostering the transformation of the given people and structures. An exit-based strategy sees renewal as coming primarily and initially from the outside through "switching," the replacement of the existing people (or at least the top people) and structures by new ones. Transform the old into the new – or throw out the old (to create a *tabula rasa*) and then import the new; that is the question.

The pure logic of exit applies only to the ideal model of a perfectly competitive market imagined in economics textbooks. And there is no human organization with "No Exit." All real world situations of decline will call for appropriate combinations of transforming the home-grown old into the new (transformation strategy) and replacing the home-grown old with the imported new (replacement strategy).

Here are some of the ways that these two logics play out in different areas.

Area	Logic of Exit ("Rather switch than fight")	Logic of Voice & Commitment ("Rather fight than switch")
Change Strategy	Replace what you have with something better. Replacement.	Change what you have into something better. Transformation.
Response to decline concerning managers	Replace inside managers with new managers from outside to solve problems.	Develop inside managers to solve problems.
Efficiency	Allocative: moving resources to the use with the best return (high mobility)	X-efficiency: getting the best return from resources in the given uses. (low mobility)
Source of change	Exit (since innovation is exogenous, change takes place through entry and exit from the organization). Rather flee than fight. Error leads to replacement from outside. Exchange what you have for something better.	Voice (since innovation is endogenous, needed changes communicated within organiza-tion). Rather fight than flee. Error leads to learning. Change what you have into something better.

Labor mobility	High mobility so changes take place primarily by hiring workers embodying new knowledge.	Low mobility so changes take place primarily by knowledge workers learning new knowledge.
Model of supplier relationships	Competition between standardized producers with feedback through the market.	Cooperation with a small number of suppliers to continuously improve product through non-market feedback.
Relations to suppliers and customers	Auction market contracting based on assumption of mobility and exit leading to greater allocative efficiency	Relational contracting based on assumption of immobility and voice leading to greater X-efficiency
Contractual relationship	Arms-length	Relational
Stability of business ownership	Liquidity of stock market shareholders	Illiquidity of closely-held business
Stability in relationships.	Low trust relationships $\Rightarrow$ highly explicit contracts with competitive arm's length exit-oriented relationships so no need to invest in building trust or loyalty $\Rightarrow$ low trust relationships.	High trust relationships $\Rightarrow$ incomplete relational contracts with voice-oriented relationships requiring investment in building trust and loyalty $\Rightarrow$ high trust relationships.
Style of interpersonal relationships.	Standardized, professionalized behavior as a means of coordinating people. Low interpersonal knowledge associated with high turnover.	Familiarity, intimacy in long-term relationships as means of coordinating people. High interpersonal knowledge associated with low turnover.
Labor training	Responsibility of worker as it increases value on labor market.	Responsibility of company since immobility allows company to benefit.
Job definition	Extensively specified job definition to limit opportunism since there is little commitment.	Job flexibility and low monitoring based on worker commitment to company
Wage determination	Rate for job determined by market.	Rate determined by seniority and assessed merit.
Response to decline concerning workers.	Reduce employment and other direct costs to maintain profits.	Maintain employment, reduce hours, and retrain workers for new product lines.

MARKETS *AND* ORGANIZATIONS: NOT ONLY MARKETS

Consider the application of the logic of exit versus the logic of commitment in an organization. The exit logic looks at an individual as a market participant – even inside an organization.[6] The individual's actions within the organization are evaluated according to how the actions affect the person's market opportunities, e.g., in acquiring more marketable skills, increasing bargaining power, and the like.

In contrast, the logic of commitment looks at the individual as a member of an organization so that a different set of factors come into play such as trust, voice, firm-specific skills, cooperation, voice, and identification with the organization. It is this whole logic of commitment and the conception of an organization other than just a nexus of market contracts that is missing in the vision of conventional neoclassical economics. Thus all the investment climate reasoning concerned with building productive organizations tends to be ignored unless it can be reduced back to market behavior.

Herbert Simon's Vision of the Organizational Economy

One person who spanned the disciplines of economics and organizational theory and who spent a lifetime investigating both markets and organizations was Economics Nobel-laureate Herbert Simon. Economists tend to have a cognitive map of the world (like Saul Steinberg's famous *New Yorker* cover) where markets dominate the landscape except for small market failures (small "lumps in a pail of buttermilk") known as "organizations" off in the distance. Having studied both organizations and markets throughout his career, Simon found that the reality in the advanced economies was almost the opposite. Instead of thick markets connecting small organizational dots, Simon saw a world of organizations with thin markets connecting them. Indeed, he objected to the very phrase "market economy."

> The economies of modern industrialized society can more appropriately be la-
> beled organizational economies than market economies. Thus, even market-driven
> capitalist economies need a theory of organizations as much as they need a theory
> of markets. The attempts of the new institutional economics to explain organi-
> zational behavior solely in terms of agency, asymmetric information, transaction
> costs, opportunism, and other concepts drawn from neo-classical economics ignore
> key organizational mechanisms like authority, identification, and coordination,
> and hence are seriously incomplete. (Simon 1991: 42)

The economic theory of contracts and agency imagines a world where
causal chains are well-defined, where consequences can be imputed, at
least probabilistically, to specific agents, where contracts can be clearly
drafted, where performance criteria can be explicitly specified and they
measure the right variables, and where fulfillment of the criteria or lack
thereof can be objectively verified. It is a world where "complexity,
uncertainty, instability, uniqueness, and value conflicts" (Schön 1983,
14) or, again, "uncertainty, complexity, and value conflict" (Hirschman
and Lindblom 1962) can be somehow controlled or ignored. In such an
imagined world, much of human activity could be carried out under
performance-based contracts.

> But such [performance-based] reward systems are effective only to the extent that
> success can be attributed accurately to individual behaviors. If the indices used
> to measure outcomes are inappropriate, either because they do not measure the
> right variables, or because they do not properly identify individual contributions,
> then reward systems can be grossly inefficient or even counterproductive. (Simon
> 1991: 33)

Simon went on to note that these considerations are not nit-picking; they
cut to the core of the rationale for organizations rather than markets.

> In general, the greater the interdependence among various members of the organi-
> zation, the more difficult it is to measure separate contributions to the achievement

of the organizational goals. But of course, intense interdependence is precisely what makes it advantageous to organize people [i.e., in organizations] instead of depending wholly on market transactions. The measurement difficulties associated with tying rewards to contributions are not superficial, but arise from the very nature and rationale of organization. (Simon 1991: 33)

The Periodic "(Re-)Discovery" of Performance-Based Contracts

One area where these issues are periodically played out is that of output-based or performance-based contracts. From time to time, private sector management "discovers" the idea of paying for performance (not just for time put in), of paying for outputs (not just inputs), and of management by objectives accomplished (not just intentions). It all sounds so obvious and so sensible that one must ask "Why didn't people think of this before?" The answer is that they did. And they discovered that it doesn't work too well – aside from fairly rude forms of labor. In areas of human effort where effort, commitment, and the application of intelligence are important, the carrots and sticks of external motivation are insufficient for sustained performance (see, for example, Chapter 11 on "Inducements" in Stone, 1997). Beyond simple and specific products, the determinants of quality are rarely susceptible to external monitoring.

One area where these issues periodically play out is in education. In the US today, parents and local politicians are "discovering" the idea of paying teachers for performance. One would hope that the substantive goal of school teachers is to awaken and foster a self-starting learning capacity in the students – but that goal is difficult for a third-party to objectively certify. Hence the measurable proxy goal of passing standard tests is used, and then teachers are pushed by educational administrators to fulfill the "performance-based" requirements by drilling students to pass the standard tests. In this way, the shoe-horning of education into the procrustean bed of performance-based contracts would probably do more harm than good to the original substantive goals of education.

What sort of activities can or cannot be farmed out to arms-length market-based private provisioners under performance-based contracts? Even in a country with highly developed markets such as the United States, there is considerable controversy about maximal private provisioning (e.g., public schools, public safety, social welfare services, public health services, prisons, and so forth). It is even more controversial in Europe. When this philosophy is mired in controversy in developed market economies, then it is very difficult to understand how private provisioning with output-based contracts could be done well in the developing countries with their much less developed markets.

Extrinsic and Intrinsic Motivation

But let us assume away the problems of identifying and measuring the relevant variables and let us heroically assume away the "uncertainty, complexity, and value conflict" that afflicts human activities. Could we *then* replace governmental and private organizations with virtual nexuses of performance-based contracts? This brings us to the question of motivation. The economic theory of agency contracts is based on "economic" motivation, the "carrots" of monetary compensation and the "sticks" of contractual penalties or termination of contracts. But this approach to motivation is based only the extrinsic motivation that can be used by the "principal" to control the behavior of the "agent." Yet it seems that extrinsic motivation works as a long-term motivator for only a rather narrow band of rudimentary activities ("ditch-digging" and piecework are classic examples). More often the intrinsic motivators of craftsmanship, workmanship, professionalism, pride, self-esteem, and a sense of vocation, calling, and organizational identification are prominent, and the extrinsic motivators of "carrots and sticks" – while still important–are more in the motivational background.

Piece rates and pay-for-performance schemes are examples of carrots in the foreground trying to get people's attention and guide their actions. An equitable salary more geared to experience and seniority would be an example of keeping the carrot of pay in the motivational background so that other more intrinsic motives might emerge in the foreground to guide action. The tight coupling of pay with performance, as implied by agency theory, is beside the point when the pay is in the background.

These considerations are quite clear in the quality-based (e.g., "Japanese") management methods that take organization seriously. For instance, Edward Deming's "New Economics" recommends to "Abolish incentive pay and pay based on performance" (1994, 28), e.g., to pay salespeople by salary rather than by commission. Deming recommends replacing a system based on close monitoring and quality bonuses with a system using (for the most part) trust based on self-esteem and pride in the quality of one's work. This approach to quality relies not on cleverly constructed pay-for-performance schedules but on switching over to a quality system driven largely by intrinsic motivators such as self-esteem and pride in one's work – in short, quality as a calling.

Simon came to similar conclusions about organizations in general:

> Although economic rewards play an important part in securing adherence to organizational goals and management authority, they are limited in their effective-ness. Organizations would be far less effective systems than they actually are if such rewards were the only means, or even the principal means, of motivation available. In fact, observation of behavior in organizations reveals other powerful motivations that induce employees to accept organizational goals and authority as bases for their actions. (Simon 1991, 34)

Simon goes on to identify pride in work and organizational identification as some of the most important motivators. These intrinsic motivators are not controlled by the purse-strings of managers. Other influential management theorists make the same point:

> 'Intrinsic' rewards…are inherent in the activity itself; the reward is the achieve-ment. They cannot be *directly* controlled externally, although characteristics of the

> environment can enhance or limit the individual's opportunities to obtain them. Thus, achievement of knowledge or skill, of autonomy, of self-respect, of solutions to problems are examples. (McGregor 1966, 203-4)

Paying someone to "identify" with the organization is like trying to "buy love." The motive corrupts and falsifies the action.

CONCLUSION

Much of the conventional western thinking about improving the investment climate is informed by a market-oriented exit-based vision of the markets-and-organizations system. This vision leaves out "half" the story and thus it yields rather one-sided policy recommendations. The market-oriented exit-based vision leads to policies that do not support and may even worsen the investment climate for the members of organizations to invest in building organizational and productive capacity.

We have also seen that in the face of decline, there are essentially two strategies for renewal: transform the old into the new (transformation strategy based on logic of commitment and voice), or throw out the old (to create a *tabula rasa*) and then import the new; that is the question (replacement strategy based on logic of exit).

If the local decision-makers are to stay in control of the country's own development, then enough of the home-grown old must be transformed into the new so that they do not "lose their footing" and become so estranged from the change process that his only response is to cling to the old. From that sound footing on the home-grown but transformed old, they can then take charge of throwing out part of the old and to appropriate and adapt the imported new to make it their own. The alternative is a process externally driven by replacement of the old with the imported new where people are "blown off their feet" and are being swept along without any real ownership of the new realities that were established outside of their control.

This analysis supplies a perspective on the current debate about global-ization. Often that debate is posed in simplistic terms of whether or not a country should be "open" to globalization. This seems to be the wrong question. Of course, a country needs to be open to whatever is compatible with and will augment its independent development. Gandhi used a good metaphor for the openness that is compatible with one's autonomy. "I do not want my house to be walled in on all sides and my windows to be stuffed. I want the cultures of all lands to be blown about my house as freely as possible. But I refuse to be blown off my feet" (Quoted in Datta 1961: 120). By building on enough transformation of their old into the new, the local change-agents could remain "on their feet" and have the self-confidence to seek out, assimilate, adapt, and own the external knowledge, experience, and relationships available to them in a globalized world.

(This paper is based on my work in the World Bank as advisor and speech-writer for Joseph Stiglitz who was then the Chief Economist (1997-1999) of the Bank.)

NOTES

1 The World Bank's advice to client countries is framed in terms of labor market policies rather than human resource management. But for the Bank's own staff there is a Human Resource Vice-Presidency rather than a "Labor Market" Vice Presidency.

2 Keynes, John Maynard (1936) *The General Theory of Employment, Interest, and Money*. New York: Harcourt, Brace & World (157). In the same vein, Hirschman is fond of mentioning "that long confrontation between man and a situation' (Camus) so fruitful for the achievement of genuine progress in problem-solving" (Hirschman 1973: 240).

3 After the WB sponsored and funded "pension reform" in Kazakhstan, more than a billion dollars has been taken by law out of workers' paychecks and fed into the "pension funds" controlled by the main financial/tribal groups in the country.

4 A private sector development team took a tour in the late 90's around Russia visiting compa-nies to help prepare the new strategy for Russia. One of their striking observations was the number of bright young people who had recently come into manufacturing after originally being in "financial engineering" but then had to leave after the financial collapse in August

1998. Here again, it was the collapse of the Bank/Fund protect-the-ruble-corridor policies and the related financial schemes that help redirect the "best and brightest" human capital into the real sector.

5   One example of this strategy to thwart foreign direct investment was the flotation of the Croatian pharmaceutical company Pliva on both the London and Zagreb stock exchanges – when a large western drug company was in hot pursuit.

6   Recall the Bank having a "labor markets" sector but no human resources sector in work with client countries.

REFERENCES

Blair, Margaret M. (1995) *Ownership and Control: Rethinking Corporate Governance for the Twenty-First Century*. Washington DC: The Brookings Institution.

Datta, Dhirendra Mohan (1961) *The Philosophy of Mahatma Gandhi*. Madison: University of Wisconsin Press.

Deming, W. Edwards (1994) *The New Economics for Industry, Government, Education*. Cambridge: MIT Center for Advanced Engineering.

De Soto, Hernando (2000) *The Mystery of Capital*. New York: Basic Books.

Ellerman, David (1998) Voucher Privatization with Investment Funds: An Institutional Analysis. *Policy Research Paper No. 1924*. Washington: World Bank. A version of this paper was published as: Lessons of East Europe's Voucher Privatization, *Challenge*. July-August 2001, 14-37.

Ellerman, David (2005) *Helping People Help Themselves: From the World Bank to an Alternative Philosophy of Development Assistance*. Ann Arbor: University of Michigan Press.

Freeman, Richard and James Medoff (1984) *What Do Unions Do?* New York: Basic Books.

Hirschman, Albert O. (1973) *Journeys Toward Progress*. New York: Norton.

Hirschman, Albert O. (1970) *Exit, Voice and Loyalty*. Cambridge: Harvard University Press.

Hirschman, Albert and Charles Lindblom (1962) "Economic development, research and development, policy making: some converging views." *Behavioral Science*, 7: 211-22.

Kagono, Tadao and Takao Kobayashi (1994) "The Provision of Resources and Barriers to Exit", in Kenichi *Imai* and Ryutaro Komiya (eds.) *Business Enterprise in Japan*. Cambridge: MIT Press

McGregor, Douglas (1966) *Leadership and Motivation*. Cambridge: MIT Press.

Simon, Herbert (1991) "Organizations and Markets." *Journal of Economic Perspectives*, 5(2): 25-44.

Stone, Deborah (1997) *Policy Paradox: The Art of Political Decision Making*. New York: Norton.

PART II

Searching and Debating Alternatives

CHAPTER FIVE

Capitalism and Radical Alternatives

Michael Kuur Sørensen

Capitalism can be defined as a system of material reproduction that is based on the accumulation cycle M-C-C*-M*. The capitalist, or nowadays the investors, invest their money (M) in constant capital, buys machines, workers (C), that together create another set of commodities C*, which when sold on the market creates a profit, that is M*. This particular accumulation cycle has been criticized for a number of reasons, most famously by Marxists, for creating antagonistic relations between capital and labor, since the former get rich by structurally exploiting the latter. However, other critiques are worth mentioning as well, such as those that have been advanced by the green movement and liberal socialists, who emphasize what can be done locally. Here we will take a look at two radical local alternatives to the problems inherent in the capitalist system.

A number of well known problems co-exist with this type of economic system:

1) The well-being of workers is determined by fluctuations in the labor market
2) Environmental degradation, pollution, depletion
3) Unhealthy food-stuffs, chemicals added which are dangerous for human consumption
4) Inequality and poverty

Over the years many alternatives have been tried out in order to counter tendencies within the capitalist system. Two cases will be presented, with a focus on local experiments trying to reject capitalism, and to create an alternative economic system. To pre-empt the conclusion, we find that they in general fail to achieve this goal, because these small group cases are linked to the overall development of the capitalist mode of production. The first of these alternatives, Community Supported Agriculture (CSA) is linked to the green movement and tries to create an alternative to the separation of the producer and the consumer in the capitalist system, and furthermore tries to present it as an alternative that can circumvent the risks to the environment, which capitalism poses. The last example is based in Ithaca, upstate New York. It is a radical experiment to create an alternative form of money, based on the idea that one hour of work in principle is worth as much as another hour of work. In other words, the group in Ithaca tries to create an equitable form of exchange of goods and services that seek to counter the drive to inequality and poverty that stems from the capitalist system.

COMMUNITY SUPPORTED AGRICULTURE

We turn to one example that can be seen as a response to the environmental and health risks in the capitalist system. We focus on what has been launched by the green movement, as the solution to the world's food problems, namely alternative ways of organizing food production locally (Hines, 2000).

This organization is characterized by an economic interaction, where there is no inherent drive for expansion and where production is oriented towards the satisfaction of basic human needs. One such organization of production is the so-called Community Supported Agriculture or CSA, where consumers provide monetary support for local farmers who in return agree to supply high quality food to the consumers (Pretty, 2001: 278). Community Supported Agriculture is a partnership between farmers and community members, working together to create a local food system. It is a system where a city or community directly subsidizes the local farmers. The consumers in the city or in the community pay a certain amount of money to a farmer in advance, and get in return a share of the output of the commodities in proportion to the money invested. Dan Wiens, a key figure in the Canadian movement, explains: "In the case of our farm, a group of 200 city people paid about 200$ the first year for a share. What a share means is that over the course of a harvest season from July to October we supply them with whatever is in the garden" (Wiens, 2005). It is not a typical market system – because the consumers are directly intertwined with the producer – they both share the risks of production; if harvest fails, both the producer and the consumer will have nothing to consume. There is an accumulation cycle but it is markedly different from a traditional capitalist cycle. In the CSA capital is accumulated in the form of constant capital (tools, machines, buildings) and the form of accumulation is much more transparent than the process in a traditional corporation. First, the surplus the CSA-structure can use as investments into new capital is transparent, since they agree on this with the consumer and set the price for each share accordingly. Secondly, there is in principle a closed circuit of supply and demand, which implies that the drive to expand is not inherent in this type of organization, and any expansion will therefore be based on more consumers signing up. The CSA structure is widespread around the world, for instance in England, USA, Japan, Germany, Austria, Denmark and Canada, which therefore makes it an interesting phenomena to examine (Boisvert, 2005: 12ff). Now why has this structure of economic organization emerged?

The industrialization of agriculture, along with the development of chemical industry from 1950s onwards, has created health problems that people have tried to liberate themselves from, by creating a type of subsistence farming that can be seen as the antithesis to the increasing separation of producer and consumer in the capitalist system. This gives a push from capitalist organization towards alternative ways of organizing production.

If capital produces commodities that are harmful for human beings, then human beings will produce products outside the capitalist system

Especially the industrialization of agriculture with large supply chains and chemical production, have made people aware of health risks attached to eating ordinary food bought in the supermarket, and it is against this awareness, that the success of the CSA structure should be found. Consumers want commodities that do not harm them, and that might be in conflict with the practices of modern agriculture. As a farmer once said: "If you don't feel sick after spraying, you haven't sprayed enough" (Beck, 1992: 42). This practice is good for capital and bad for human beings. The externalities of the capitalist production cycle are not linked to moral obligations between producer and consumer; hence the producer can make an effort to cheapen the goods, since it is a means to increase the rate of profit and to be competitive in the market, against other producers of food-stuffs. The consequence is that the consumers or customers lose confidence in the capitalist food-industry.

The consumers are increasingly afraid of eating the food-stuffs produced by capitalist agriculture, because the ingredients in the products are harmful for human reproduction. It is now common knowledge that the industrialization of agriculture has produced health risks to society and the nature it is embedded in (NNF, 2006). In Denmark there has recently been a number of scandals in the public sphere concerning food security; for instance the discovery that some catering-firms were selling 10 year old meat; not suitable for human consumption (DR, 2006a). Or that the Danish foodstuff-company "*Tulip*" has been compromising its food security (DR, 2006b). Another example also taken from the public debate in Denmark is a study that showed that many glasses of Olives, Feta-Cheese and Sun-dried tomatoes were contaminated from their plastic cap with cancer producing chemicals (Fødevarestyrelsen, 2005). In general, the capitalist enterprises that rely on the market want food-products to preserve their commodities as long as possible, because they then can stay on the market for a long period of time. This practice makes it necessary to add chemicals and other products which are dangerous for human beings. This is conducive to the formation of socio-economic experiments like the CSA structure.

This alienation, in the sense of being afraid of what we put into our mouths, creates demand for healthy products within the capitalist system. This is both the strength and the weakness of the CSA structure, as we shall see.

The consequences of increased health hazards in food production is an increased demand for healthy products

The limitations of the CSA structure as a general model for society arise from an unexpected source, namely from capitalism itself. The basic problem is that the initial money given to the farmer is obtained through wages in the capitalist system. The consumers that pay this money could use it for similar products if the price was lower and the products equally healthy. Secondly, Capitalism, relying on economies of scale is simply better at creating cheaper products, and also cheaper healthy products than a CSA structure.

Consumers in a capitalist system, when aware of the health risks produced by capital, can through a change of demand, change capital. In 1999, 87 percent of all consumers in Denmark bought organic products, and about 2/3 of all consumers have bought organic milk or vegetables (Husmer, 2004: 57). The report also concludes that the demand for ecological products have increased tremendously the last 30 years. Of the respondents, only a few (1 percent) answered that they had been buying organic products for more than 30 years. 22 percent replied that they had been buying organic food for more than 7 years, and about 30 percent replied that they had been buying organic products in less than 2 years (Husmer, 2004: 58). In 1994, over half of the Danish consumers were willing to pay 10 percent extra for organic foods. In 1995, 80 percent of the consumers were willing to pay a special environmental tax if it could guarantee more healthy food in the stores (Husmer, 2004: 85). In other words, there is a lot of demand that capitalist firms can respond to.

Capitalist dynamics can adapt and learn from the problems that concern the consumers, and therefore start producing healthy food at a lower price than with the low-scale production of the CSA structure. Investments and profits simply allow for productivity increases, which cannot be undertaken without additional capital that is difficult to obtain in a CSA structure.

If consumer demand rises, so does the capitalist companies' interest in producing healthy food

Hence, the organic market in Denmark is dominated by capitalist players like Arla (Husmer, 2004: 57) and the former CSA, Årstiderne (the Seasons), rather than the local CSA structures. Interestingly the 'Seasons', a major Danish organic-food producer, changed from a CSA structure to a capitalist firm early on (Harttung, 2004). These large companies have begun to accommodate to the fear that the separation of producer and consumer have caused, by for instance indicating where the milk bought in a supermarket comes from – even pointing out the exact farmer that produce the milk to remind the consumer of the close connections with the producer. Another interesting development in connection with this is that consumers begin to doubt the validity of organic products, when they are produced by capitalist firms (DR, 2007). About 9 percent of the respondents replied that they do not trust the organic-marked products originating in Denmark, and in regard to foreign organic food, the number was 38 percent (Husmer, 2004: 63).

Therefore, we can here observe that a dialectic has been formed between the integration of normative interaction (CSA), but with a higher cost for consumers, vis-à-vis a lower cost of production and the subsequent separation of producer and consumer (capitalism).

When capital has regained its legitimacy by producing commodities that are not hazardous to consume, then some consumers with less resources favour that organization. There is both a push away from capitalism, and a pull back to capitalism. This explains on the one hand the resilience of the capitalist system, but also the weakness inherent in it, which produces a desire to opt out of capitalism.

BASING ECONOMIC INTERACTION ON ONE HOUR FOR ONE HOUR

We now turn to another alternative to the capitalist system, which is different from the CSA structure described above. The idea which we shall follow below is to create another type of exchange between human beings that is based on an equitable form of transaction. This system exists on an experimental basis, but is also a structure that has been viewed as potentially liberating for human beings, by giving the promise of equitable interaction. Equating one hour of labour with another hour of labour, could in theory counter the inequality in the capitalist system, poverty, and consequently provide well-being for workers.

The Ithaca HOURS is a local issued money-bill that represents the value of one hour of work in a particular community. In this system one aims for a principle of equality; that one person's hourly work equals another person's hourly work. Poul Glover, the founder of this system, explains:

> There is no law against printing time... so we have been printing labor money; labor is the foundation of wealth, without people to make things of stuff, there is nothing to trade. So this is again part of the revolution in the understanding of the money in respect given back to labour that mere capital seeking endlessly to increase its numbers does not respect. (Glover, 2005)

When you have done something in X number of hours you receive an equivalent number of HOURS to spend somewhere else. People have an hour grant, which they can cash in somewhere else. In practice, the system runs like this:

> A bookstore owner accepts HOURS and uses them for food, jewellery, and her mortgage at the local credit union. The Science centre sells memberships and

admissions for HOURS and uses them to hire a book cataloguer. The cataloguer spends them on Spanish lessons. The Spanish teacher uses them at the farmers market. A craftsman who makes fine paper out of cattails earns HOURS by providing the paper for the two-HOUR note (Meadows, 2006).

Money is issued as people sign up for the money – which means that money is backed by real labour. HOURs are created on the basis of the HOURs needed.

This idea assumes that labour is not differentiated, and demanded to a greater or lesser extent. In practice, there is differential demand for a dentist vis-à-vis an unskilled person, which proves to be a practical problem in Ithaca. Far from being equal, that is, one hour for one hour, one dentist hour in Ithaca, equals three cleaning hours. Paul Glover, who took the initiative writes:" ...dentists, massage therapists and lawyers charging more than the $10.00 average per hour are permitted to collect several HOURS hourly" (Glover, 2006). With this kind of inbuilt asymmetry, the idea of equating hours of work with one another loses its purpose. In practice, the system is not based on one hour for one hour; the system is flawed. In Ithaca they also made the hour-bills convertible into dollars (1 hour = $10), that is:

> One HOUR is worth ten dollars. That's roughly the average wage in Tompkins County, New York. The idea is that one person's time is as valuable as anyone else's, so an HOUR can be exchanged for an hour's work, whether that work is farm labor or dentistry. There's nothing to prevent professionals from charging several HOURS per hour, of course, and a babysitter might accept a quarter-HOUR per hour. (Meadows, 2006)

In short, it is questionable if this type of organization that in theory is based on equality is more than an ideal without a corresponding practice.

A more gentle evaluation of the inequality that was introduced into the HOUR system, would argue that the inequality 3:1 is still much more equal than the exchange of labour one finds in the capitalist system. In

the capitalist system, dentists get wages that exceed the 3:1 ratio in relation to unskilled labour, and in this sense the system still counters some
of the inequality that is present in cut-throat capitalism. It amounts to
a soft socialist system, based on small inequalities due to the differences
amongst mental and physical labour. In short, it is not a perfect system,
in line with its own principles, but then again the achievement of perfect
equality might be too high a goal to set in the first place.

There are other problems associated with this type of money which
we will show below. One problem for this principle of interaction is the
asymmetry between manufacturing and the service sector. A manufacturer
might increase productivity per hour and be able to make 800.000 items
for sale in that hour, which cannot be sold or even traded directly within
the immediate community, since the market is too small. At the same time
there are limits to the productivity increases in the service sector. Since
productivity is going up inside the factories constantly, the hourly work
necessary to produce a given quantity of commodities is falling (Pierson,
2001:85). As Pierson has noted:

> In many services, it is essentially the labour effort itself that we wish to consume.
> Such activities are resistant to the processes of standardization and replication
> that is essential to efficiency gains in manufacturing. It is extremely difficult in
> most services to generate the large, continuous increase in productivity typical of
> manufacturing. (Pierson, 2001: 84)

The consequence is that while manufactured products tend to become
cheaper and cheaper with increasing productivity, services tend to become
more expensive. Here we have the general asymmetry in the way things
are, which creates resistance for the ideal of an equitable interaction of
one hour per one hour. In other words, since we still have manufacturing
jobs in the capitalist system, it becomes difficult to superimpose this type
of exchange on the economic sphere. The consequence could be that
mainly service type industries will be involved in this system, and not
manufacturing. Since there are practical implementation problems with

this structure, it is limited as to how important the HOUR system is for people in the community as an economic means for exchange. This is one of the reasons why the Ithaca-HOURS are *not used* much in practice as indicated below, since it is not a practical instrument for economic transaction under these circumstances.

The HOUR-system is of relatively little importance in the material reproduction for the people that utilizes them – people still rely mainly on the capitalist system for their material well-being (Jeffrey et al, 2004: 42). In other words, something is hindering the equitable idea to materialize in practice.

The use of the HOUR-system is of a marginal importance for the material reproduction of a community

More than one third of the people using Ithaca-HOURS have a yearly income of above $50.000 (Jeffrey et al, 2004: 46). The use of Ithaca HOURS is almost of no importance in a strictly economic sense, since over 70 percent of the respondents (N=42) answered that they had only used HOURS equivalent to $500 the last 12 months (Jeffrey et al, 2004: 48). And since the sum of $500 per year is not sufficient to satisfy the most basic human needs, the system is far from being of economic importance in the community as a whole. Half of the respondents answered that they typically use Ithaca HOURS less than 4 times a month (Jeffrey et al, 2004: 49). Therefore, a situation emerges where the material well-being and the attractiveness of the capitalist system, still provides a motive for people to leave the Ithaca-HOURS structure and to re-enter or to remain in the capitalist system. The capitalist system simply produces many things that they themselves would like to obtain, but which would be impossible to generate under a local Ithaca-HOURS based system. In other words, this idea is fragile because the technological drive of capitalism creates products which people like, and which require the global organization of production. The dynamic character of capitalism is the creator of numerous innovative and fashionable products – such as computers, cars, USB-drives, CD's, TV's, airplanes, trains, etc – which would not be possible to produce at the local level on the basis of the Ithaca-HOURS based system. Marx's old idea that it was difficult to transcend capital within a capitalist society seems true, at least for this type of alternative economic system. Marx would argue that the desire to overcome material necessity is a greater incentive for human beings than to be secluded from the rest of the world. If one wants to seclude oneself in a monk-like existence, then one must also be willing to accept the consequences, which implies to have none of the things that cannot be produced at the local level. In Ithaca the HOUR-system merely functions as an ideological phenomenon for the well-educated part of the population.

The HOUR-system is a source of local identity formation in the Ithaca community

Since HOURS are of minimal material importance, it can be hypothe-sized that non-material aspects of the HOUR-system are more important. Jeffrey Jacob et al (2004) concluded in a case study survey that the forma-tion of the Ithaca-HOURS should be seen in the context of the value this currency holds as a cultural phenomenon, rather than as a strictly economic phenomenon. As one respondent answered in the study:" *Just knowing it's there makes me feel good about living in Ithaca*" (Jeffrey et al, 2004: 43). Over 50 percent of the respondents answered that the Ithaca-HOUR system improved their quality of life (Jeffrey et al, 2004: 50). The average user of Ithaca HOURS is well-educated, close to the median income, parent, married, middle-aged and votes for the Green Party.(Jeffrey et al, 2004: 47). In short, it is a middle-upper class phenomenon, with no immediate prospect for human liberation. It remains a luxury for rich people that already are well off in the capitalist system to experiment with this kind of social utopia.

As with the CSA structure, we find that the potential for liberation with this structure is highly limited, since it is not practical to implement on a wider societal scale. The HOUR-system has a rather bleak record and usually breaks down fairly soon after its initiation. Less than 20 percent of the HOURS-based systems, inspired by the Ithaca experiment, have proved to be viable, which shows the fragile situation of such a system in the context of the capitalist system (Lepofsky & Bates, 2005: 4).

The lesson learned from the HOUR experience is that it is reality that conditions the idea and not vice-versa. Reality fights back on the idea to create equitable relations when there is an unequal division of labor in reality. This practical failure of this system makes capitalism resilient to the challenges it poses.

AND HOW DOES THIS RELATE TO MARX?

The general conclusions presented here differ in some aspects from the paradigm presented by Marx and Engels in the Communist Manifesto, that is based on two irreconcilable forces in society: "Oppressor and oppressed, stood in constant opposition to one another, carried on an uninterrupted, now hidden, now open fight, a fight that each time ended, either in a revolutionary re-constitution of society at large, or in the common ruin of the contending classes" (Marx & Engels, 1848: 483). In their view, it would be impossible to modify the capitalist relations between capital and labor, because this system, per definition, creates antagonism between them. However, the argument advanced here is that it is useful to map and to examine the strong and weak points, because it creates an awareness of possible alternatives, and because these alternatives can function for a period, and thereby soften the traditional problems connected with capitalism that we identified in the beginning of the chapter.

If antagonism is taken for granted, and if antagonism is inherent in the organization of the capitalist system, why should we even care to solve it? These radical alternatives, flawed as they are, can be seen as a counter-movement to the problems that are inherent in the capitalist system.

CONCLUSION

In the beginning of this chapter we listed five problems that we argued as being inherent in the capitalist system, and we examined how different alternatives have been created as reactions to these problems. Community Supported Agriculture was presented as an alternative to the way in which food has been produced under the capitalist system and should be seen as a way of coping with the chemicalization of food. The Ithaca HOUR system was an alternative against the inequitable way in which economic transactions are occurring in the capitalist system.

Concerning the case of Community Supported Agriculture, we could observe that this structure has been created as a reaction against the industrialization of agriculture and the chemicalization of food-stuffs. However this structure is limited as a solution to this problem, since the capitalist system can adapt to the change of demand towards healthy food-stuffs, which is the reason why capitalist companies are now just as much involved in producing healthy foodstuffs, as the people involved in community supported agriculture.

The Ithaca HOUR experiment also showed us that a fundamentally different type of economic organization has to be practically possible, if it is to have any effect on the way in which human beings interact. Because it was not practically possible the ideals of the HOUR system were systematically circumvented or not used at all. This is a token of the fact that this type of transaction system is more an ideological phenomenon than a practical alternative to capitalism.

However the mere existence of these alternatives are also a token of the fact that people try to modify capitalism with diverging success, and that its drive to create inequality is as unstable as the solutions presented above because people actually want changes.

We are in a situation where the capitalist system produces a push for people to change some aspects of the system, and at the same time the capitalist system has some qualities that undermine these alternatives over time.

To acknowledge that the solutions to the problems of capitalism are conditioned by the development of that system itself is conducive to understanding and modifying capitalism.

As long as we have a capitalist system, the way to accompany human liberation is to adapt to that system and to reform it, so that it deals with the problems inherent in it. As long as another system is not practically possible (as a complete solution) – as we have seen with the HOUR system and Community Supported Agriculture – capitalism in a reformed manner is the best we have. Alternatively, this reform could be envisioned as a kind of mixed economy where one could imagine several types of sectors co-existing alongside each other. There could be room for a sector of the economy that is somewhat subsidized by the state, and which is allowed to experiment with economic alternatives. This could be incorporated into the idea of worker self-management, so that the workers in a large chunk of the economic structure have democratic alternatives to the traditional sector of capitalist production.

REFERENCES

Beck, Ulrich (1992) *Risk Society*. London: Sage Publications.

Boisvert, Isabelle et al (2005) "Promoting Community Supported Agriculture in Denmark – Promoting Organic Ideals through Local Food Links" at http://www.kursus.kvl.dk/shares/ea/03Projects/32gamle/_2005/CSA%20in%20Denmark.pdf p.12ff.

DR (2006a) "10 År Gammelt Kød På Lager", available at http://www.dr.dk/Nyheder/Indland/2006/04/05/202913.htm, accessed the 13th of April 2006.

DR (2006b) Kontant "Fordærvet Kød Hos Tulip", available at http://www.dr.dk/DR1/kontant/2006/03/28173822.htm, accessed the 13th of April 2006.

DR (2007) "Forbrugerrådet: Sprøjtegift i Øko-Æbler er tilsat bevidst", available at http://www.dr.dk/Nyheder/Penge/2007/09/28/102120.htm accessed 28 sep. 2007

Fødevarestyrelsen (2005) "Skruelåg Afgiver for Mange Skadelige Stoffer til Fede Madvarer", available at http://www.foedevarestyrelsen.dk/Nyheder/Pressemeddelelser/Arkiv/2005/skruelaag.htm, accessed the 13th of April.

Galtung, Johan (2004) *Transcend & Transform – An Introduction to Conflict Work*. London: Pluto Press.

Glover, Paul (2006) "*Creating Community Economics with Local Currency*", available at http://www.ithacahours.com/intro.html 22/04-2006.

Glover, Paul (2005) "Interview", available at http://www.suesupriano.com/article.php?&id=90 accessed 23/4-2006.

Harttung, Thomas (2004) "NOFA-NY Annual Winter Education Conference" January 31, available at http://nofany.org/hottopics/harttung.htm

Hines, Colin (2000) *Localization – A Global Manifesto*. London: Earthscan.

Husmer, Lis et al (2004) "Miljø og Forbrugeradfærd." Miljøprojekt Nr. 870, Miljøstyrelsen, Denmark.

Jeffrey, Jacob et al (2004) "The Social and Cultural Capital of Community Currency an Ithaca HOURS Case Study Survey." *International Journal of Community Currency Research*, 8(1): 42-56.

Lepofsky, Jonathan & Bates, Lisa K. (2005) "Helping Everyone have PLENTY: Addressing Distribution and Circulation in an HOURS-based Local Currency System." *International Journal of Community Currency Research*, 9(1): 1-20.

Marx, Karl & Engels, Friedrich (1848) *The Communist Manifesto*. Marx/Engels Collected Works, vol. 6, London:Lawrence & Wishart.

Meadows, Donella H (2006) "Ithaca Creates Its Own Money", available at http://www.sustainabilityinstitute.org/dhm_archive/index.php?display_article=vn544ithacaed accessed 11/11 2007

MetroXpress (2006) Mandag d. 24 April: 20.

NNF (2006) "Gift i Maden", available at http://www.nnf.dk/default.asp?mId=893&aId=25231 accessed 20th of March.

Pretty, Jules (2001) "Saving our small farms and rural communities", in Goldsmith & Mander (eds.) *The Case Against the Global Economy*. London: Earthscan.

Ugebrevet A4 (2002) August 26, Nr. 16.

Wallerstein, Immanuel (2004) *World-Systems Analysis – An Introduction*. Durham: Duke University Press.

WeekendAvisen (2006) *"Nødudgangen"*, downloaded from 21-25 May 2006, http://www.weekendavisen.dk/apps/pbcs.dll/article?AID=/20060505/SAM-FUND/605040355/0/TEMA.

Wiens, Dan (2005) interview in *"Sustainable Farming"*, November 22.

CHAPTER SIX

The Mondragon Co-operatives Going Global?

Gorm Winther and Michael Kuur Sørensen

INTRODUCTION

The Mondragon Co-operatives have since the late fifties shown an impressive growth record in terms of job-creation and economic growth. Still today, where the co-operative corporation is at the verge of passing 84.000 employees and co-owners working for the corporation, it has shown a steady growth in terms of employment. Looking at the early historic records, the Mondragon experience was not just a question of growth; it demonstrated that co-operatives fare well in comparison with conventional companies in the Basque region and in Spain (Thomas and Logan, 1982; Hoover, 1992; Whyte and Whyte, 1991). The overarching question is whether this has to do with the managerial philosophy and the co-operative distinctiveness, or whether some other unknown variables are at play. This paper can of course not answer this question unambiguously, yet we can for the reader without prior knowledge present the co-operative model before and after the Co-op's were incorporated in the Mondragon Co-operative Corporation (MCC). Furthermore, we can present the literature on comparative performance research done in the earlier days of the co-operatives and some new data for the last ten years. Since the seventies and the eighties, empirical research on comparative economic performance has not been implemented.

Yet, some critics of the Mondragon model have raised a concern of whether the co-operatives are as participatory as their ideals; this is often taken for granted among researchers and management abiding to a co-operative management philosophy. We lack knowledge on workers perceptions of their work-places and of the company where most are co-owners. Only one case study compares this in a Mondragon co-operative and a conventional company; we do not have much empirical evidence on the issue of power distribution between occupational groups in the MCC (Kasmir, 1996). The methodology introduced by Tannenbaum in the late sixties regarding control in organizations and the distribution of power between occupational groups has hitherto not been applied in empirical studies on workplace relations in the MCC (Tannenbaum, 1968). If possible, this approach would probably give better evidence than Kasmirs anthropological study based on observations and qualitative methods.

The workers are in labor-sociological studies often not being asked about their satisfaction with co-operatives; instead, it is management and key personnel. The case study in question in a Basque town raised the issue of conflicts between management and labor in co-operatives. Severe industrial disputes were rare in the Mondragon co-operatives, but during the years antagonisms have occurred due to concerns of becoming corporate. This may suggest a negative impact from globalization, and it is not just the power distribution problem we see at play here. The initial principle of genuine worker ownership, where all workers co-own, is to an increasingly degree being replaced by contract and part-time positions based solely on wage earning instead of income sharing. This is explained by the issue of an initial co-operative network of companies transforming into a corporation and becoming global. The question is whether this impacts the comparative performance of the MCC to regional and national data. This paper indicates that in terms of a productivity proxy, the MCC does not fare as well as before, where the co-operatives mainly operated in the region and in Spain.

Nevertheless, this is not to say that techno-structural power relations were not present earlier, but that the problems have deepened due to globalization and sharpened competition in the market place. The question about creating owners and non-owners to an increasing degree undermines the co-operative principles. Part-time labor is not a new tendency. Nonetheless, it used to be an exception explained by booming periods with demand increases growing faster than the pace of possible inclusion of new worker-owners.

Another important issue is related to globalization itself and the pressure on a network of co-operatives to go global. The question is whether this has a negative or a positive impact on the performance of the co-operatives. There are a number of stumbling blocks in this process, which the MCC also face.

This article will present the philosophies of the co-operatives from 1956 to the nineties. It will present the ownership model and organizational principles before and after the Mondragon Co-operatives became a corporation. Performance studies conducted back in the early eighties and newer data collected during the last ten years are also presented. Finally, it is recommended that further research be conducted for an analysis of the causalities behind recent development in economic performance.

IN SEARCH FOR ALTERNATIVES – WORKER OWNERSHIP AND PARTICIPATION

Discussing alternatives to corporate global Capitalism, we may resort to either micro organizational or systemic principles being an actual alternative to the principle of Capital hiring labor. When Capital hires labor we see social coordination mechanisms based on subordination and concentration of wealth accumulated as incomes for savings and investments. The distributional aspects of this are an unequal distribution of incomes (value added). In the short run marginal income, after consumption needs are met, accumulates wealth under control of capital possessors. Accumulated wealth also has power implications, when the holders of land and real assets hire other factors of production in order to increase value added – labor is subordinated to Capital. The aspects of this in a larger perspective then are an unequal distribution of income, wealth and power, and needless to say, when transforming this to the global scene, we have reproduced the basic principle of Capitalism from the national scale to a larger scale.

A central issue when discussing alternative economic systems is to transform dehumanized labor as a mere factor of production to a democratic relation – if labor hires Capital or own Capital, what types of ownership and organization do we then talk of? In an evolutionary context, we may either see embryonic structures toward a full realization of this alternative, or we may within the framework of Capitalism already see ownership structures and organizations actually representing labor hiring Capital. Seen as a dichotomy, the first mentioned employee owner-ship represents a first step but not a full step, if we take the distributions into account. Employee Stock ownership plans (ESOPs) as leveraged or non-leveraged plans could be one example of tools creating egalitarian ownership structures. Such plans can take the form of employee buy-outs or take-overs. Profit sharing schemes represent another approach of egali-tarian measures in the realm of income distribution. If such schemes are deferred plans, we are in essence talking about another form of employee ownership, especially if the assets co-owned are workplace assets to the employee.

One may regard pension funds or wage earners funds as employee owner-ship, nonetheless, we are here talking about an indirect type of ownership, because the fiduciary principle introduces managers or administrators taking care of the funds, while management of the funds resorts to the members of a board, not appointed by employees contributing to the funds. Wage earners funds in relation to economic democracy were only seen in Sweden in the eighties, but they never quite fulfilled the vision of Rudolph Meidner on economic and industrial democracy. Meidner's idea was that all companies with more than 50 employees should yearly issue new shares to funds representing workplaces. As wage earners capital grew, more power could be handed over to the workers – in the end wage earners could then control up to 52% of all stock. Workers' self-management or workplace democratization was not an issue in either of the cases. The reforms in Sweden on "economic democracy" was never implemented the way Meidner foresaw. Wage earners never owned significant shares of the stock market, and the workers never got a real say in company decisions. In 1992 the right-wing government abandoned the funds (Pontusson & Kuruvilla, 1992).

Workers' co-operatives are also a form of employee ownership, where the distinctive feature is the principle of workers' democratic control (one person – one vote), while employee stock ownership schemes most often do not imply democratic control, i.e. the worker owners can vote their stock as a block of minority shares or they can vote in accordance with the principle of votes being equal to the amount of shares held. A democratic employee stock ownership scheme does not necessarily mean that democratic control is impossible – democratic ESOPs have been conceptualized (Ellerman, 1992). Nevertheless, democratic schemes are seldom seen globally.

Self-management on a national scale is seen as a special model of socialism, implemented by the Yugoslav communists under the leadership of Josip Broz "Tito" and inspired by Edward Kardelj. In theoretical writings on the Yugoslav model, it was obvious, that the inspiration came as much from anarchism, utopian socialism and the parts of Marxism that advocate a decentralized model taking its point of departure in the younger Marx's writings on alienation and the older political Marx's writing on the Commune of Paris. (Djilas 1954; Kardelj, 1979; Horvat, et al., 1975; Horvat 1982).

The characteristics of the Yugoslav system after 1950 and after several reforms represented a genuine attempt to practice co-operative principles at a national scale. The law on associated labor from 1976 introduced management and income sharing principles in basic organizations of associated labor (BOALs). BOALs comprised from 20 up to 500 workers and each organization had its own democratically elected workers council formally in charge of the operations although a techno-structural hierarchy prevailed. According to the Tannenbaum approach to the distribution of power sociological studies have suggested that this was unequally distributed: the workers councils had power on interest-related decisions, while professional management and key personnel often dominated strategic and technical decisions (Hunnius, 1975 in Horvat et al.). Larger organizations like the Work Organizations of Associated Labor (up to 1000 workers) and Composite Organizations of Associate Labor comprised several BOALs.

The question is then whether such constructions – whether at macro, meso or micro level – can survive or have a future in a globalized market capitalist social setting. Worker co-operatives' performance records represent mixed evidence – some would claim mostly positive. The paradox seems to be that while co-operative banking and insurance represents large scale operations (ICA, 2008) workers co-operatives do not.

Latin American and Carribean socialism may represent a step toward a strengthening of local initiatives, import substitution and the encouragement of workers in the private sector to form co-operatives. According to journaliststic reporting, increasing co-operative initiative defines the development strategies of the Bolivarian Revolution in Venezuela. Moreover, cases like Bolivia and Argentina represent a growing acknowledgement of the potentials of co-operatives and micro-finance as vehicles for promoting an alternative development path to globalization. From the 1990s, the co-operative sector of the Cuban economy has to an increasing degree been able to operate independently of state control.

GLOBAL INTEGRATION.

In the era of Globalization (Hirst and Thompson, 1996) an important issue is whether hitherto known national characteristics of ownership and organizational governance can be reproduced at a global scale. Obviously, large corporations in the Galbraithian sense (Galbraith, 1967, 1982, 2005) have a lead in this respect. The "global market place" is based upon the hazards of the anarchistic market. Free mobility of capital and access to cheap resources and cheap labor enhances the operations of the corporation. In terms of power relations, the techno-structure and the huge corporation comprise a subtle conditioned power (Galbraith, 1982 : 24 ff.) that is more than compensatory power. In terms of socio-political relations, the corporation is the main player in political national life as well as in global politics. The institutional arrangements are to a higher degree pertinent to the interests and operations of the corporations.

Hitherto at the national level, co-operative companies and co-operative systems have evolved by establishing national or regional supporting structures or networks that shelter the co-operatives and improve the options for larger scale operations. Moreover, these structures facilitate entry of new co-operative firms to markets through planning, finance and feasibility studies. Creating access to Capital in closed financial circuits is one way to buttress co-operatives' access to financial leverage – creating funds or co-operative banking can overcome what Jaroslav Vanek called "the dilemma of the collateral" (Vanek, 1970). Commercial banks are reluctant to finance co-operatives due to their democratic characteristics, profit sharing and lack of external investors. The question is whether laissez- faire markets and institutional set ups for traditional corporations fit the co-operatives. Or to quote the late Branko Horvat, when he addressed Swedish employers back in the eighties and was asked why worker-managed firms had trouble outperforming conventional companies. The answer was as trivial as thinking of the capitalist firm being implanted in the feudal mode of production. Such firms' requirements of free mobility of labor and free contracting did not fit to feudal institutions, as will labor-managed firms requirements not fit into the settings of corporate Capitalism (Horvat, 1974).

Looking into national experiences with self-help movements and education to think co-operatively, co-operative systems established educational institutions for workers, farmers and consumers, as well as other supporting structures. This is in essence the most important stepping stone to the establishment of a co-operative democracy. The consciousness among workers about the co-operative idea and the willingness to embark on a co-operative job as a co-owner of the company does not show up like a "bird phoenix" – in essence, it was a "long pull" at the national level, that lifted the working mans competencies and knowledge in order to participate as a co-operator.

Hence, to overcome the problem of a slower birth rate of co-operatives in the global economy, and to deal with the issue of co-operative systems going global, more international co-operation is needed. This process is much more time consuming in terms of establishing co-operatives in other countries based on genuine co-operative principles of control, ownership and participation in decision-making. The traditional corporation, however, has its playground facilitated by policy measures through conditionalities on rolling back the frontiers of the state and liberalizations established by institutions like the IMF and the World Bank (Stiglitz, 2003; Ellerman, 2006). Liberalized markets are in no way competitive in the concept's theoretical meaning. Instead, liberalization alludes to the business man or CEO of huge corporations attempts to operate without regulations and control. Monopolies, duopolies, oligopolies, cartels and trusts create welfare losses. It is spurious to label these companies as being competitive in the theoretical sense. As an apologetic theory, it has the pleasing consequence that extreme laissez-faire gives the huge corporation freedoms to be in the forefront controlling the markets where they operate.

The rule of the game here is poisonous for co-operative principles to be established. Co-operative networks can adopt a corporate structure if the network is big enough to be a dominant player in the international marketplace. But the structures from traditional corporations are then adopted by the co-operative. Two phenomena are a problem here – first, economies of scale call for larger daughter companies or larger units operating within the company. This is noxious for democratic and participatory decision-making, while smaller organizations provide a better underpinning for these decision-making processes. Second, expert systems already presented by Weblen and later Galbraith (Weblen, 2001; Demsetz, 1968) pointed to the fact that technocrats reproduce the same power structures which are based on autocracy as seen in conventional corporations. This is not a new insight. It was also present in the earlier stages of the history of co-operatives and workers' self-management. However, as the division of intellectual and managerial labor become more sophisticated in the era of globalization, the distance between blue and white collar workers, between managerial/intellectual and ordinary work deepen to such a degree that it is phoney to talk about participatory democracy or workers' control.

It seems that co-operative systems going global have to rely on their historical experiences and have to take another road than corporate capitalism. This includes international supporting structures of the same type as seen at the national level earlier in History.

THE ROOTS OF THE MONDRAGON CO-OPERATIVE EXPERIENCE

The Mondragon co-operatives represent an attempt to create a model based on 100 % worker ownership and workers' participation in decision-making according to principles of democratic control. From five "founding fathers" initiative to install the first co-operative in 1956 producing oil stoves and paraffin heaters and until today, the MCC's growth record on employment is impressive. Employment in 2006 amounted to 83.600. In Spain alone employment was some 68.000 with some 37.000 in Euskadi. Mondragon was in 2006 Spain's seventh largest corporation and the co-operatives went global in the 1990s. Today the MCC has 65 plants in Brazil, China, the Czech Republic, India, Italy, Marocco, Mexico, Portugal, Romania, Slovakia, Turkei, the UK and The US (Mondragon, 2007). The new element in this is the presence of hired labor in these plants and offices – the Mother corporation in Spain has not succeeded in transferring the pure co-operative model to these countries. The

Mondragon co-operatives represents most sectors in the economy as illustrated in figure 1 below.

The corporation represents a unique network of industrial sectors supported by its own financial system organized in the co-operative bank (Caja Laboral Popular), its own distribution group, training centres for worker-owners and its own university and Research centre.

Figure 1: The Mondragon Co-operative Corporation (MCC)

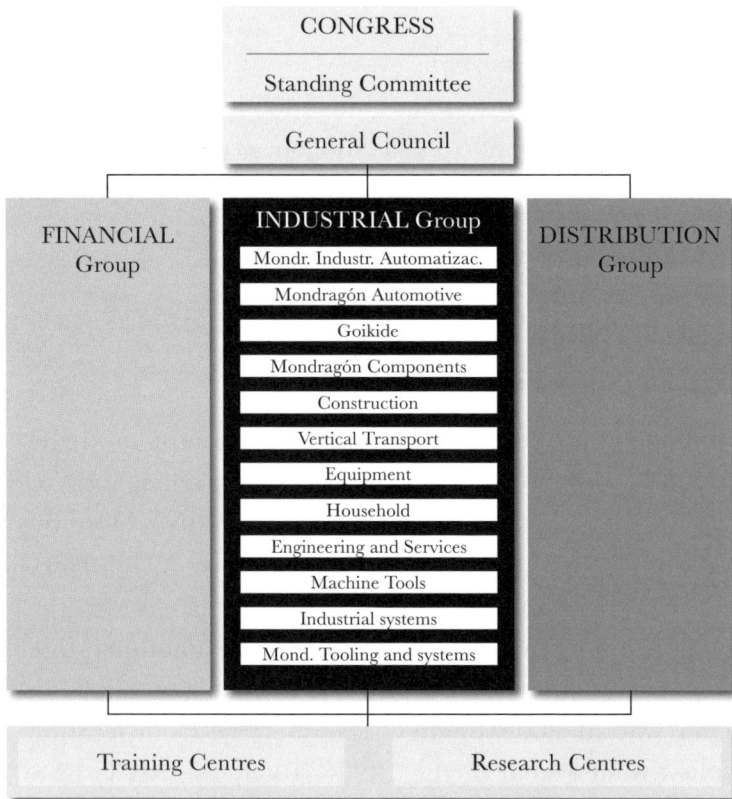

(Source: http://www.mcc.es/ing/estructura/estructura.html)

It all started in the town of Mondragon (Arrasate) in the Basque region of Spain. A catholic Priest Jose Maria Arizmendi had studied the economics of the Marxian critique of Capitalism as well as the laissez-faire doctrine of Adam Smith, and had found that ideas rooted in the 18th century utopian socialism as well as catholic social doctrines fitted better to the conditions of Euzkadi and fascist Spain in the 1950s. He started a polytechnical school in the town of Mondragon in 1943, and with five graduates, all with a working class background, the first co-op Ulgor was established in 1956. As a social innovator, Arizmendi claimed that local initiatives and co-operation could be the lever needed to create growth and local prosperity. In essence, his philosophy was what differentiated people in their attitudes towards life. Those who abide to self-help principles and change the course of events themselves will be better off than those who choose a passive life waiting for the results of other peoples' initiative (Mondragon, 2008). Despite his reluctance, when it came to Marxian centralism and classical liberalist notions of Manchester Capitalism and free markets, he was enthusiastic for the political Karl Marx, who in his inaugural address to the international working men's association in 1864 proclaimed:

> But there was in store a still greater victory of the political economy of labor over the political economy of property. We speak of the co-operative movement, especially the co-operative factories raised by the unassisted efforts of a few bold "hands". The value of these great social experiments cannot be overrated. By deed instead of by argument, they have shown that production on a large scale, and in accord with the behests of modern science, may be carried on without the existence of a class of masters employing a class of hands. (Marx, 1964)

The ideological roots of co-operatives are multi-faceted and as such the catholic social doctrines undoubtedly had a profound impact on the making of the Mondragon Co-operatives. Pope John the 23. wrote in his encyclical "Mater et Magistra" on Christianity and Social progress (1961): "Accordingly, we paternally exhort our beloved sons, craftsmen and members of co-operatives throughout the world, that they fully realize the dignity of their role in society, since by their work, the sense of responsibility and spirit of mutual aid can be daily more intensified among the citizenry, and the desire to work with dedication and originality be kept alive."

Nonetheless, Arizmendis philosophy looked back to the ideas of socialist Robert Owen, who in his "Report to the County of New Lanark" pleaded for a local community organized as a federation of self reliant agricultural co-operative village societies controlled by benevolent landowners and members of the co-operative. Seeking social justice Owen, himself an industrialist managed a cotton Mill in New Lanark, improved the living conditions of workers and their families. He advocated a plan for agricultural villages to create prosperous communities consisting of 300 to 2000 members (Owen, 1975).

Industrial co-operatives never really got off the ground in Great Britain. Instead consumers' co-operatives proved more viable. The Rochdale Pioneers are a group of Christian Socialists inspired by Owen who established the world's first consumers co-operative in Rochdale in 1844. The principles that ruled the co-operative at the time still globally characterize co-operatives. The Rochdale principles are simple (International Co-operative Alliance, 2008):

- democratic control of members according to the principle of one person – one vote
- open membership and limited liability for members covering losses
- profit sharing /dividends paid to members in accordance with labor input or trade with the company.
- limited withdrawal of capital
- education

These principles were elaborated further into the Arizmendi system of the Mondragon Co-operatives.

THE MONDRAGON CO-OPERATIVE PRINCIPLES.

However, the Mondragon co-operatives have proved that Industrial co-operatives are viable: most countries have worker co-operative sectors, and in some cases the co-operatives fared well (Jones and Svejnar, 1985; Defourney et. al. 1985).

The classic worker co-operative is mostly organized on the basis of democratic control, limited liability and limited withdrawal of capital, but looking at Mondragon, it is more correct to say that the organization, management and finance is a mix of collective and individual principles. The principle of democratic control as expressed in the Rochdale principles is still present in the Mondragon Co-operatives. Education is the glue that binds the co-operative principles together. It is mandatory that worker members know about the co-operative idea. In the early days, Labor subordinated Capital, decision-making was democratic and management was participatory. Members were co-owners of the corporation and the participatory approach was sought through self-managed teams.

Describing the co-operative bodies the Mondragon co-operative Corporation (MCC) still describes itself in this way:

> - **The member**. Members must complete a trial period in their jobs, generally lasting between six months and one year, after which, as co-operative members, they are free either to confirm or reject the offer of permanent membership.
>
> - **The Co-operative**. Based on a system of shared management, the co-operatives constitute the basic elements of MCC. Each retains its own organisational structure, individual legal personality and independence.
>
> - **Support Co-operatives**. The result of an association of grass roots co-operatives, their aim is to support the co-operatives in specific areas of management. Known also as 'co-operative co-operatives', they also have their own members (their own workforce) and encompass the following fields: financial, welfare, training and research.
>
> - **Divisions and Subgroups**. Associations constituted within the framework of MCC between co-operatives operating in the same area, with the aim of taking

advantage of certain common services and economies of scale. They co-ordinate the management of their respective co-operatives in accordance with their own individual strategic framework.

- **General Assembly**. The supreme body of the co-operative and a vehicle for expressing the social will of the members.

- **MCC Co-operative Congress**. The aim of the Congress is to establish the strategic criteria by which the Corporation is to be administered, through the planning and co-ordination of its business units. It is comprised by 650 members delegated by the various co-operatives.

- **Governing Council.** This is the body which represents and governs the co-operative. Its members are elected by the General Assembly.

- **Management Council**. The body which co-ordinates the functions of the management team and advises the Governing Council. It is made up by the general manager and the executive members.

- **Management**. The executive management team of the co-operative, appointed by the Governing Council.

- **Social Council**. The body which represents the members to the co-operative's internal institutions. The number of members on the board is established in accordance with the total number of members in the co-operative.

- **Monitoring Commission.** Auditors appointed to ensure correct compliance with accounting principles and any other areas which require their consideration (Source: http://www.mcc.es/ing/cooperativismo/expemcc/organos.html)

The general assembly of worker-owners democratically elects the governing council, which consists of both professional management and elected representatives. An interesting organ is the social council that is the participatory element in decision making, while the general assembly and the governing council is the control element. The social council report to both the management and the elected organs expressing employee interest related decisions at the operational level of decision making. Earlier the co-operatives had a *watch dog council* elected by members at the general assembly – it seems that this democratically elected body of 3 members has been substituted by professional auditors. The idea behind the watch dog council was the overall control and inspection of management and other governing bodies (Thomas and Logan, 1982)

All workers should in principle co-own the assets and all newcomers can join a co-operative. However in recent years there has been an increase of hired labor without co-ownership in the co-operatives. This is especially true in the case of daughter companies outside the Basque region of Spain, where the co-operative network initially was established. In case of a lack of capital, newcomers can borrow money to be paid back later. The income distribution among worker-owners is not entirely egalitarian as the ratio from the highest income to the lowest is 4.5 to 1.

Regarding profit sharing, its distribution goes into individual accounts in the bank Caja Laboral Popular, to be paid when the worker-owner leaves or retires (70%). These savings must be paid upon departure and they constitute the capital the co-operative bank can work with when funding new ventures and expanding existing ones. The collective part of profit sharing (30%) is earmarked for re-investments and collective consumption (Thomas and Logan, 1982). At Mondragon co-operatives, the workers own the profits of their production. The individual 70 percent is allocated to the members IICA "*individualized internal capital accounts.*" The IICA is a membership fee to become an associated member (equivalent to around $5.000) where $4000 of this initial amount is used to create an IICA. Every year profits will be added relative to the share of capital one has deposited. If there are losses in the co-operative the accounts similarly get smaller. In other words, each member has a personal stake in the capital accumulation process. The IICA is in principle a loan to the co-operative which the worker can get out when he or she decides to retire or to find employment outside the network of co-operatives.

OTHER CO-OPERATIVES AND SUPPORTING STRUCTURES

There is no doubt that the Mondragon co-operatives' growth record in the early years was impressive. Similar experiences are seen in other countries, but it is worthwhile noticing that co-operatives that fare well are most often consumers' or suppliers' co-operatives rather than workers' co-operatives. In Denmark consumers' co-operatives (Brugsen) is seen in the trade of retailing, while suppliers' co-operatives (andelsbevægelsen) are seen in agriculture and to a less degree in fishing industries. As mentioned above, there are worker co-operative sectors in Southern Europe with performance data suggesting that worker co-operatives in certain sectors operate competitively in sectors like for instance crafts and construction, where economies of scale are less possible to utilize. In Denmark, the worker co-operative movement has been a limited success and confronting Danish workers' co-operatives with the Rochdale Principles, it suffices to say that Danish co-op's are not worker managed and worker-owned, but under the control of unions and other associations rooted in the Social democratic movement. Yet, looking at the long term viability of workers' co-operatives and other types of co-op's, the key to an explanation is national supporting structures sheltering the co-operatives from a hostile business climate geared to suit conventional corporations and companies based on capital control. In essence, co-operatives are not based on control of capital but on the members' needs, i.e. membership is open, control is democratic and the needs of the members go before the goal of profit maximization in the neo-classical sense (Winther, 1988).

Supporting structures take the form of enterprise networks, banks and offices comprising financial services and funding, planning, projection and stimulation of entry of new co-op's into the network, marketing, research and development, training, education and labor force development. By sheltering the co-op's into a coherent system, the potential for growth and development are larger than in the case of co-operatives competing alone in the marketplace (Vanek, 1970: 311-327; Vanek, 1977: 171-185).

In the Mondragon co-operatives workers' co-operatives comprise all sectors, also high tech. companies and sectors that can utilize economies of scale. One success indicator has been the co-operative bank "Caja Laboral Popular" founded in 1959 and which today has branches all over the Basque region of Spain. The bank's financial holdings today are some 11 billion Euros, and they have shown an impressive growth from some 300 million in the early eighties (Mondragon, 2008). The bank and other organizations are organized as second degree co-operatives, another expression for multi-purpose co-operatives. Referring again to the co-operatives as need-based organizations, there could of course be cases where several interests are at play. There could be both consumers interests and workers interests or even perhaps all three types of interests adding suppliers interests – in that case democratic control engages interests on an equally composed footing, i.e. if it is a multi purpose co-op consisting of consumer and worker members, control is shared between the two. The Caja serves the interests of the co-operatives, the customers in the bank and the employees of the bank. Hence, all interests are represented at the board of the banks. Other multi purpose structures in the Mondragon network are for instance "Lagunaro", that manages the Corporation's own social security system, "Eroski" a food retailing group of companies with both consumers and workers as stakeholders, "Saiolan" a training centre for entrepreneurship and the development of new ventures (Jakobsen, 2001), the Mondragon University and other education and training companies operated by the co-operatives, "Ikerlan" a research and development centre and at large comprising all fields of life, schools, kindergartens and co-operative housing are also second degree co-operatives. Life in and around the town of Mondragon is co-operatively organized.

HISTORICAL DATA ON COMPARATIVE PERFORMANCE

Yet, supporting structures, especially financial ones, are the underpinning for securing economic viability in the long run. Proponents of the participatory or labor-managed firm in theory and practice often stress another important virtue. Intrinsic factors for best practices and optimal performance are often not included in micro-economics. Economic incentives are important, but labor-psychological factors related to a democratic workplace are as important. Profit sharing is an important incentive, if it results in higher annual labor income than in conventional firms. Additionally, the abolishment of main antagonisms between labor and capital decreases agency costs and removes alienated perceptions among workers. A motivated well-paid work-force that has the feeling of ownership, and participation, may work better or harder in terms of the quality, intensity and duration of labor supplied (Vanek, 1970: 233-254). That could be one further factor behind the impressing growth figures experienced by the Mondragon co-operatives.

Looking into data published in the 1980s, the Mondragon record was astounding. From 1956 to 1986 21.000 new jobs were created, and while in 1976 to 1986 Euzkadi saw 15.000 unemployed, the Mondragon co-operatives increased employment with some 4.200 employee owners. In 1986, the unemployment figure for Spain was 20%, while it was 0.6% in Mondragon – yet no worker-owner was ever fired, because workers went back to the school bench in order to gain new competences to be utilized in other co-op's. Comparative performance indicators showed that output grew faster than in the rest of Spain, and especially comparative productivity figures and profitability figures suggested, that Mondragon fared well, when compared to the rest of Spain or Euzkadi. From 1971 to 1979 the value added per person was higher than in the industry in the rest of Spain for the years (1972, 1973, 1975 and 1977), where data were available, and in terms of value added per factors of production and per fixed asset, it was higher in 1972. Absenteeism was lower in the period from 1965 to 1975 (Bradley and Gelb, 1981; Thomas and Logan, 1982)

Globally speaking comparative research on co-operatives and employee owned companies suggests similar trends. Employee ownership companies in the US with a participatory organization often outperform their comparable companies – it seems that the extraordinary incentives related to co-operatives, employee ownership, profit sharing and participatory management most often is associated with a competitive edge and comparatively speaking a better performance than companies without these structures (Conte and Svejnar 1990; Tyson and Levine, 1990; Winther and Marens, 1997).

NEW DATA ON COMPARATIVE PERFORMANCE

Since the performance studies in the early 1980s, no new empirical studies have been conducted. From the early 1990s, the Mondragon co-operatives were re-organized and have become incorporated as the MCC. Especially in the era of globalization, the MCC has evolved into "group capitalism" – not so much in the regions initially being the base for the evolvement of the Mondragon co-operatives, as in the countries where "daughter companies" were established.

In 1988 with the advent of the new market reforms initiated in the EU to heighten competition between EU countries, the co-founder of the MCC, José Maria Ormaechea argued, that the co-operatives had to become more competitive in order to survive the increased market pressure (Cheney, 1999: 48). The enormous growth of the MCC-complex has been justified by the need for a larger capital base in order to compete with other giant multinational corporations (Cheney, 1999: 76).

The result of these pressures pushed the co-operatives to become a formal corporation, the MCC, in 1991 (Clamp, 2000: 560), which have further centralized power to management and have begun the practice to hire non-members. Nevertheless, it is difficult to assess if these decisions were taken in anticipation of future problems, or if they were merely an arbitrary change of management discourse. One factor that favours the former explanation is that one of the founders of the co-operatives, namely Jose Maria Ormaechea has been in favour of the centralization efforts.

Workers, who are not members, and who therefore have neither democratic influence nor the right to appropriate a part of the profit, are increasingly employed in the co-operatives. *In fact over half of the current staff working in the co-operatives are non-members – which in numbers in 2006 meant over 35.000 of the 70.000 employees. In other words, the democratic structure has been cut in half.* With the corporate structure, the MCC adopted hierarchies and techno-structures placing the employees in the same subordinated relation to management as in conventional companies (Kasmir, 1996; Mondragon Cooperatives, 2006).

The problems that the Mondragon co-operatives have faced in the 1990s, ending up relying increasingly on non-owners, indicate the democratic structure will enter a problematic phase, when they grow and have to compete with other big players in the capitalist system. *Nonetheless, looking back to the co-operative principles of Rochedale and the principles developed by Arizmendi, the Mondragon co-operatives have degenerated into a partially employee owned corporation with partial co-operative principles.*

The MCC describes this situation as explained by the move to go global:

> Due to the rapid growth of the organisation over the last ten years, during which the workforce has increased from 25,322 in 1992 to 83,601 in 2006, just over half of our current staff are not co-operative members. Non-members are mainly concentrated in the distribution sector outside the Basque Country and in our industrial plants located both outside the Basque Country and abroad.

> In our traditional area of activity, i.e. the Basque Country, the creation of new jobs has also risen sharply. Today 80% of the workforce in this area are members. However, many non-members are only temporary non-members, since the majority become members within a two or three year period.

> However, outside the Basque Country, either in Spain or abroad, thousands of new jobs have been created in accordance with the non co-operative system. This is due to: the lack of adequate co-operative laws in the areas into which we have expanded; the fact that many new companies have been set up as part of a joint venture with other partners; and, above all, the fact that the creation of co-operatives requires the existence of co-operative members who understand and are committed to the co-operative culture, something which is impossible to obtain over a short period of time and in such a wide variety of locations. (Source: http://www.mondragon.mcc.es/ing/contacto/faqs6.html)

The MCC still portrays itself as a corporation that has grown at an impressive rate over time and in relation to initial figures. However, using the same comparative approach as in empirical studies in the 1970s, the evidence seems mixed. Using national income data as indirect deflators, a productivity proxy value added per employed suggests, that the MCC in the period 1997 – 2007 had lower averages than the economy of Euzkadi (Gross domestic product per employee) and the economy of Spain (Gross national income per employee). In both comparisons, the MCC were excluded in the computations. Figure 2 below demonstrates that it is not just that the MCC had lower productivity figures. For the 1997- 2001 period the MCC saw negative Growth, while Euzkadi had positive Growth in value added per employee.

Table 1 shows in terms of annual average employment growth, that the MCC still grows considerably faster than both the region (6.8%) and the rest of Spain (4.3%).

Table 1: Comparative Average annual growth value added,
employment and productivity*

	Mondragon Value Added	Spain GNI	Diff.	Euzkadi GDP	Diff.
1997 – 06	9.7%			7.2%	2.5%
1999 – 05	8.3%	7.7%	0.6%		
	Employment				
1997 – 06	10.4%			3.6%	6.8%
1999 – 05	9.0%	4.7%	4.3%		
	Productivity				
1997 – 06	-0.6%			4.0%	-4.6%
1999 – 05	-0.6%	2.9%	-3.5%		

* The periods, where data were available were not the same. The time series for Spain were shorter (6 years) than for Euzkadi (9 years). Accordingly, the differences in growth are read in column 4 (Spain) and column 6 (Euzkadi).

Sources: Mondragon Co-operative Corporation annual reports 1997 – 2007, National Income Accounting for Spain, Instituto National de Eustadistica, National Disposable Income in current prices 1995 – 2006, the EU Labor Force Survey on Spain 1999 – 2005 (Persons in employment by countries, age group, period and sex) and economic accounts and Employment Market, EUSTAT

In terms of value added the growth lead is more modest – this then explains why the productivity proxies for Euzkadi and Spain show a better performance than for the MCC and it may also explain why the Mondragon productivity is lower, as seen in Figure 1. The value added seems to be less and growing at a lower speed. The findings here are contrary to the findings of Thomas and Logan for the period 1971 – 79, who found that for the years 1972, 1973, 1975 and 1977 the value added per person was higher than for Spanish industry; however, we are comparing to the whole economy of Spain and not only to the industry.

Figure 2: Comparative Productivity figures for the MCC, the rest of Euzkadi and Spain

Comparative Productivity Data

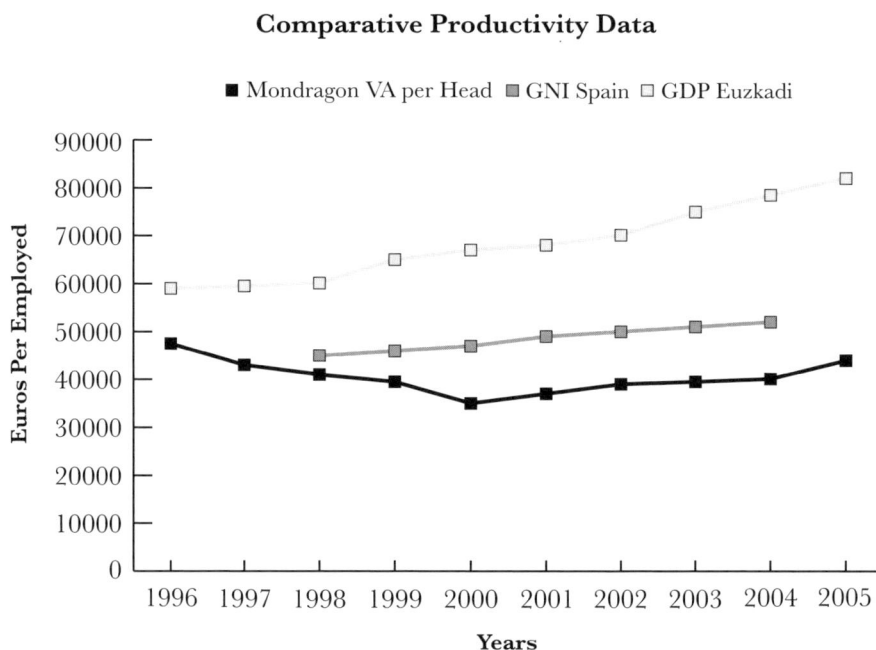

GNI: Gross national Income per employed and GDP, Gross Domestic Product per. Employed. The national income figures GNI and GDP are accumulated value added in the economy. GNI is the GDP – (depreciation + net income flows to/from the rest of the world), while GDP is the production value (revenues) less material inputs. (Sources: Mondragon Cooperative Corporation annual reports 1997 – 2007, National Income Accounting for Spain, Instituto National de Eustadistica, National Disposable Income in current prices 1995 – 2006, the EU Labor Force Survey on Spain 1999 – 2005 (Persons in employment by countries, age group, period and sex) and economic accounts and Employment Market, EUSTAT).

Conjecturing on causalities in a longitudinal perspective, at least two hypotheses come into mind. First, the issue of Mondragon going global to transforming economies and developing economies – productivity figures in these economies are not direct comparable to the Basque region of Spain and the aggregated Spanish economy. In 2006 18 % of employment was outside of Spain. Second, the co-operative principles adopted earlier in the Mondragon co-operatives in Spain have not yet been "exported" to the daughter companies abroad. It is not that managerial echelons of the MCC are not aware of this problem. It is discussed without a solution being found yet. It takes time to educate, and in some cases local reluctance and lack of knowledge is a hindrance for the dissemination of co-operatives. The incentives that may explain a former co-operative's success may not be able to unfold in the daughter companies abroad.

How participatory are the Mondragon co-operatives?

Second, we have the other problem suggested by Kasmir's observational case study of a Mondragon co-operative in comparison with a conventional company. It seems that employees in Mondragon in one company do not feel particularly more motivated than employees in a comparable conventional company. I found similar attitudes among employee owners in five Washington State Employee Ownership companies (Winther, 1999). Quite often social scientific research do not include worker perceptions on the relation to management – it may be that the techno-structure as described by Thorstein Weblen (1921) and John K. Galbraith (1967, 1983) persistently remains to exist also in the MCC, where no empirical study has been conducted yet on perceptions among employees and management on the distribution of influence among occupational groups.

When the MCC went global and got incorporated, the structures of the huge corporation may have meant that the workers to the Mondragon co-operatives have less influence on the day to day operations than before. Again such a development could explain a constraint on the inherent potentials of democratic ownership and control present in unique co-operative structures characterizing the earlier phases of the Mondragon development.

This is as mentioned not to say that circles in the MCC are not aware of the problem of going global without including workers abroad as owners of the MCC. A one day Conference on the Mondragon co-operatives led to a question to the researchers: What can we do, can we go back to the teaching of Arizmendi or are there other solutions to the problem of staying co-operative?

> The MCC itself is aware of the problem a co-operative network going global faces: Being aware of this problem, the Co-operative Congress (General Assembly of all MCC co-operatives), which was held in May 2003, approved a resolution regarding 'Membership Expansion' which urged the organisations responsible for this area to study and develop formulas which would enable non-member employees to participate in the ownership and management of their companies, similarly to that which occurs in co-operatives.
>
> In this sense, we already have a successful precedent. We are referring to a project set in motion in 1998 by the Eroski Distribution Area which, through the company Gespa, offered non-member employees the opportunity of participating in the capital and management of their place of work – a participation formula which was met with enthusiasm by the majority of non-member employees of the Eroski Group.
>
> The Strategic Plan for the period 2005-2008 contemplates the gradual application in our main subsidiaries of a "participative enterprise" model that will channel worker participation in company ownership and management and which by 2008 will involve 30% of the workforce. (Source: http://www.mondragon.mcc.es/ing/contacto/faqs6.html)

What we said above on the evils of a corporate structure included in a co-operative network is acknowledged in leading circles in the MCC. It seems that access to education, capital and other supporting structures in the same way as in the first decades of the development of Mondragon co-operatives are necessary, although perhaps more costly than in conventional corporations.

However, conjecturing why the comparative data turns out so bad, leaves room for the hypothesis that abandoning the democratic organization, caused a loss in comparative efficiency. With the loss of employee commitment, lower motivation and lower productivity result. Further research is imperative to address the issue about the influence of workers with lower productivity in countries where Mondragon was established. In general we need a comparative study of the MCCs performance vis-à-vis traditional corporations. Furthermore, research on the techno-structure, the power relations and worker participation in the co-operatives in Euzkadi and Spain is imperative.

REFERENCES

Blinder, Alan (1990) *Paying for Productivity – A Look at the Evidence*. Washington D.C.: The Brookings Institution.

Bradley, Keith and Gelb, Allan (1981) "Motivation and Control in the Mondragon Experiment." *British Journal of Industrial Relations*, 19(2): 211-231.

Cheney, George (2000) *Values at Work, Employee participation meets Market Pressure at Mondragon*. Ithaca: Cornell University Press.

Clamp, Christina A. (2000) "The Internationalization of Mondragon." *Annals of Public and Cooperative Economics* 71(4): 557-577

Conte, Michael and Svejnar, Jan (1990) "The performance Effects of Employee Ownership Plans" in Allan Blinder (ed.) *Paying for Productivity – A Look at the Evidence*, Washington D.C.: The Brookings Institution.

Demsetz, Harold (1968) "The Technostructure Forty-six Years Later." Reviews, *Yale Law Journal*, 77(4): 802-818

Djilas, Milovan (1957) *The New Class, an Analysis of the Communist System*. New York: Frederich A Praeger.

Edvard, Kardelj (1978) *Democracy and Socialism*. London: The Summerfield Press.

Ellerman, David (2006) *Helping People Helping Themselves*. Michigan: University of Michigan Press.

Ellerman, David (1990) *The Democratic Worker Owned Firm, a Model for the East and West*. Boston, London: Unwin Hyman.

Estrin, Saul, et al (1985) "The Effects of Workers Particiaption on Enterprise Performance: Empirical Evidence from French Cooperatives." *International Journal of Industrial Organization*, 3(2): 197-217.

EUSTAT Euskal Estatistika Erakundea/The Instituto Vasco of Estadística), the Basque statistical bureau 1997 – 2007.

Galbraith, John K (2004) *The Economics of Innocent Fraud, Truth of Our Time*. Boston: Houghton Mifflin.

Galbraith, John K (1983) *The Anatomy of Power*. Boston: Houghton Mifflin.

Galbraith, John K (1967) *The New Industrial State*. Boston: Houghton Mifflin.

Hirst, Paul and Thompson, Grahame (1996) *Globalization in Question – the International Economy and the Possibilities of Governance*. Cambridge: Blackwell Publishers.

Hoover, Kenneth R. (1992) "Mondragons Answer to Utopias Problems." *Utopian Studies*, 3(2): 1-20.

Horvat, Branko (1982) *The Political Economy of Socialism – a Marxist Social Theory*. Armonk, New York: M.E. Sharpe.

Horvat, Branko (1974) "Varför har inte arbetarstyrda företag redan slagit ut kapitalistiska?" *Ekonomisk Debatt* 5.

Horvat, Branko; Markovic, Mihailo; and Supek, Rudi (1975) *Self Governing Socialism: A Reader*. White Plains, New York: International Arts and Sciences Press.

Hunnius, Gerry (1975) "Workers' Self-management in Yugoslavia", in Branko Horvat, et al (eds) *Self Governing Socialism: A Reader*. New York: International Arts and Sciences Press.

Instituto National de Eustadistica, National Statistics institute, Spain 1999 – 2005

International Cooperative Alliance (2008) *Global 300 List 2007, The World's Major Co-operatives and Mutual Businesses*, available at http://www.ica.coop/.

International Cooperative Alliance (1937) *The Present Application of the Rochdale Principles of Co-operation*, available at http://www.ica.coop/coop/1937.html.

Jakobsen, Gurli (2001) "Cooperatives and Training Dimensions in Entrepreneurship." *INUSSUK Arctic Research Journal*, 1: 137-146

Jones, Derek and Svejnar, Jan (1985 "Participation, Profit Sharing, Worker Ownership and Efficiency in Italian Producer Co-operatives." *Economica* (52)208: 449-65.

Kasmir, Sharryn (1996) *The Myth of Mondragon, Cooperatives, Politics and Working-Class Life in a Basque Town*. New York: State University of New York Press.

Levine, David and Tyson, Laura (1990) "Participation, productivity and the Firms Environment", in Blinder, Alan (ed): *Paying for Productivity – A Look at the Evidence*. Washington D.C: The Brookings Institution.

Marx, Karl (1964) Inaugural Address of the International Working Men's Association *Documents of the* First International. *The General Council of the* First International, *1864-1866. The London Conference 1865. Minutes*, published by the Foreign Languages Publishing House, Moscow, for the Centenary of the First International in 1964

Mater et Magistran *Mother and Teacher* Pope John XXIII, 1961 Encyclical Letter of Pope John XXIII issued on May 15, 1961, Catholic Social Teaching, available at http://64.233.183.104/search?q=cache:2gkH71qBxFMJ:www.osjspm.org/major doc_mater_et_magistra_official_text.aspx+Mater+et+Magistra%E2%80%99+o n+Christianity+and+Social+progress&hl=da&ct=clnk&cd=2&gl=dk

Mondragon Corporacion Cooperativa December (2008) http://www.mcc.es/ing/index.asp

Mondragon Corporacion Cooperativa (2006) http://www.mondragon.mcc.es/ing/con-tacto/faqs6.html,

Mondragon Cooperation Cooperativa, Annual Reports 1997 – 2007.

Owen, Robert (1975) Report on the County of New Lanark, in *"A New View of Society and Other Writings"*, partly reprinted in Horvat et Al (eds.) *Self Governing Socialism: A Reader*, White Plains, New York: International Arts and Sciences Press.

Pontusson Jonas and Kuruvilla Sarosh (1992) "Swedish Wage-Earner Funds: An Experi-ment in Economic Democracy." *Industrial and Labor Relations Review*, 45(4): 779-791.

Stiglitz, Joseph (2003) *Globalization and its Discontents*. New York: Norton & Company

Tannenbau, Arnold (1968) *Control in Organizations*. New York: Mcgraw-Hill.

Thomas, Henk and Logan, Chris (1982) *Mondragon – an Economic Analysis*. London: Allen and Unwin

Vanek, Jaroslav (1977) *The Labor-managed Economy – Essays*. Ithaca: Cornell University Press.

Vanek, Jaroslav (1970) *The General Theory of Labor-managed Market Economies*. Ithaca: Cornell University Press.

Veblen, Thorstein (2001)[1921] *The Engineers and the Price System*. Kitchener. Ont.: Batoche Books.

Whyte, William & Whyte Kathleen K. (1991) *Making Mondragon, the Growth and Dynamics of the Worker Co-operative Complex*. Ithaca: Cornell Industrial and Labor Relations Report.

Winther, Gorm (ed.) (2001) "Participatory ownership and Management in Greenland and other Arctic Regions." *Inussuk Arctic Research Journal*, 1: 7-34

Winther, Gorm (1999) "Theory O – is the Case Closed?" *Economic and Industrial Democracy – an International Journal*, 20(2): 269-295.

Winther, Gorm (1995) *Employee Ownership – a Comparative Analysis of Growth Performance*. Aalborg: Aalborg University Press.

Winther, Gorm (1988) *Erhvervsudvikling I Grønland – en Selvforvaltet Fiskeindustri*. Aalborg: Aalborg University Press.

Winther, Gorm and Marens, Richard (1997) "Participatory Democracy May Go a long Way – Comparative Growth Performance of Employee ownership Firms in Wash-ington and New York States." *Economic and Industrial Democracy – an International Journal*, 18(3): 393-422.

Chapter Seven

South American Alternatives to Neo-liberal Globalization: the Cases of Brazil and Bolivia

Steen Fryba Christensen

After Latin America's generalized shift to neo-liberal development strategies in the 1980s and 1990s (Stallings, 1992), the often poor development results produced by neo-liberal strategies have now led to the adoption of a number of alternative strategies in different South American nations.

In the debates on South American development strategies, views differ regarding the extent to which different South American nations have or haven't left the mainstream neo-liberal path of the 1990s[1]. In this chapter I analyze the recent development strategies of Bolivia and Brazil and argue that they have chosen alternatives to a mainstream neo-liberal development strategy.

The analysis aims at characterizing the options of these two countries and at explaining how and why they differ. It is my hope that this will provide a valuable contribution to research on current South American development strategies from the research domain within International Political Economy (IPE) that focuses on the interaction between domestic politics and the world political economy (Lawton, Rosenau and Verdun, 2000: 6) in the current phase of globalization. The assumption underlying this interest in "specific" globalization analysis is that the situations of different countries that take part in the globalization process vary widely and that this variety must be taken into account in order to understand specific responses to (neo-liberal) globalization.

The adoption of neo-liberal reform policies across the board in Latin America in the years just before and after the end of the Cold War (1989) should be understood as a historical and contextually specific phenomenon. The international context has now changed, and there is a tendency to go in new directions. However, national responses at the present moment differ substantially more than in the neo-liberal 1990s. Brazil and Bolivia exemplify these differences. In the analysis, I have dedicated most space and attention to the Brazilian case because Brazil is often seen as a clear-cut case of neo-liberal continuity as opposed to Bolivia. This makes the Brazilian case more complex in terms of discussing Brazil's current policy as an alternative to the neo-liberal strategy of the 1990s.

Neo-liberal globalization and the "Globalization Thesis"

The globalization thesis suggests that there is no alternative to neo-liberal globalization which is understood as a combination of strict fiscal and monetary policies, a reduction in the size of the state, privatization of state companies, deregulation of financial flows and economic openness. According to the globalization thesis a nation cannot opt out, and, if it does there is a big risk that there will be seriously negative development consequences (Ferrer, 1997: 45). However, some analysts disagree with the argument that there is a lack of alternatives to neo-liberal globalization as well as to the argument that this supposed lack of alternatives is exclusively due to economic globalization. Aldo Ferrer argues (ibid.) that neo-liberal globalization simply is not an appropriate policy in the Latin American context. At the same time, the tendency towards neo-liberal globalization has been strengthened by the politics of leading developed states and international financial institutions that have exerted pressure on developing countries e.g. through conditional lending policies of the IMF and not just by market pressure. This argument is valid. A conclusion we should draw from this when analyzing actual development strategies in South America and in other parts of the developing world is that *it is not enough to focus on the dimension of state-market relations and the dimension of class aspects* when analyzing the impacts of globalization on national development strategies. *We should add a North-South dimension* alongside these two dimensions and analyze international political aspects.

In the following, I first analyse the Bolivian case and then the Brazilian case. I briefly explain the shift to neo-liberal development strategies and then go on to analyze how a change in economic, social and political circumstances led to the adoption of different alternatives to the neo-liberal strategies of the 1990s. I seek to explain the variation in strategies as being based on differences in national economic structures and the results experienced after the introduction of neo-liberal reforms.

NEO-LIBERAL REFORMS: THE CASE OF BOLIVIA

Bolivia's adoption of a neo-liberal strategy came about in a gradual manner but was initiated in 1985, briefly after the introduction of democracy in 1982 (Christensen, 2006a). Prior to the conversion to neo-liberalism, Bolivia had pursued a strategy of state-led development in the ISI (import substitution and industrialization) family (Morales, 1994: 130), which aimed at diversifying and industrializing the economy that was based on agriculture and mining. As a result, Bolivia managed to diversify its economy by developing a small industrial capacity and developing the energy sector. However, by the late 1970s, Bolivia's foreign debt exposure left it in a weak position to withstand worsened conditions in international credit markets in the early 1980s. A significant reduction in Bolivia's export prices added to these problems (Loza, 2002). These restrictions had a strongly negative impact on economic growth (Gamarra, 1994: 104), hurt the output in the industrial sector (Auty and Evia, 2001: 187-188) and provoked a major contraction in GDP per capita (Christensen, 2006b: 5). The crisis destabilized the military government, and widespread protests from miners, peasants and urban protesters opened up for democratic elections in 1982 and the withdrawal of the military government (Torcuato di Tella, 1990: 77). The unstable economic and political situation led to a major shift in development strategy in an attempt to adjust to the financing constraints and assure renewed growth with a neo-liberal strategy. The government pursued cuts in public employment, froze wages, initiated a series of privatizations (Gamarra, 1994: 105) and eliminated subsidies in product and capital markets (Petras and Veltmeyer, 2005: 183) and thereby left behind the state-led ISI-model.

The challenge posed by foreign indebtedness and weak state finances led to a further withdrawal of the state in 1990, moving Bolivia further in the direction of neo-liberal globalization. Bolivia opened up for foreign investments in the economically strategic mining and energy sectors (Morales, 1994: 136-142), signed a trade and investment agreement with the United States (Gamarra, 1994) and in 1991 it entered ICSID (Garrido, 2007), the international body for settlement of investment disputes that is part of the World Bank structure. In short, Bolivia was pursuing strategies in accordance with the "Washington Consensus" largely due to the development constraints of the country and in an attempt to reassure foreign private investors while cooperating with the US and international financial institutions by adopting the policies promoted by them.

The policies involved a shift in the control over key sectors in the Bolivian economy from state control to private control, often by foreign multinational companies. This tendency was cemented, when in 1994, during the government of Sánchez de Lozada, the Law of Capitalization was introduced. This law led to the privatization of the last strategic state companies (Petras and Veltmeyer, 2005: 185).

The neo-liberal path had some positive social results, e.g. a reduction in urban poverty from 52.6% in 1989 to 48.7% in 1999 (CEPAL, 2007a: Anexo estadístico, cuadro 4). However, in 1999, Bolivia experienced a drop in per capita GDP and in the period between 2000 and 2003 GDP per capita remained stagnant (CEPAL, 2005: 357) as Bolivia was hit by financial instability and worsening export prices (Loza, 2002). The response to these developments was a deepening of neo-liberal reforms. However, the combination of a deepening of reforms and the economic downturn led to rising poverty. At the national level, poverty figures went from 60.6% in 1999 to 63.9% in 2004, but the increase in poverty was even greater in urban areas (CEPAL, 2007a: Anexo estadístico, cuadro 4), and social inequality widened (ibid., cuadro 12). As a result, Bolivia remained the second poorest country in South America in 2005 (CEPAL, 2007c: 86) with little development and high dependence on the exports of primary goods, particularly gas and oil.

This development provoked popular dissatisfaction and led to a rising tide of demonstrations against the policies of the Bolivian government. This "tide" of contestation started with demonstrations against the privatization of the city of Cochabamba's public water company in 2000, and reached its height in late 2003 when the government sought to let the multinational company LNG Pacific export natural gas to California. The demonstrations against the privatization of water in Cochabamba centred on price hikes on water for private consumption and for farmers. In the case of the demonstrations against natural gas exports to California, the main problem was that people believed that these exports would only benefit domestic and foreign elites but not the broad population (Petras and Veltmeyer, 2005: 187-194). In both cases, the government reacted with harsh repression (ibid.). *The protests became widespread making it clear that the government and its neo-liberal policies had lost backing and legitimacy.* A wide range of indigenous, rural and urban groups took part in the protests that eventually caused the president to resign (Verdesoto, 2004). According to Evo Morales, leader of the political party MAS (Movement Towards Socialism) that was established in 2002 and won the presidential elections in 2005, the protests should be seen as a sign of a unified national movement against the gas policy and the neo-liberal development model and for a more inclusive social order and national control over gas deposits (Christensen, 2006a: 7). The neo-liberal belief system and the policies associated with it were in other words being challenged. This development shows the continued relevance of Karl Polanyi's thinking on the "double-movement" and the importance of counter-hegemonic popular struggles. These struggles were broad-based popular struggles focused on inter-class, inter-ethnic and North-South issues (ibid.).

However, this line of argument has been challenged by left-leaning analysts such as James Petras (2006: 10). In April 2006 he argued that Morales' "policies are oriented toward an integration of Bolivian development with the interests of Western capitalist countries. In this and other respects, the Morales regime is following in the footsteps of his neo-liberal predecessors, not least his pro-big business outlook and his obedience to IMF fiscal, monetary and budgetary imperatives" and in 2007, after the nationalization of Bolivia's energy resources, he further argued (2007: 3) that Morales' "'revolutionary nationalization' of petrol and gas was little more than a tax increase on the rate paid by the multi-nationals (MNC) to the state. Not a single MNC was expropriated." In Petras' view then, cooperation with the IMF and acceptance of MNCs in Bolivia's energy and other natural resource sectors mean that the Morales government can be seen as a government of neo-liberal continuity. I do not agree with this argument. Instead, I find that the Morales government represents a break with the neo-liberal strategy of the 1990s. I analyze this break in the following sections.

After the outbreak of socio-political instability and contestation in the first years after 2000, the Bolivian president, Gonzalo Sánchez de Lozada, and his follower, Carlos Mesa, were forced to step down from presidential power. In the 2005 presidential elections the indigenous leader Evo Morales became president on an electoral platform that called for making the state the engine of development, nationalizing Bolivia's strategic natural resources, and making Bolivia a more socially just country, including a constitutional reform to assure greater representation of indigenous groups (Christensen, 2006a: 8). In short, the electoral platform of MAS and Morales was an open criticism of the neo-liberal economic model from a position which emphasized the need for an economic model characterized by more national control, social fairness and a more active role for the state in assuring such outcomes.

Morales and MAS took over power on January 1'st, and on the symbolic international workers' day of May 1'st 2006, the Morales government introduced a bill of nationalization that, although it did not confiscate existing foreign investments in the energy sector, introduced a hike in taxation in the energy sector to 82 % and established majority ownership for the Bolivian state company YPFB (Christensen, 2006a: 9), thereby assuring a substantial increase in the tax revenue of the government along with a majority control of companies in the key sector of energy.

In June 2006, the government introduced its plan for national development. This plan emphasized that the state should gain a new role as key actor in the reactivation of the economy. It should pursue policies aimed at reducing poverty and bringing hunger to an end, both through job creation and redistributive policies and improved access of the broad population to public goods such as water, health care and schooling. While these goals were to be reached at the same time as assuring macroeconomic stability, the plan was seen as a way to end centuries of colonialism as well as bringing the neo-liberal policies of the last decades to an end.

Distancing itself from the neo-liberal model and policies, Bolivia joined the Bolivarian Alternative for the Americas (ALBA) in April 2006 (Sader, 2007: 1). Alba had been started up by Cuba's president Fidel Castro and Venezuela's president Hugo Chávez in 2004 as an alternative to the Free Trade of the Americas (FTAA) proposition sponsored by the US government. In its self-understanding ALBA stands for solidarity between peoples and for social justice. Bolivia's entry into ALBA can be seen as a symbolic shift in its foreign policy towards cooperation with its Latin American neighbours and away from the close relationship with the United States and its policies.

With regard to the relationship to Cuba and Venezuela, there were concrete signs and acts of solidarity with Bolivia. Cuba sent a large group of doctors to perform cataract operations on Bolivians and donated a number of eye clinics and basic hospitals during 2006 (Morales, 2006). Venezuela, amongst other things, gave financial assistance to Bolivia to construct two coca-processing plants that were to produce coca-tea for exports to Venezuela (Romero, 2007). In this way, Bolivia was taking an autonomous position on the issue of coca-production which the United

States is strongly opposed to. This autonomous stance was again underscored in May 2007, when Bolivia decided to withdraw its ICSID membership, arguing that the ICSID seemed to be biased in its rulings favouring MNCs and the interests of the advanced countries (Weisbrot, 2007). The government's autonomous stance was further cemented when on the symbolic day of May 1'st, it presented a new decree that nationalized the privately owned oil refineries, of which Brazilian Petrobras controlled the two largest. This gave Bolivia's state-owned YPFB monopoly over oil exports from Bolivia (ibid.: 6) and created friction with Petrobrás. However, the Brazilian president Lula ordered Petrobrás to accept Bolivia's offer of US$112 million for the two refineries (La Jornada, 2007) and thereby strengthened Brazil's chances of building up a regional leadership role in South America (Christensen, 2007: 139-158).

In the area of social justice, in October 2006 the Bolivian government introduced the "Juancito Pinto" project that would give a small cash subsidy to poor families on the condition that their children go to school. The project was to be financed by energy taxes (Pamplona, 2006). In this way the government wanted to show a direct link between its energy policy, and thereby also its policy towards multinational companies, and the social benefits provided by the Juancito Pinto project. In November 2007, the Bolivian Congress approved a new social program known as the "Dignity Income" that would transfer 2,400 bolivianos, the equivalent of US$26, to people aged 60 and above. This policy substituted Bonosol (or "Solidarity Subsidy") of 1,800 bolivianos given to people aged 65 or above (Observatório Político Sul-Americano, 2007).

Furthermore, a large number of concrete law initiatives, many of them quite controversial in Bolivia, were developed as part of the process of the Constituent Assembly. One Article called for independence between state and religion, moving away from Bolivia as a Catholic state and towards a situation were indigenous religions would be equal to Catholicism. Another Article proposed to give indigenous communities' justice systems status as ordinary justice while yet another article recognized the coca leaf as a factor of social cohesion and cultural patrimony of Bolivia (ibid.). All of these articles aim at the inclusion of indigenous rights and recognition of indigenous cultures.

The policies are controversial and much opposed in the richer regions of Bolivia where there are strong movements towards breaking free of Bolivia. This shows the strong political polarization in Bolivia at the current moment (ibid.).

In conclusion, Bolivia has pursued macroeconomic stability under the Morales government, although there has been no complete confiscation of MNC property, and Bolivia still aims at having a capitalist economy in which MNCs are welcome to invest, even in strategic sectors, *it does seem that there has been a significant shift away from the neo-liberal policies of the 1990s in Bolivia*. The nationalization of energy, the entry into ALBA, and the decision to leave ICSID and a number of other policies suggest an autonomous policy towards the US, and a policy of challenging interests of powerful economic actors. Similarly, policies aimed at the inclusion of the poor and of indigenous groups seem more determined under the MAS government than ever before. In this process of policy change, the state has played a key role. The same can be said about the role of politics. Thus, the democratic process with the election of Morales and MAS in 2005, and the counter-hegemonic popular struggles prior to the elections were important causal factors behind the change in policies. However, in spite of the crisis provoked by neo-liberal policies and the struggles against them, capitalism and democracy are proving to be resilient in Bolivia, although the current situation of political polarization shows that it is quite difficult to reach a generally accepted order that is widely seen as legitimate.

NEO-LIBERAL REFORMS: THE CASE OF BRAZIL

The introduction of a neo-liberal development strategy happened later in Brazil than in Bolivia. Brazil had pursued a quite successful strategy of import substitution and industrialization (ISI) between 1930 and 1990, reaching a relatively advanced level of industrial development and having turned into the 8th largest economy in the world (Cervo, 2003b: 16). The strategy was based on allowing the state play a central role in regulating the economy through the provision of incentives and protection to the private sector, state ownership and a substantial level of foreign direct investments in the industrial sector (Lima and Hirst, 2006: 23). By the late 1970s, the Brazilian growth success ran into trouble, and Brazil faced a severe balance of payments crisis that led to a severe economic recession in the first three years of the 1980s (Abreu, 2004: 4). This development was similar to what we saw in Bolivia's case. However, as economic growth returned (BCB, 2006: 16), the basic orientation was maintained through-out most of the 1980s, giving Brazil the reputation for being the "laggard" in Latin America in terms of introducing liberal reforms (Abreu, 2004: 7).

However, in the late 1980's, Brazil faced a new balance of payments crisis. This led to a new economic downturn and to the belief that the ISI strategy had been exhausted and that Brazil needed to change its develop-ment strategy both in terms of economic and foreign policies (Lima and Hirst, 2006: 22-23). As a consequence, Brazil introduced a neo-liberal re-form agenda similar to Bolivia's in the 1990s. This change in development strategy was based on a particular interpretation of the functioning of the world system and of Brazil's place in this system. According to the domi-nant view, the international system that emerged with the end of the Cold War was a deeply changed system. The logic of the globalization process had led to deep changes in the functioning of international relations that challenged the autonomy of the state and its ability to control the process of development (Cervo, 2002: 7). The view of the policy-making elites was that as the world had changed, Brazil needed to change itself and its strategy of development in order to assure a "competitive insertion" in the world economy (Pereira, 1996: 164). Brazil had to leave behind old-fashioned nationalism and state-directed development (ibid.: 161-165) and opt for a liberal strategy of open integration in order to avoid isola-tion from the international mainstream and to promote a competitive par-ticipation in the international economy (Vigevani and Oliveira, 2007: 62).

There simply were no better options due to the external constraints that Brazil faced. The prestigious liberal economist Marcelo de Paiva Abreu defends the position that the constraints on Brazil's freedom to pursue an independent line of policy were overwhelming. He argues (Abreu, 2004: 4) that the "scope for choice imagined by those who criticized the policies because they were allegedly based on "conformism with constrained development", or because they were those of a "second class power", or based on ideas of a "conceptually 'small Brazil'", simply did not exist. In short, the scope for choice for Brazil was generally viewed as very narrow due to its development crisis and constraints from the context of globalization and from the country's foreign debt. In such a situation the correct response according to the dominant view at the time was to seek the "confidence" of powerful external actors by pursuing neo-liberal economic policies and a foreign policy aligned with the leading global powers (Guimarães, 2003: 122; Lima, 2005: 33-34). Brazil's president (1994-2002) Cardoso's view was in line with this dominant conception of Brazil's situation and development possibilities. He argued that the dependency relations between the South and the North had changed by the 1990s. In the new situation there were only two possibilities for countries in the South. They could either become an integrated part of a democratic, technological and scientific competitive game where they would need to invest heavily in research and development and join the information economy, or they could become isolated from the modern economy and thereby lose importance and become irrelevant in the global economy. An insistence on national autonomy would not help here; what was needed was to make great technological advances, increase productivity in the economy, and improve the level of education of the population in order to avoid falling behind in this new phase of capitalist history. The Third World could either fall behind in a Fourth World of isolation and desperation or become integrated in the world economy in a subordinate position to the First World (Cardoso, 1996: 12). The goal for Third World countries was therefore to avoid falling behind by opting for integration in the world economy. This idea was understood from a neo-liberal point-of-view and therefore meant that a liberal integration with reduced state intervention in the economy was the answer.

A decisive move in the neo-liberal direction was taken during the government of Fernando Collor de Mello (1990-1992). Collor's government pursued strict fiscal and monetary policies, removed export subsidies, started a privatization process of state companies, and liberalized imports through a process of gradual tariff reductions and the removal of the import licensing system (Palma, 2000: 18). All of these policies were part and parcel of the neo-liberal policy agenda of the "Washington Consensus." As Wilson Peres notes (2006: 69), the loss of faith in the ISI strategy also led to a gradual loss of legitimacy of industrial policies in Latin America and to the new vision that the state should have a subsidiary role in the economy. According to this view, the role of the state was to assure economic stability while the market should assure economic development (Cervo, 2003b: 16-19), since the state and directed industrial policies were seen as being generally ineffective compared to a market-led approach. The neo-liberal direction was maintained throughout the 1990s and arguably deepened during the first presidency of Fernando Henrique Cardoso (1995-1998) with an acceleration of the privatization of state companies (Lacerda, 2000: 133). The Cardoso government's strategy was to privatize state companies, reduce state debt and to open up to international competition in order to assure international competitiveness (Cervo, 2002: 7; Souza, 2002: 22).

Cervo (2003a; 2003b) has criticized the strategy of the Cardoso government for being subservient to the US and suggested that the strategy of open integration lacked an adequate strategy for insertion in the global economy. Some analysts differ with regard to the issue of Brazilian subservience as they argue that Brazil's regional integration policy at the level of Mercosur aimed at balancing relations with the EC and the US and that Brazil was the only country in Latin America to openly resist US free trade initiatives in the region (e.g. Albuquerque, 1998). Cervo agrees (2003a) that Brazil did pursue such a balancing strategy but that nevertheless the general policy was subservient to the US. The weaknesses of this strategy led to an unsustainable path of Brazil's external economic accounts as it did not assure a sufficiently competitive economy (ibid.). Economic growth was mainly a result of growing domestic consumption whereas extra-regional exports did not show dynamism (Souza, 2003: 188). The strategy thus led to a surge in imports and to a rising dependency on foreign capital inflows (Cervo, 2002: 22) in order to finance the explosive growth in the current account deficit in spite of the acceleration of privatizations. This development turned out to be unsustainable and provoked a major devaluation in 1999 and led to relative economic stagnation in 1998-99 along with major difficulties in getting foreign debt and state debt under control. These new severe constraints on Brazil's development were then met with new reforms characterized by a further tightening of fiscal policies in a context of rising unemployment (Bielschowsky, 2006: 12), much like the response given to this type of problem in Bolivia.

Faced with the critical situation provoked by financial instability in the late 1990s, the Cardoso government started to strengthen its criticism of the asymmetrical character of globalization and to argue for more fair rules e.g. in international trade (Lafer, 2004: 135-137). Similarly, the Cardoso government initiated the first South American presidential summit in 2000. The main focus in the first of these summits, that still continue, was to promote the integration of infrastructure, particularly in the area of energy. This initiative can be seen as a move towards a renewed emphasis on the role of the state in planning economic development.

THE LULA GOVERNMENT'S DEPARTURE FROM NEO-LIBERALISM

> Structural adjustment in Latin America is atomising many state capacities and is generating new social movements and political parties which may in time come to challenge the thrust of neoliberal orthodoxies, such as the Lula phenomenon in Brazil. (Gill, 1993: 12)

As this citation shows, there were already hopes in the early 1990s that Lula and his supporters could challenge the thrust of neo-liberal ortho-doxies in Brazil if he and the Workers' Party (PT) were to be successful in gaining presidential power. When Lula and the PT finally succeeded in gaining power in Brazil in 2003, it was with a highly critical attitude towards the neo-liberal strategy pursued in Brazil in the 1990s. Already in his inaugural speech on January 1st 2003, Lula criticized the policies of his predecessors for their neo-liberal orientation. He argued that the policies had not been appropriate for Brazil. Instead they had created an intensification of economic inequality and deprivation in the population and had left Brazil vulnerable towards global financial markets and had posed threats to national sovereignty. A fundamental point of criticism of Cardoso's policy approach was that the government had been "lack-ing a true national development plan, and truly strategic planning" Lula argued (Lula, 2003).

The electoral triumph of Lula and the Workers' Party in the presi-dential elections in 2002 therefore created expectations of a shift in Brazil's development strategy. Analysts differ on how to view the actual development strategy pursued by Lula and the PT during his presidency in the period 2003-2006, though. Some analysts find that Lula's strategy predominantly represents a shift in development strategy (Lima and Hirst, 2006), while others believe that Lula's administration has continued pur-suing and even deepened the neo-liberal agenda (Coggiola, 2004; Rocha, 2007).

Rocha (2007) finds that the Lula government has been pursuing a renewed version of the Washington Consensus that combines strict mac-roeconomic fiscal and monetary policies with business-friendly reforms and targeted social policies. From her perspective the new policy line should be seen as a deepening of neo-liberalism and she argues that this policy line will lead to a continuation of an economic model characterized by social inequality, low economic growth, an emphasis on the primary sector of the economy, and the continuation of the problem of external vulnerability. In spite of such criticisms, as well as the opposite criticism of the government's lack of fiscal discipline, the Lula government has been relatively successful in promoting economic growth and social inclusion. This has contributed to the new victory of Lula and the PT in the 2006 elections where the PT was particularly supported by the poor regions in Brazil. A recent survey from March 2008 found that Lula had a 55 % approval rating, the best result of any Brazilian president since 1990 (Bragon, 2008).

In the following section I will discuss to what extent Lula's presidencies mainly represent neo-liberal continuity or if they mainly represent a policy shift. I argue that although a number of aspects of the development strategy can be seen as a continuation of the neo-liberal policies pursued in the 1990s, there are a number of significant policy changes that should be taken into account when characterizing the development strategy pursued by the Lula government. I will argue that on balance the development strategy represents an important change in certain aspects of economic policy and foreign policy when compared to the neo-liberal 1990s.

Economic policy

The main element of continuity is that the Lula government has maintained a fiscally stringent policy. In fact, the Lula government has pursued an even more stringently orthodox policy line than the Cardoso government in this policy area. As an example, the government "voluntarily exceeded the IMF's budget surplus targets – 4.25 percent versus the IMF's 3.75 percent" (Desposato, 2006: 29). The high target for the primary budget surplus was maintained for some years, and in fact an even bigger primary budget surplus of 4.84% of GDP was achieved in 2005. This shows the high degree of commitment to fiscal stringency that has characterized the Lula government (BCB, 2006: 77 and 82). This very strict fiscal policy stance represents a shift in the PT's orientation. When it was in the political opposition in the 1990s, the PT criticized such strictness and expressed reservations regarding the repayment of the foreign debt and the state debt. It should be noted, though, that Lula and the PT in 2002 campaigned on a policy of respecting contracts – and thus the repayment of the foreign and domestic state debt. This position was spelled out in Lula's "Letter to the People" in June 2002 (Lula 2002a). This change in policy posture on the fiscal front is likely to have helped the PT to gain the elections in 2002. It seems that the Brazilian population has consistently supported policies committed to respecting Brazil's debt obligations.

Fiscal and monetary strictness was part of the overall globalization strategy of the Lula government, and it was motivated by the belief that such policies would be needed to reduce the "country risk" (BCB, 2005: 12-14) and thereby improve credit conditions and the conditions for economic growth. This corresponds closely to the emphasis given to gain "confidence" in international financial markets during the 1990s. The Lula government has been vastly more successful in achieving a reduced external vulnerability than the Cardoso government, and this success has been assured with a set of policies that differ in important ways from the neo-liberal approach to a competitive integration in the world economy pursued by the Cardoso government.

This is not to say that policies generally have differed substantially between the two governments. For instance, there has also been continuity in the policy of seeking to attract FDI and to maintain a relatively liberal foreign trade policy. A good example of the strategy of attracting FDI is the policy of public-private-partnerships (PPP) that aims at attracting private foreign direct investments in infrastructure projects. This policy is motivated on the one hand by a need to improve infrastructure, and on the other hand by the severe fiscal constraints facing the Lula government. Brazil has also not challenged foreign investors as in the case of Bolivia's policy of nationalizing energy resources.

In spite of the significant examples of continuity just mentioned, the Lula government has also pursued a range of policies that qualify as a shift in policy orientation. This shift has been coupled with a new belief that globalization can be shaped and that in spite of the powerful constraints it is faced with, the state has a key role in assuring a successful development path for the country, and it retains an important transformative capacity in the economic area. A second aspect of this policy shift can be found in the foreign policy orientation where the Lula government has moved away from the hypothesis of shared interests with the global North. What characterizes the Lula government is a much more activist and sovereignty-oriented approach to development and to international relations and its attempt at creating a national development plan based on strategic planning.

This move towards a more pro-active and strategically oriented state has been at the heart of the Lula government's highly complex and multi-faceted development strategy.

The strategy of the Lula government is characterized by a renewed emphasis on the state's strategic planning and on industrial policy. In this strategy, the government has emphasized the goal of reducing external vulnerability by boosting exports. According to Abu-El-Haj (2007: 109-110), a neo-mercantilist consensus already emerged at the end of the Cardoso administration between the leading industrial organizations and state agencies such as the national development bank BNDES. The new orientation gained coherence and definition in the Lula government's development plan (Brazilian government, 2003: 1-3), the so-called PITCE program. In this program, the government laid out its guidelines for industrial, technological and foreign trade policies, and argued for a combination of macroeconomic orthodoxy, policies aimed at stimulating innovation, the expansion of exports, and stimulation of economic sectors with a capacity of developing competitive advantages. It was argued that this would open the way for an improvement in the performance of the most dynamic economic sectors in international trade. In this way, the PITCE program represented a return to sector-oriented industrial policies that had been all but left behind in the 1990s. The program singled out four industrial sectors, namely capital goods, pharmaceutical products, software and semiconductors and points towards three technological areas which are seen as promissory: bio-mass, biotechnology and nanotechnology (Ministry of Development, Industry and Foreign Trade, 2004: 9).

The PITCE program can be seen as the initial element in a strategy aimed at restoring the role of industrial development in promoting Brazil's development. The appointment of Luciano Coutinho as the new president of Brazil's National Development Bank (BNDES) in 2007 was one more step in the direction of prioritizing industrial development, particularly in the most advanced areas. In an interview shortly after his appointment, Coutinho called the development strategy of the 1990s a poorly planned policy of openness that led to the destruction of a large part of the most technologically advanced industries in Brazil, and to a major fall in the participation of the industrial sector in Brazil's GDP, and he argued that it will be his foremost goal to turn this development around (Pinto, 2007a: 12). The Brazilian government and Luciano Coutinho thus take an activist Schumpeterian position aimed at using industrial policies in a strategic effort to develop a modern and efficient national economy that is internationally competitive in certain advanced industrial sectors.

The BNDES partakes in this effort along with a number of new institutions that have been formed during Lula's presidency. Amongst these new institutions are Apex-Brazil that promotes Brazilian exports, and Embrapa Agroenergy that promotes the development of bio-fuels based on agricultural products. Similarly, the government has created a ministry for long term strategic planning. All of these institutional innovations have been carried out with a view of promoting national social and economic development.

FOREIGN POLICY

It is in the foreign policy area that the greatest shift in policy can be found. From the conformist and cooperative strategy of the 1990s that emphasized relations with the US and the EU along with sub-regional integration at the level of Mercosur, Brazil's foreign policy under the Lula administration has changed to a strategy that Cervo has called "sovereign affirmation" (Almeida, 2006: 11 and 13). *The foreign policy of the Lula government has three characteristic elements:* a determined defence of Brazilian interests, activism and humanism. In pursuing these elements, Brazil has sought to gain a more prominent role in terms of setting the international political agenda to assure a better representation of the interests and concerns of the developing world and of promoting Brazil's economic development. Lula's Brazil thus seeks to change the globalization process actively through political means whereas Cardoso's Brazil mainly sought to adapt to the constraints imposed by globalization.

Foreign minister Celso Amorim stresses (2007: 233-238) that apart from being an instrument in the development strategy of Brazil, the Lula government's foreign policy also has a humanitarian dimension. In line with this, Lima and Hirst (2006: 22) argue that the "inclusion of the social agenda as a major topic of foreign affairs was one of the first and most important innovations" in the foreign policy of the Lula government. This humanitarian and social aspect of Brazil's foreign policy can be observed in initiatives such as the establishment of a cooperation scheme with South Africa and India, IBSA. The three countries have sought to increase economic links and to introduce policies aimed at the reduction of poverty in the developing world. This is part of the Lula government's attempt to address growing development asymmetries associated with the process of globalization and to defend the marginalized groups and reduce social injustice (Seitenfus, 2007: 18). It can also be observed in Brazil's bilateral relations with Bolivia, where the Lula government has defended Bolivia's right to nationalize energy resources in spite of the costs this has meant for Brazil's Petrobrás (Christensen, 2007).

The IBSA initiative actually can be related to all of the three characteristic elements of the foreign policy of the Lula government. Above, I have argued that it was part of Brazil's emphasis on stressing the importance of the social agenda in its foreign policy. It is also part of Brazil's activist foreign policy approach under the Lula government. With regard to this, the foreign policy has been characterized by a new emphasis on diversification of Brazil's foreign economic relations by establishing cooperation, trade and investment agreements with a host of developing countries. Emphasis has been given to the biggest developing countries. China, India, South

Africa and Russia are of particular relevance here (Mercadante, 2006: 41). Seitenfus (2007: 18) shows this tendency towards greater emphasis on cooperation with the developing countries in a comparison of the destination of Lula's and Cardoso's foreign visits. Thus between the start of 2003 and March 2006, Lula was on 34 trips to developing countries (excluding South America) and on 30 trips to developed countries whereas Cardoso in his eight years was only on 13 trips to developing countries (excluding South America) and on 39 trips to developed countries. When including the visits to South America (ibid.: 19), one notices a relative balance between Lula's trips to developing countries, developed countries and South American countries. In Cardoso's case there is balance between visits to developed countries and South American countries, but much fewer trips to developing countries.

The negotiations and agreements with countries in the global South have helped Brazil achieve a more diversified export structure geographically. This has meant a reduction in its relative dependency on the developed countries, and as a consequence, an increase in its autonomy. Apart from being a conscious strategy of developing a more balanced insertion in the world economy, the emphasis on economic links with the South can also be seen as a response to the growing economic weight of parts of the developing world in the world economy.

In this overall strategy of emphasizing and expanding links with the developing world, Mercosur and South America have been the explicit priority of the government (Amorim, 2007: 118). Integration in South America is seen by the government as the key to strengthening Brazil's sovereign presence in the world and as a way to make Brazil increasingly important on the world stage as the leading country in South America (Lima and Hirst, 2006). The Brazilian government sees its role as a leader of South America as a way to aggregate power and become a pole in a multi-polar world system. The way this should be achieved is through a strategic alliance with Argentina as a basis for using Mercosur as the foundation for integration at the wider South American level (Guimarães 2003 and 2006). The critics of the government disagree with this strategy and believe that the government should emphasize its links with the developed countries more and that the government's policy is too accommodating towards its South American neighbours. The weak response of the Brazilian government to Bolivia's nationalization of Petrobras-owned oil refineries is an example of an overly ideological policy that does not defend the interests of Brazil, according to the critics (Christensen, 2007). However, the government defends itself by arguing that its policy is pragmatic and in the long-term interest of Brazil since its accommodating and solidarity-oriented policies in South America are useful both in terms of Brazil's construction of a leadership position in the region and in its economic expansion.

South America and Latin America overall are indeed rising in importance for Brazil on the economic front. Thus, in 2006 the Latin American Integration Association (LAIA), which includes Mercosur, came to be Brazil's biggest export market, surpassing the EU (SECEX/MDIC, 2007: 20), and exports to South America are the dominant element in Brazil's Latin American exports.

The different alliances Brazil has sought to promote with its South-South policy have instrumental goals in assuring an increase and a diversification of Brazil's exports that can contribute to the economic development of Brazil and they have proved relatively successful. Thus, Brazil's exports in dollar value more than doubled between 2002 and 2006, from US$ 60,362 million in 2002 to US$137,470 million in 2006 (BCB, 2007: 114), with manufacturing exports accounting for more than 60% of the total (SECEX/MDIC, 2007: 17) and an impressive 86.3% of the exports going to LAIA countries (BCB, 2007: 117). This has assured a major trade surplus and an impressive reduction in the relative weight of foreign debt obligations (SECEX/MDIC, 2007: 16). Also, the high percentage of manufacturing exports to the Latin American region and to other developing countries has been helpful in strengthening the manufacturing sector in Brazil.

The IBSA initiative also represents an example of the determined defence of Brazilian interests as it can be seen as a forerunner of the G20 coalition that was established briefly before the Cancún meeting in the WTO's Doha Round of international trade negotiations in September 2003. The members of G 20, which are all from the developing world, include India, China and South Africa along with most South American countries. The group was established as a way for the developing country members to influence the international trade rules in the agricultural sector and thus to change global governance structures in a favourable direction. The main aim is to encourage developed countries and regions, particularly the United States and the EU, to open their markets to agricultural exports from the developing countries and to refrain from using export subsidies in the agricultural sector. Such an opening of developed country markets is believed to be useful in terms of helping to reduce poverty in the developing world, and thus forms part of the social agenda promoted internationally by the Lula government. According to Celso Amorim, the establishment of the G 20 in 2003 helped Brazil and other developing countries avoid a bad agreement in the WTO trade talks (Amorim, 2007). Such a decided effort to reach international trade agreements that would benefit Brazil has also been pursued strongly at the level of the negotiations of a Free Trade Agreement of the Americas (FTAA). During his presidential campaign in 2002, Lula called the FTAA, which was proposed by the Unites States, a project of annexation and not of integration (Oliveira, 2003). The problem with the FTAA, from the perspective of the Brazilian government, is that it would get in the way of an active industrial policy and would provoke deindustrialization along with an increase in external vulnerability and poverty, as happened with the neo-liberal agenda of the 1990s (Guimarães, 2006).

Thus, the Lula government seeks to combine political and economic power in a realist fashion through coalition building with Southern partners and stronger economic links with the South with particular emphasis on South America. The aim is to strengthen Brazilian economic development, to assure a more balanced globalization, and procure greater Brazilian influence on the international political stage. In short, Brazil seeks to live up to its potential as a powerful nation in the concert of nations. The size of Brazil's economy, territory and population means that this aim is realistic if Brazil is successful in dealing with its problems.

The Lula government's global change agenda, with its emphasis on the aim of reducing global development asymmetries and reducing poverty and problems of hunger, has been criticized by the opposition in Brazil. Critics fear that the government's style, with its open criticism of the developed countries, could prove to be counterproductive for Brazil's development (Lafer, 2004: 139-145). Ricardo Seitenfus, on the other hand, defends Brazil's foreign policy and argues that the symbolic dimension in Lula's change agenda has been received well on the international stage (Seitenfus, 2007: 19).

It is thus clear from Lula's very strong criticism of the neo-liberal policies prescribed by the developed countries in the 1990s that his government is taking a critical and activist position on the international stage as opposed to the more adaptive and defensive policy of his predecessors.

Brazil's break with neo-liberalism during the Lula government is thus particularly strong with regard to the North-South dimension when compared to the foreign policy orientation of the Brazilian governments between 1990 and 2002.

Summing up, I would argue that Brazil's foreign policy orientation in combination with its trade policies and domestic development policies form a complex package of policies aimed at creating the right conditions for sustained economic growth and poverty reduction in Brazil.

This strategy has been relatively successful as it has helped assure improved economic growth and the stabilization of the economy. It is important to stress that in spite of its emphasis on *'credible'* and strict macroeconomic policies the government has in fact pursued an agenda aimed at reducing social disparities in a country characterized by a high level of social inequality. According to Guimarães (2003), social inequality is one of Brazil's biggest challenges. The solution to this problem, however, is not mainly to be found in the area of social policies but in the area of job creation. Therefore, the reduction of external vulnerability and the building of a strengthened productive capacity have been central to the social orientation of the Lula government. In spite of this, social policies have been an important feature of the policies of the Lula government. I will illustrate this below by looking at the *Bolsa Familia* program and the minimum wage policy of the Lula government.

SOCIAL POLICY

The most salient social policy initiative under the Lula government is the *Bolsa Familia* program which the Lula government instituted in 2003. *Bolsa Familia* is a cash transfer program which targets poor families. Transfers are conditioned on school attendance of these families' children. The program has been greatly expanded during Lula's presidency. In 2003 some 3.6 million families were included in the program. By 2005 the number had risen to 8.7 million (Mercadante, 2006: 123), and today some 11 million families are included in the program (The Economist, 2008 April 17).[2] In 2007, the program was thus expanded to also include almost 2 million young people between the ages 15 to 17. This program is generally considered to be an important reason for the government's popularity, but it has also been criticized for contributing to a too large tax load that weighs down the private sector and holds back economic activity and growth. Finance Minister Guido Mantega, however, defends the policy and argues against those who favor fiscal spending cuts, also in this area. According to Mantega, the government's social programs contribute to reducing social inequality and by injecting more money into the economy they contribute to strengthen demand in the domestic market. As domestic demand rises, it increases the demand for those domestically produced manufacturing goods that are difficult to export. Thereby, the social programs contribute to a new model of economic growth in Brazil according to Mantega. He calls it the "social developmental model." This model is characterized by sustained growth, a growing market of mass consumption and, finally, Brazil's dynamic export performance that has created large trade surpluses and helped stabilize the economy (O Estado de São Paulo, 2007).

The same arguments are brought forward to defend the minimum wage policy of the Lula government that is another policy aimed at reducing social asymmetries and exclusion. In the first three years of the Lula government, the minimum wage increased 20.6% in real terms (Mercadante, 2006: 128), and at the end of 2006, after the election of Lula as president for a second term, a new policy was instituted in this area determining that the minimum wage should grow at the speed of the inflation plus the rate of growth in the period 2008-2011. Likewise, it was to be adjusted by 5.3% in real terms in 2007. Again, besides reducing inequality in Brazil, the increased real wages for poor wage earners was seen as a way to inject billions of Reais into the economy and thereby contribute to economic growth based on the domestic market (Folha Online, 2006).

The claim of the government is that this so-called "social developmental model" shows that they are creating change and social improvements through their overall policy orientation. In this way, they try to legitimize what some analysts see as strict "neo-liberal" policies and a continuation of a "neo-liberal developmental model."

These policies have been quite successful in terms of economic growth and the reduction of Brazil's extremely high level of social inequality. A study from Ipea shows that the gini-measure of inequality in family income was reduced from 0.593 in 2001 to 0.566 in 2005 (Barros, Carvalho, Franco and Mendonça, 2007: 15). At the same time vigorous economic growth, coupled with relatively strict fiscal policies, have led to a reduction of the GDP/public debt coefficient from around 55% in 2002 to 42.2% in early 2008 (The Economist, 2008). Brazil is experiencing an exceptional period of economic growth coupled with reduced inequality and greater economic stability and may have broken the instability of the period between the late 1970s and 2002.

CONCLUSION

Bolivia and Brazil both embarked on neo-liberal strategies as a response to financial crises and economic depression in the final years of the 20th century. In both countries the view was that there was no alternative to neo-liberal reforms due to economic globalization and political pressure from international financial institutions and leading states such as the US. Neo-liberal adjustment was therefore seen as a way to maximize national economic development opportunities by way of cooperating with global powers and accepting their recommendations in terms of development strategy. The belief underlying this strategy of "passive adjustment" was that the two countries lacked alternatives. To there was no real scope for choosing other strategies than a strategy of open integration in the global economy and the withdrawal of the state. In this strategy, foreign direct investments played an important role as a dynamic factor in the economy so policies aimed at attracting FDI were introduced. Both Bolivia and Brazil sought an international insertion that emphasized economic ties with the developed countries, although Brazil saw sub-regional integration in Mercosur as a way to balance relations with their main economic partners the US and the EC.

However, Bolivia and Brazil both experienced renewed problems with external vulnerability and economic stagnation in the late 1990s and in the beginning of the 2000s. The disappointing results led to the adoption of new development strategies in both countries.

In Bolivia's case the poor development results led to political instability and social mobilizations against neo-liberal reforms were repressed violently. However, counter-hegemonic forces forced two presidents to step down before Evo Morales was elected on a platform that promised to fight against neo-liberalism and US domination, for nationalizations and strengthened social policies, and for constitutional reform that would ensure better representation of indigenous groups. After winning the election, the Morales government went ahead with nationalizations in the energy sector and other sectors, although without an all-out confiscation of private property from the MNCs that were typically dominated by foreign capital.

In this way a combination of protests from counter-hegemonic forces against neo-liberal policies and the democratic elections that led Morales to power led to a break with the neo-liberal strategy of the 1990s. Apart from nationalizations and increased spending on cash transfers to poor sectors of the population, the Morales government also made important changes in foreign policy. The entry into ALBA and thus coalition with countries such as Venezuela and Cuba is an important example of a more autonomous foreign policy than the more US-aligned policies of the 1990s. Another example was Bolivia's exit from the World Bank's ICSID, where Bolivia argued that this organ that judges international investment related conflicts was biased and tended to systematically favour MNCs from developed countries over the interests of less-developed countries. Bolivia's relatively radical strategy can be explained by the historical experiences of poor development results associated with neo-liberal reforms that made an impoverished population fight against continued neo-liberal policies. Bolivia's backward economic structures, where industry is weak and energy resources form the backbone of the economy, help explain why Bolivia ended up nationalizing energy resources against the interests of economic elites and foreign MNCs. Although the Bolivian government has not pursued a radical policy of outright confiscation of property, the policy line of the Morales government has led to strong political polarization in Bolivia and it has not been possible to stabilize the country politically.

In Brazil's case the neo-liberalism of the 1990s has been attacked discursively by the current Lula government that came to power on an electoral platform that promised change without breaking contracts. Lula and the Workers' Party were elected on this platform as a consequence of the disappointing development results associated with the neo-liberal strategy of the 1990s. Some argue that Lula's government has continued neo-liberalism or even deepened this direction with business-friendly policies. The Lula government has not pursued radical reforms that would go against the interests of economic elites and foreign investors. I believe that these aspects of continuity should be understood in the light of Brazil's economic structures that are characterized by a substantially more developed industrial sector than in Bolivia's case. Brazil has thus sought to reduce external vulnerability by seeking to establish the "confidence" of international financial markets and a positive image amongst foreign investors more generally as a way to protect and strengthen its industrial capacity. However, in the analysis I have argued that although the policies of the Lula government can be seen as a continuation of macro-economic orthodoxy and other policies characteristic of the neo-liberal model of the 1990s, the overall policy orientation has undergone significant changes that make it reasonable to speak of the development policy of the Lula government as an alternative to the strategy pursued in the 1990s.

There are two main aspects that characterize this change in policy. First, the state has regained much of its centrality. It has not done so through nationalizations, but rather through strategically oriented in-dustrial policies aimed at sectors where Brazil either already has, or is believed to have, a good chance of developing competitive advantages when assisted by strategic state policies. In this way, strategically planned development is back in Brazil after having basically been left in the 1990s. There is a new belief in the transformative capacity of the Brazilian state. The issue of international economic diplomacy, and more generally an activist foreign policy, is the second area where the Lula government has introduced important changes. In this area, the Lula government is characterized by a much more activist and affirmative foreign policy that at times is openly critical of the foreign policies of leading powers such as the United States. The strategy is no longer one of relatively passive align-ment with the United States. Instead, the Lula government emphasizes relations with other developing countries, particularly the most economi-cally dynamic and politically powerful countries such as India, China and South Africa. These relations have been strengthened through economic agreements that improve Brazilian business opportunities and exports and through coalition building. With regard to coalition building, the G20 is a tool used by Brazil and other developing countries to concentrate power and gain a stronger negotiation position in the WTO, with the aim of influencing the global governance of trade and related economic issues in a direction that is beneficial to Brazil's (and those of other developing countries) development possibilities. Brazil is also engaged in a strategy of uniting South America with Brazil as a regional leader. This policy has two goals, namely to strengthen Brazil's economy and to make Brazil more influential politically on the international political scene. Also Brazil faces difficult challenges in this realm, particularly due to competition for influence in the region with the United States, it does seem that it has made important progress in this area. As with the neo-liberal policies of the 1990s, these foreign policies are also being pursued with a view of improving Brazil's economic development.

It does seem that the current strategy is more successful than the neo-liberal strategy of the 1990s. The current strategy has reduced external vulnerability significantly, and economic growth is now increasing in spite of the downturn in the US, largely on the basis of strong domestic demand. Poverty and economic inequality have been reduced. According to finance minister Guido Mantega, Brazil is introducing a new development model, namely a "social-developmental model" characterized by stable economic growth, job creation and reductions in economic inequality. This model has not been pursued through a major break with neo-liberalism, but the two types of changes in development strategy mentioned above have been instrumental in assuring some success for this new model, and in creating conditions that make its future success more likely. The elements of con-tinuity, such as orthodox macro-economic policies and a relatively liberal economic set-up have been part of the overall policy orientation of the Lula government and have contributed to its success. The new policy ori-entation can be said to combine elements of orthodoxy and heterodoxy in the economic sphere along with an affirmative and creative foreign policy approach, and it has been developed through a prism of finding policy solutions that "fit" the circumstances. The policies pursued by the Lula government thus fit Brazil's circumstances as a large industrial economy with serious problems of social inequality and external vulnerability much better than the strategies of the 1990s. On the basis of Brazil's suc-cess with the alternative strategy pursued by the Lula government, Brazil today enjoys political stability and dynamic economic growth through a strategy that has not directly challenged powerful market players but has found a better way to engage them.

NOTES

1   Mainstream neo-liberalism is exemplified by John Williamson's famous list of policy suggestions for Latin America known as the "Washington Consensus" (Williamson, 1990). The ten points on the list are: 1. Fiscal discipline. 2. Reorientation of public expenditure. 3. Tax reform. 4. Financial liberalization. 5. Unified and competitive exchange rates. 6. Trade liberalization. 7. Liberal rules for foreign direct investments. 8. Privatization. 9. Deregulation. 10. Secure property rights.

REFERENCES

Abreu, Marcelo Paiva de (2004) *The political economy of high protection in Brazil before 1987.* IADB-INTAL, Working Paper SITI-08A, Buenos Aires.

Abu-El-Haj, Jawdat (2007) "From Interdependence to Neo-mercantilism: Brazilian Capitalism in the Age of Globalization." *Latin American Perspectives, Issue 156,* 34(5): 92-114.

Almeida, Paulo Roberto de (2006) "Uma nova 'arquitetura' diplomática? – Interpretações divergentes sobre a política externa do Governo Lula (2003-2006)." *Revista Brasileira de Política Internacional,* 49(1): 95-116.

Amorim, Celso (2007) *POLÍTICA EXTERNA BRASILEIRA Volume II: Discursos, artigos e entrevistas do Ministro Celso Amorim (2003-2006).* Ministry of Foreign Affairs, Brasília.

Auty, Richard M. and Evia, J.L. (2001) "A Growth Collapse with Point Resources: Bolivia", in Richard M. Auty (ed) *Resource Abundance and Economic Development.* New York: Oxford University Press.

Barros, Ricardo Paes de; Carvalho, Mirela de; Franco, Samuel and Mendonça, Rosane (2007) *A Queda Recente da Desigualdade de Renda no Brasil.* Discussion Papers 1258, Instituto de Pesquisa Econômica Aplicada (IPEA). Brasília.

BCB (2007) *Informe Annual 2006.* Central Bank of Brazil, Brasília.

BCB (2006) *Informe Annual 2005.* Central Bank of Brazil, Brasília.

BCB (2005) *Informe Annual 2004.* Central Bank of Brazil, Brasília.

Bielschowsky, Ricardo (2006) "Vigencia de los aportes de Celso Furtado al estructuralismo." *REVISTA DE LA CEPAL,* 88: 7-15.

Boletim OPSA (2007) *Boletim OPSA, 04, jul./ago 2007.* Downloaded from OPSA's homepage (Observatório Político Sul-Americano, IUPERJ, Rio de Janeiro) in November 2007.

Bragon, Ranier (2008) "Aprovação a Lula atinge 55 % e bate recorde desde Collor." *Folha de São Paulo*, 31/03/2008.

Brazilian government, (2003) *Diretrizes de Política Industrial, Tecnológica e de Comércio Exterior*. Brazilian government (Presidency), Brasília.

Campos, Iris Walquíria and Pinto, Paulo Silva. (2007) "Plano B." *INDÙSTRIA BRASILEI-RA*, 73: 10-16.

Christensen, Steen Fryba (2007) "The influence of nationalism in Mercosur and in South America – can the regional integration project survive?" *Revista Brasileira de Política Internacional*, 50(1): 139-158.

Christensen, Steen Fryba (2006a) "La Política Energética de Bolivia y las Relaciones entre Bolivia y Brasil" pp. 1-24 in *Sociedad y discurso, No. 10, 2006*. Downloaded on January 22, 2008 from http://www.discurso.aau.dk/dec%2006%20no10/Sociedad%20 y%20discurso%20Nr.10-final/Steen.pdf.

Christensen, Steen Fryba (2006b) "An Analytical Framework for Studying Weak but Not Failed States: The Case of Bolivia", in *proceedings from the Conference Power, Politics and Change in Weak States* held by GEPPA on March 1-2 2006 in Copenhagen.

CEPAL (2007a) *Panorama social de América Latina 2007*. CEPAL, Santiago.

CEPAL (2007b) *COHESIÓN SOCIAL: Inclusión y sentido de pertenencia en América Latina y el Caribe*. CEPAL, Santiago.

CEPAL (2007c) *Anuário estadístico de América Latina y el Caribe, 2006*. CEPAL, Santiago.

CEPAL (2005) *Estudio Económico de América Latina y el Caribe 2004-2005*. CEPAL, Santiago.

Cervo, Amado Luiz (2003) "A POLÍTICA EXTERIOR: DE CARDOSO A LULA." *Revista Brasileira de Política Internacional* 46(1): 5-11.

Cervo, Amado Luiz (2002) "RELAÇÕES INTERNACIONAIS DO BRASIL: UM BAL-ANÇO DA ERA CARDOSO. *Revista Brasileira de Política Internacional* 45(1): 5-35.

Coggiola, Osvaldo (2004) *Governo Lula: da esperança à realidade*. Xama, São Paulo.

Desposato, Scott W. (2006) "From Revolution to *Rouba Mas Faz?*" *ReVista. Harvard Review of Latin America* (Spring): 29-32.

Di Tella, Torcuato S. (1990) *Latin American Politics: A Theoretical Framework*. Austin: University of Texas Press.

Ferrer, Aldo (1997) *Hechos y ficciones de la globalización: Argentina y el Mercosur en el sistema internacional*. Fondo de Cultura Económica, Buenos Aires.

Ferrer, Aldo (2003) "Globalisation, Argentina and Mercosul", in Helio Jaguaribe and Álvaro de Vasconcelos (eds.) *THE EUROPEAN UNION, MERCOSUL AND THE NEW WORLD ORDER*. London: Frank Cass.

Fiori, José Luís (1997) *Os moedeiros falsos*. Editora Vozes, Petrópolis.

Folha Online (2006) "Salário mínimo de R$ 380 vai injetar 8,5 bi na economia em 2007." *Folha Online*, December 12th 2006.

Gamarra, Eduardo A. (1994) "Crafting Political Support for Stabilization: Political Pacts and the New Economic Policy in Bolivia", in Acuña, Carlos H., Gamarra, Eduardo A. and Smith, William C. (eds.) *Democracy, Markets, and Structural Reform in Latin America*. Boulder: Lynne Rienner.

Garrido, Mario Hubert (2007) "El Gobierno rechaza un arbitraje sobre las inversiones internacionales en el país" in *Prensa Latina, May 18 2007*. Accessed on the internet on May 21 2007 from http://www.rebelion.org/noticia.php?id=51032

Gill, Stephen (1993) "Gramsci and Global Politics: Towards a Post-Hegemonic Research Agenda", in Gill, Stephen *GRAMSCI, HISTORICAL MATERIALISM AND INTERNATIONAL RELATIONS*. Cambridge: Cambridge University Press.

Guilhon Albuquerque, José Augusto (1998) *U.S. and Brazil Bilateral Foreign Relations as a Major Obstacle to Hemispheric Integration*. Version presented in October, 1998, Ottawa. NUPRI/USP paper. Downloaded from NUPRI on August 12 2005 at http://143.107.80.37/nupri/wpn9861.htm.

Guimarães, Samuel Pinheiro (2003) "The International Political Role of Mercosul II", in Helio Jaguaribe and Álvaro de Vasconcelos (eds.) *The European Union, Mercosul and the New World Order*. London: Frank Cass.

Guimarães, Samuel Pinheiro (2006) *Brasil na era dos gigantes*. Contrapontos, Rio de Janeiro.

Hay, Colin; Marsh, David (2000) "Introduction: Demystifying Globalization", in Colin Hay and David Marsh" (eds.) *Demystifying Globalization*. New York: St. Martin's Press.

Hugueney, Clodoaldo (2003) "Brazilian Foreign Policy at the Beginning of the Twenty-first Century", in Helio Jaguaribe and Álvaro de Vasconcelos (eds.) *The European Union, Mercosul and the New World Order*. London: Frank Cass.

Hurrell, Andrew (2006) "Hegemony, liberalism and global order: what space for would-be great powers?" *International Affairs*, 82(1): 1-19.

Izique, Claudia (2006) "Tanque quase cheio." *INDÚSTRIA BRASILEIRA*, 66: 26-29.

La Jornada (2007) "Lula ordena a Petrobras aceptar la oferta de Bolivia por sus refierías", in *La Jornada*, 11-05-2007.

Lacerda, Antônio Corrêa de (2000) "Desenvolvimento e inserção externa da economia brasileira", Antônio Corrêa de Lacerda (org.) *DESNACIONALIZAÇÃO: MITOS, RISCOS E DESAFIOS*. Editora Contexto, São Paulo.

Lafer, Celso (2004) *A Identidade Internacional Do Brasil E A Política Externa Brasileira: Passado, Presente E Futuro*. Editora Perspectivas, São Paulo.

Lawton, Thomas C; Rosenau, James N; Verdun, Amy C. (2000) "Introduction: Looking Beyond the Confines" in Thomas C. Lawton, James N. Rosenau and Amy C. Verdun *Strange Power: shaping the parameters of international relations and international political economy*. Ashgate, Aldershot.

Lima, Maria Regina Soares de (2005) "A POLÍTICA EXTERNA BRASILEIRA E OS DESAFIOS DA COOPERAÇÃO SUL-SUL." *Revista Brasileira de Política Internacional, janeiro-junho*, 48(1): 24-591.

Lima, Maria Regina Soares de and Hirst, Monica (2006) "Brazil as an intermediate state and regional power: action, choice and responsibilities." *International Affairs*, 82(1): 20-41.

Loza, Gabriel T. (2002) "Bolivia's commodity price shock" in *CEPAL Review*, 76: 167-183.

Lula, Luíz Inácio 'Lula' da Silva (2002) *Carta ao povo brasileiro*. Declaration presented on June 22, 2002 during the presidential election campaign. Downloaded from the internet October 14, 2005 from: http://www.globalizacion.org/democrasiasur/documentos/BrasilLulaCaraPovoBrasil

Lula, Luíz Inácio 'Lula' da Silva (2003) Address to the Congress by the President of the Federative Republic of Brazil, Luiz Inácio Lula da Silva, on the occasion of his inauguration – *A New Course for Brazil*. Downloaded from the internet on October 14, 2005 from: http://www.mre.gov.br/ingles/politica_ext.../discurso_detalhe.asp?ID_DISCURSO=206

Lula, Luíz Inácio 'Lula' da Silva (2005) Declaração à imprensa do Presidente da República, Luiz Inácio Lula da Silva, por ocasião da visita official ao Brasil do Presidente dos Estados Unidos da América, George Wl Bush. http://www.mre.gov.br/portugues/politica_externa/discursos/procura3.asp

Lula, Luíz Inácio 'Lula' da Silva (2007) "Discurso do Presidente da República, Luiz Inácio Lula da Silva por ocasião de visita à sede da representação da FAO para a América Latina e o Caribe", April 26, 2007. Downloaded from the internet on June 22, 2007 from: http://www.mre.gov.br/portugues/politica_externa/discursos/discurso_detalhe3asp?I

MAPA (2006) *Plano Nacional de Agroenergia: 2006-2011*. Ministry of Agriculture, Brasília.

MDIC (2004) *O Futuro da Indústria de Bens de Capital: a perspectiva do Brasil*. Ministry of Development, Industry and Foreign Trade, Brasília.

MDIC (2006) *O Futuro da Indústria: Biodiesel*. Ministry of Development, Industry and Foreign Trade, Brasília.

Mendonça de Barros, José Roberto and Mendonça de Barros, Alexandre Lahóz (2005) "A revolução do agronegócio/agroindústria com base na economia do conhecimento" in João Pulo dos Reis Velloso: *O Desafio da China e da Índia: A Resposta do Brasil*. José Olympio Editora, Rio de Janeiro.

Mercadante, Aloizio (2006) *BRASIL: PRIMEIRO TEMPO. Análise comparativa do governo Lula*. Planeta, São Paulo.

Morales, Juan Antonio (1994) "Democracy, Economic Liberalism, and Structural Reform in Bolivia" in Acuña, Carlos H., Gamarra, Eduardo A. and Smith, William C. (eds.) *Democracy, Markets, and Structural Reform in Latin America*. Boulder: Lynne Rienner.

Morales, Evo (2005) "I Believe Only In The Power Of The People", in *ZNet/Activism*. Downloaded from the internet on July 03, 2007 on http://www.zmag.org/content/print_article.cfm?itemID=9389&sectionID=1

Morales, Evo (2006) "Capitalism Has Only Hurt Latin America", Spiegel interview with Evo Morales in *Der Spiegel 35/2006 – August 28, 2006*. Accessed on February 8'th 2008 from http://www.spiegel.de/international(spiegel(0,1518,druck-434272,00.html

Observatório Político Sul-Americano (2007) *Boletim OPSA, 2007* (6). Downloaded from the internet on Janary 22, 2008 on http://observatorio.iuperj.br/pdfs/27_boletins_Boletim_nov_dez.pdf

O Estado de São Paulo (2007) "'A diferença é que hoje se divide o bolo enquanto ele é produzido' (Entrevista Guido Mantega, Ministro da Fazenda)" in *O Estado de S. Paulo, October 14th 2007*.

Oliveira, Amâncio Jorge de (2003) "O governo do PT e a Alca: política externa e pragmatismo." *ESTUDOS AVANÇADOS 17* 48: 311-329.

Palma, Gabriel (2000) *The Magical Realism of Brazilian Economics: How to Create a Financial Crisis by Trying to Avoid One*. CEPA Working Paper Series III. New School for Social Research, New York.

Pamplona, Nicola (2006) "Imposto banca bolsa-escola boliviano." *O Estado de São Paulo,* 26-10-2006.

Pereira, Luiz Carlos Bresser (1996) *Crise Econômica e Reforma do Estado no Brasil: Para uma nova interpretação do Estado no Brasil*. Editora 34, São Paulo.

Peres, Wilson (2006) "The Slow Comeback of Industrial Policies in Latin America and the Caribbean." *CEPAL REVIEW* 88: 67-83.

Petras, James and Veltmeyer, Henry (2005) *Social Movements and State Power: Argentina, Brazil, Bolivia, Ecuador*. London: Pluto Press.

Petras, James (2006) "Centre-Left" Regimes In Latin America", posted on *countercurrents.org*. Downloaded in November 2007 at http://www.countercurrents.org/petras080406.htm.

Petras, James (2007) "Latin America: Four Competing Blocks of Power", posted on *countercurrents.org*. Downloaded in June 2008 at http://www.countercurrents.org/petras280407.htm

Pinto, Paulo Silva (2007a) "A reindustrialização como meta." *INDÚSTRIA BRASILEIRA,* 77: 10-15.

Pinto, Paulo Silva (2007b) "O que esperar dos encontros." *INDÚSTRIA BRASILEIRA,* 74: 30-33.

Rocha, Geisa Maria (2007) "Celso Furtado and the Resumption of Construction in Brazil as an Alternative to Neoliberalism." *Latin American Perspectives* 34(5): 132-159.

Romero, Simón (2007) "Venezuela Rivals US in Aid to Bolivia." *The New Your Times,* 23-02-2007.

Sader, Emir (2007) *ALBA: From Dream to Reality*. Article downloaded on June 13, 2008 from http://www.globalpolicy.org/empire/challenges/general/2007/0517albareality.htm

Saraiva, José Flávio Sombra (2005) "Dois anos da Política Externa de Lula." *Boletim Meridiano,* 47(52-53): 19-20

SECEX/MDIC, (2007) *Brazilian Trade Balance: Consolidated Data, January-December 2006*. Secretariat of Foreign Trade and Ministry of Development Industry and Trade, Brasília.

Seitenfus, Ricardo (2007) "O Brasil e suas relações internacionais." *Carta Internacional.* (Março): 11-21.

Singer, Paul. (1985) *Repartição da renda: Pobres e ricos sob o regime militar*. Jorge Zahar editor, Rio de Janeiro.

Souza, Amaury de (2002) *A AGENDA INTERNACIONAL DO BRASIL: UM ESTUDO SOBRE A COMUNIDADE BRASILEIRA DE POLÍTICA EXTERNA*. CEBRI, Brasília.

Souza, Amaury de (2003) "Brazil in a Globalising World" in Helio Jaguaribe and Álvaro de Vasconcelos (eds.) *The European Union, Mercosul and the New World Order*. London: Frank Cass.

Stallings, Barbara (1992) "International Influence on Economic Policy: Debt, Stabilization, and Structural Reform", in Stephan Haggard and Robert R. Kaufman (eds.) *The Politics of Economic Adjustment: International Constraints, Distributive Conflicts, and the State*. Princeton: Princeton University Press.

Strange, Susan (1996) *The retreat of the state: The diffusion of power in the world economy*. Cambridge: Cambridge University Press.

The Economist (2008) "Brazil: The delights of dullness." April 17th 2008.

Verdesoto, Luis (2004) "¿Hacia dónde va Bolivia?" *Nueva Sociedad* 191: 38-49.

Vigevani, Tullo and Oliveira, Marcelo Fernandes de (2007) "Brazilian Foreign Policy in the Cardoso Era." *Latin American Perspectives,* 34(5): 58-80.

Weisbrot, Mark (2007) *A New Assertiveness for Latin American Governments*. Downloaded from the internet on June 17 from http://www.cepr.net/index.php/op-eds-columns/op-eds-columns/a-new-assertiveness-for-latin-american-governments/

Williamson, John (1990) "What Washington means by Policy Reform", in John Williamson (ed.) *Latin American Adjustment: How Much Has Happened?* Washington: Institute for International Economics.

CHAPTER EIGHT

Alternative Approach to Well-being Attainment and Measurement

Li Xing & Mammo Muchie

INTRODUCTION
Revisiting development and underdevelopment

Since its inception in the 1950s, the notion of development has been an equivalent term with "progress" and "modernization." Nowadays it has become an analogue of "economic growth". In this sense, development denotes a movement away from something that is considered to be "underdeveloped." Since the word "underdeveloped" was invented in comparison with the development level of the West at the end of World War II,[1] the majority of the world population had suddenly degraded into a status of "underdevelopment." The dichotomy between development and underdevelopment was thus established behind the thinking: to develop is to think oneself as underdeveloped and is to escape from a condition called underdevelopment.

Since then, all non-Western countries have been more or less in a process to "develop" or to "catch up." The *Petit Robert* dictionary contains the following text under the general heading of "development": "Developing country or region, whose economy has not yet reached the level of North America, Western Europe, etc. Euphemism created to replace underdeveloped" (Rist, 1997: 8). The basic assumption of development, regardless of its definition, is of a linear teleology vis-à-vis the standard criteria of measurements: economic growth and expansion, wealth accumulation, mass production and consumption. One is considered as being "developed" if it can meet these measurements.

These measurements reflect the thinking which dominates development theories, practices and policies. They have become institutionalized discourses of the powerful global agencies such as the World Bank and the IMF. These discourses, whether economic, political and sociological, are rooted in a basic paradigm – commonly referred to as the modernization paradigm. Seen from this paradigm, development is an evolutionary process; and development and underdevelopment are differences between rich and poor nations in terms of visible economic, political, social and cultural gaps. The alleviation of *observable* poverty is seen as the objective of development

Hence, the *notion* of the mainstream ideology of development is entirely based on neoclassical economic theories which suggest that the sole goal of economic activity is to maximize profit and that individual preferences are the most important aspects of human being. It also implies that a modernization process to bridge these gaps by means of a follow-up imitation through which less developed countries will gradually assume the material living standard of the Western industrialized nations. In light of this implication, development is seen as a universal process as well as a characteristic of human societies rather than a concrete historical process taking place in specific societies during specific periods.

It is generally recognized that the neoclassical economics is derived from Adam Smith, who founded the discipline of economics in his *Wealth of Nations* in which he sketched the theory of general equilibrium characteristics of a market economy – the pursuit of private gain can be socially productive under conditions of free competition. Interestingly enough, Smith was also a professor of moral philosophy at Glasgow University whose publications included *The Theory of Moral Sentiments*. Besides Smith, many of the celebrated nineteenth-century economists, from Thomas Malthus and John Stuart Mill to Francis Edgeworth and Alfred Marshall, also took moral considerations seriously (Cooper, 2000: 163). However, there is unfortunately a mismatch between the modern professional economics emphasizing competition, productivity, efficiency, the free market and moral-ethical frameworks of social justice, collective values as well as human development. To be short, it is the separation between economics and ethics, because economics and the market are seen as ethically value-free.

Globalization and well-being

In the past two decades, forceful national and international developments in market-oriented reforms have been sweeping around the world, spreading from the northern to the southern, and from the western to the eastern hemispheres. These movements have changed relations in the national and international political economy between capital-to-labour, capital-to-capital, and capital-to-state, in which transformations are taking place in favour of the capital. Consequently, economic and social relationships in accordance with international norms of productivity, capital returns and competitiveness are redistributing resources from "non-productive" sectors (welfare, health, education, social and cultural activities) to "productive" ones (financial market, trade).

The question over globalization – whether the increasing levels of international trade, finance, investment and cultural communication have positive or negative impact on advancing human well-being for the majority of world population – is still being debated. It is our point of departure that development in the era of rapid globalization has not delivered well-being to all nations and peoples. On the opposite, it has actually increased hunger and poverty in many development countries[2]. The neoliberal discourses of globalization that: 1) economic growth and increased trade achieved through deregulation and privatization automatically increases the wealth of communities and humanity; and 2) increased foreign investment in developing countries promotes their productive capacities and development improving the well-being of the poor, have proved false. On the contrary, globalization has actually increased the well-being of transnational corporations that have perpetuated it (Anderson and Cavanagh, 2000: i).

A published *Special Report*[3] from The International Forum on Globalization (IFG) concentrates on the three decades of globalization's rapid growth and finds that the outcomes for the poor were exactly the opposite of what is claimed by globalization advocates. In fact it concludes that the effects of globalization have contributed to increased poverty, increased inequality between and within nations, increased hunger, increased corporate concentration, decreased social services and decreased power of labor vis-à-vis global corporations. The findings of this report correspond to the conclusions of numerous research literatures on this issue.

Numerous issues of UNDP *Human Development Report* also admit that "Human development is the end – economic growth a means. So, the purpose of growth should be to enrich people's lives. But far too often it does not. What we have seen in the past decades clearly show that there is no automatic link between economic growth and human development" (UNDP, 1996: 1). Therefore, it is the time to question the entire discourses of globalization paradigm, to reconceptualize the meaning of development, and to reconstruct well-being measures by putting human and society at the centre rather than market and economics. In connection with the studies on the impact of globalization, it is proposed here that such impact must not be narrowly studied on the basis of monetary data. Rather, it should be analyzed and measured from social perspectives as well.

Objectives and methodological considerations

The key theoretical incentive of this paper is to seek how Amartyr Sen's contribution on the conceptualization of development is to be taken forward. Sen has brought us an appropriate starting point for further research with his broad alternative development thinking. This paper is part of the on-going endeavours by many scholars in an attempt to contribute to the discussion of social well-being. It has three objectives: 1) to offer a framework of understanding the notion of well-being as essential part of social development; 2) to signify the limits of conventional measures of well-being attainment and performance; and 3) to propose an alternative interdisciplinary approach to constructing well-being measures.

Methodologically, what we intend to do is a process of deconstruction and reconstruction of theories and applications, i.e. to break down the established way of thinking and practice, and to recreate a new worldview and interpretation of the truth and reality in order to find alternative methodological epistemology and policy implications. We are challenging the conventional quantitative and objective measures that are entirely based on the monetary dimensions of well-being, income and consumption. However, what is proposed here is to add the non-monetary elements as well as the subjective dimensions, such as emotion, capacities in maintaining social-cultural-political coherence as important indicators of measuring well-being. Thus, well-being is associated not only to material well-being, but also to *subjective well-being*[4] in terms of social relations, freedom, security, self-confidence and happiness, etc. It is a bottom-up approach to the understanding of well-being and progress.

The overall objective is to formulate conceptual framework and a fresh approach for ranking the different countries in the world not merely on the number of individually reckoned well-being attainments but on the determination of the structural social capacity for sustaining and making such attainments irreversible. It is an attempt to make a contribution to this research area in which main literature on human development generally starts from individual human well-being as a measure for ranking how well countries are doing. It intends to add the structural variables for well-being /ill-being production/destruction that express the significant systemic features that are not often apparent in development studies literature and journals.

FROM AMARTYA SEN TO NEW IDEAS ON DEVELOPMENT AND WELL-BEING MEASURE
Development as freedom

As an Indian economist, Sen's award was widely appreciated after a series of prizes given to American economists, whose works were largely focused on narrow issues, such as the financial markets. The heart of Sen's unconventional writings (1985, 1999a), especially his *Development as Freedom* (1999b), combines moral philosophy with development economics. These two issues are traditionally seen as separate ones by professional economists. Sen's concept of development incorporates economic, social and political considerations to enhance the freedoms that people enjoy, i.e. an individual's ability to choose to lead the life he/she wants and to freely interact with world (Sen, 1999: 74). In Sen's own words, he points out that:

> What people can positively achieve is influenced by economic opportunities, political liberties, social powers, and the enabling conditions of good health, basic education, and the encouragement and cultivation of initiatives. The institutional arrangements for these opportunities are also influenced by the exercise of people's freedoms, through the liberty to participate in social choice, and in the making of public decisions that impel the progress of these opportunities. (Sen, 1999: 5)

Based on Sen's comprehension, development entails the expansion of five essential substantive human freedoms: political freedom, economic facilities, social opportunities, transparency guarantees and protective security. It is not only the promotion of each freedom but also the connection between them that is the core of development (Sen, 1999: 40). Individual freedom from Sen's perspective is a social commitment, meaning that the exercise of such freedom is inseparably connected with social, economic and political institutions. Different kinds of freedom interrelate with one another and freedom of one type can greatly promote freedom of other types. For example, substantial freedoms are not guarantees of happiness, good health and social security which need to be supported by instrumental freedoms, such as economic opportunity to use resources, political choices about laws, social questions about arrangement of health care, transparency guarantees and the security of a social safety net.

Sen is among others advocating *freedom* as the key to an ethical under-standing of development and as the overarching norm of development. It includes the eradication of starvation, undernourishment, escapable morbidity and premature mortality. It also takes account of freedom that is associated with being literate and numerate and with enjoying political participation and decision-making process. Freedom, according to Sen, should not be regarded either as a means to achieve economic develop-ment or as an objective that can be compromised or upgraded/degraded in the name of promoting economic wealth.

Democracy and economic development

Another conceptual contribution of Amartya Sen is on the notion of democracy. Many may not necessarily agree with him on his arguments (1999c) about the relationship between democracy and development, but his concept of democracy as well as his idea on the functions and the uni-versal value democracy is of great inspiration. Unlike conventional liberal understanding of democracy, the universal value of democracy, seen from Sen, must not be identified with the principle of majority rule. Democracy is an inherent part of his "development as freedom" concept. There are three essential aspects which democracy can enrich people's lives:

> First, political freedom is a part of human freedom in general, and exercising civil and political rights is a crucial part of good lives of individuals as social beings. Political and social participation has *intrinsic value* for human life and well-being … democracy has an important *instrumental value* in enhancing the hearing that people get in expressing and supporting their claims to political attention (including claims of economic needs) … democracy has *constructive* importance, in addition to its intrinsic value for the lives of the citizens and its instrumental importance in political decisions. (Sen, 1999c: 10)

Hence, democracy is defined her in terms of 1) *political freedoms* (political participation, civil rights, free speech and elections; 2) *social-cultural opportunities* (education, cultural value and health care); 3) *economic needs and participation* (trade and production). Based on this understanding, democracy is seen as being able to play a constructive role in promoting economic development and to generate personal well-being as well as public resources for social well-being.

Rethinking the conventional well-being measures

Thus, Sen is making a conceptual challenge to what is normatively taken for granted in the comprehension of economic development and especially in the understanding of development measurement. In our view including many other scholars', the flaws of most conventional monetary measures – economic data such as Gross Domestic Product (GDP), Gross National Product (GNP), Purchase Power Parity (PPP) are numerous: 1) they fail to give a real picture when using them for across-country comparisons due to the wide differences from country to country in terms of exchange rate anomalies, differentials in tariff and tax rates, as well as subsidies to consumption goods; 2) these data put an emphasis on the market value of economic production, that is the rate at which resources are converted to commodities and consumptions together with other paid services and activities. For example, the expansion of military budgets, expenditures on prisons, wars and crime including prevention expenditures, as well as environmental costs (the destroying of forests and the toxic dumpsites) seem to make GNP and GDP data impressive; 3) they do not take account of tradable goods and services that do not enter the market, for example, self-sufficiency, female contribution to households, elders unpaid tutoring of youth, care for the sick and elderly, voluntary work of civic societies, etc, and other social aspects, such as family and community coherence, emotional well-being, social stability.

Although higher economic growth or more increase in income is a significant component of development and is important in measuring development and technological level, it is neither the only part nor the essential part. For instance, good health, adequate education, greater longevity, the ability to influence the political decisions or the freedom to choose alternatives cannot be adequately reflected by these data. This is because these data are too narrow to the extent that they are unable to shed light on the existence of some basic human needs and the real condition of individuals in a country. Here are some examples:

1) *Monetary indicators have little or no correlation with actual benefits to the well-being of the poor or the marginalized groups.* The United States, the so-called "the largest liberal democracy" with the highest GNP/GDP per capita, is witnessing the rise of economic inequalities among the population due to the monopoly of capital and concentration of wealth. 500 giant monopolies accounted for 92 per cent of all income in 1994. During the 1980s, according to UNICEF's *The State of the World's Children* 1994, an additional four million children fell into poverty although the wealth generated by the country's economy expanded by one-fifth. According to *The State of America's Children's Yearbook* 1994, the percentage of child poverty affected 22 percentage of all children by 1992, and infant mortality rates for black children increased more than double those for white children (Watkins, 1995: 4-5). In the United Kingdom the number of people who live on less than half the average income reached 12 million, which more than double the number in 1979 (Watkins, 1995: 4-5). So, even in many developed countries within the North with high GDP and GNP per capita, the distribution of income and wealth is extremely uneven causing some people live in a misery situation.

2) *Monetary indicators tend to have a wrong focus.* The minimum economic well-being standard set by the World Bank is a-dollar-a-day, which implies the dividing line between basic well-being and poverty. By the Bank's calculation based on this standard, 23% of the world population (1.2 billion people) living in poverty. However, the flaw of such a measure is that it is such a generalization that it fails to

reflect the price differences among developing countries in purchasing goods and services. The focus of this measure also creates
a misperception that an individual's well-being depends on his/
her own resources and abilities or on the external "assistance". It
ignores the constraints of a person's environment that impose on
him/her by nature or by policy or by the capitalist world system.
For example, it could be far better for people in underdeveloped
countries to live in an environment free of war and malaria than
to have a-dollar-a-day living standard.

3)   *High income cannot fully explain well-being status.* Afro-American males
have a lower life expectancy than males in China and parts of India,
although their average real income is far higher. It was the mass-
based health care system (the three-tiered system[5]), implemented
by China under Mao, rather than increased income that had
helped to increase the nation's longevity and overall demographic
improvement (Li, 1999 and 2002). World Bank *Development Report*
(1981) stated that China's economic structure and national income
per person were similar to that of other low-income countries, but
the physical quality of life of majority of the Chinese people was
strikingly better than in most other low-income countries. Chinese
life expectancy increased from 36 years in 1950 to 64 years in 1979
was claimed by the World Bank as outstandingly high for a country
at China's per capita income level.

Therefore, the mainstream monetary measures of well-being attainment
cannot be seen as representative indicators, and they can even be ab-
surd in the case of a serious economic crisis in which GDP data can still
increase even though the well-being of the majority of the population
and communities decreases. Hence, they need to be added, refined or
reconstructed by taking into consideration other critical elements.

RECONCEPTUALIZATION OF
WELL-BEING AND ITS MEASURES

> To feel depressed, cheated, bitter, desperate, vulnerable, frightened, angry…. to
> feel devalued, useless, helpless, uncared for, hopeless, isolated, anxious, and a fail-
> ure; these feelings can dominate people's whole experience of life, coloring their
> experience of everything else. (Wilkinson, 1997: 215)

Social well-being

In our proposed alternative conceptualization of well-being, it is important to differentiate social well-being from both individual well-being and
the aggregate of individual well-beings. Social well-being refers to the
ability of a society to generate and sustain (including the degree of depth,
culture, norm and commonsense) the society's system-scale attainments. It
includes the capacity of the institutional structures in place and the quality of the provisions of four types of well-beings entitlements (described
below) to all the citizens starting from the least advantaged (Rawls, 1971):

1) basic well-being (e.g., food, shelter, clothing, the goods for
   self-respect)
2) additive well-being (e.g., health, education, identity expression,
   culture)
3) freedom from subtractive and divisive well-being (e.g. environmental degradation, violence, crime, coercion, deception, genocide,
   ethnic-cleansing, lynching, slavery, psychological torture, forced
   displacement and migration, rape and abuse)
4) multiplicative well-being (e.g., ease of mobility, degree of comfort,
   ease and participation in creative and public life, spiritual fulfillment, confidence and growing self-respect and psychic health)

Basic well-being covers the indispensable physical conditions, such as expected longevity, adequate nourishment, shelter and absence of morbidity possible, in the context of an ecologically sound environment which

223

retains its integrity even as people continue to draw the means for their physical functionings from it. Freedom from subtractive and divisive well-being is attained via the political and social functionings which make possible ease and degree of living by the population with a sense of security especially with freedom from the invasive actions by the state, organized crime networks and other agents of well-being subtraction and division. It implies the absence of restriction on the agency of freedom for the population to participate in public life as well as on the population's immunity from violence, deliberate deception, and discrimination on the ground of belief, religion, ethnicity, culture, race, gender, age or sexual orientation. Above all it implies a convivial environment for living from subtractive intrusions, which damage psychological well-being and increase society's threshold of psychological distress. Individuals, groups and whole populations should be in a position to live without shame about their position in society for having any self-defined identity so long as such identity creates no particular negative externality on the freedom to others. It also implies harmonizing human well-being development with the reduction of harm to the environment such as the atmosphere, lithosphere/geosphere, biosphere, and the hydrosphere.

Additive and multiplicative well-being refers to derivative and higher order achievements often made possible by a given population's collective intellectual, spiritual and aesthetic qualities institutionalized as a prevailing commonsense and value for a given society. Such non- primary attainments manifest through having knowledge, resources and confidence to handle problems of life and living. They imply intellectual fulfillment through contribution to human knowledge. They suggest aesthetic fulfillment through the expression of creative faculties, and spiritual fulfillment measured by the success of a population's psychological health. The latter is enhanced through the participation of a population using the free time attained by societies for well-being development in order to further and expand leisure, recreation and the higher pursuits of life.

Social well-being achievement can be defined as the foundation for continuous social innovation and learning for the preservation and deepening of the four well-being components and their workings as well as the degree to which these have been embedded in a country's histories, institutions, values, norms, interests, morals, politics and intellectual life. A country where the above well-being functionings have become part of the societal commonsense, routine, norm, moral sense and culture, with a conscious and well-informed population ready to resist any encroach- ment towards subtractive tendencies, can be said to have built a credible basis for social well-being attainments as well as further enhancement. Thus social well-being suggests the existence of a sufficiently habituated and embedded political, moral and intellectual public culture to resist attempts to subvert/ erode covertly and overtly such well-defined well- being attainments. It implies a shared belief and coherence amongst all competing and/ or cooperating actors on the need to preserve maintain and sustain institutional arrangements and policy direction to continue deepening and refining these achievements with further learning and innovation.

In line with other progressive and critical approaches

The way that we approach to social well-being shares similar thinking with the way ecological economics' approach to *sustainability*. Neoclassical expansionists treats the economy as "an independent, self-regulating and self-sustaining system whose productivity and growth are not seriously constrained by the environment", and they believe that "humankind has achieved mastery over relevant parts of the natural world and through technology will be able to compensate for the depletion of any important natural resources" (Rees, 1999: 28-29). By contrast, ecological economists sees the economy not in isolation but "as an inextricably integrated, com- pletely contained, and wholly dependent subsystem of the ecosphere," and the economy is thus seen as a highly ordered, dynamic system main- tained by available energy imported from the ecosphere (Rees, 1999: 30). Seen from this perspective, industrial metabolism (the Western mode of production transforming nature into goods and service) becomes an extension of biological metabolism (returning waste to nature). In line with this type of thinking, a society's sustainable development is conceptualized as such:

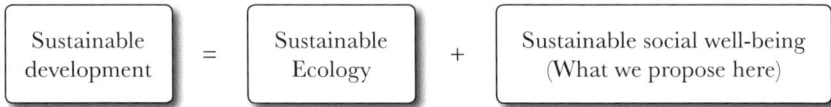

Sustainable development	=	Sustainable Ecology	+	Sustainable social well-being (What we propose here)

Another similarity can be seen from the new methodological epistemology being applied in the area of *health studies*. Health can also be defined in non-medical terms as "being confident and positive and able to cope with the ups and downs of life" (Stewart-Brown, 1998: 1608). It can also be associated with social dimensions – social health. It is now widely accepted that illness in terms of mental and psychological problems cannot be expressed fully by descriptions of medical disease such as size of infarction, tumour load, and forced expiratory volume. According to many medical scientists, in studying health problems "Psychosocial factors such as pain, apprehension, restricted mobility and other functional impairments, difficulty fulfilling personal and family responsibilities, financial burden, and diminished cognition must also be encompassed" (Muldoon, et al.1998: 542). This area of research termed "health related quality of life" has become an integral variable of outcome in clinical research as a result of understanding the various effects that illnesses and treatments have on patients' daily life and life satisfaction (Muldoon, et al.1998: 542). In terms of social health measurement, indicators can include infant mortality, child abuse, suicide, drug abuse, drop-out rates, divorce, family violence, etc.

RECONSTRUCTION OF WELL-BEING ATTAINMENT AND MEASUREMENT

The concept of social well-being focuses on bringing an understanding of a population's quality of life status by putting a premium on the quality of social relationships and inter-citizen interactions based on five inter-related and mutually reinforcing factors:

a) The attainment of the four well-being components and the functioning they impart to citizens starting from the least advantaged in society;

b) The establishment of such attainments as part of the society's commonsense, routines, values, tradition, culture and norm;

c) Social arrangements anchored in a morally interrogated, politically and intellectually reflexive pedigree, which remain sufficiently robust to withstand any attempt to reverse these attainments;

d) The existence of a recognizable degree of coherence and ethical worth of the institutional arrangements and the competing actors in society to anchor well-being development on a sustainable trajectory and commitment;

e) The existence of a shared belief, myth or metaphysics to enhance and consolidate such social well-being attainments with continuous social innovation, democratic dialogue, knowledge and learning.

In effect, social well-being measures the capacity of a society's institutional arrangements for resisting invasive activities which subtract human well-being. It is not the number of years people live, but the quality of living including their psychological well-being that the concept tries to capture and measure. Social well-being attainment thus refers to the ideas, social practices, culture, and attitudes achieved by a given society in expanding and multiplying well-being freedom, well-being agency, well-being functioning and well-being capability not only at the individual level in the Sen's sense, but also at the societal/social level in the sense of achieving a bottom line for social well-being achievement anchored in the social structure of a given society.

Social well-being attainment depends largely on the strength of a society's shared norms and the coherence of its political societies (political parties), civil society (traditional and professional associations) and economic society (business and industrial establishments). Two principles need to emerge as a shared belief for institutions and agents to manifest coherence: a) they learn not to do to others what they do not desire or find appropriate to be done to themselves, and b) their thinking, feeling, speaking and doing are not contradictory or incoherent making possible undesirable moves to use rhetoric, semantics and public relations to organize deception, manipulation, myths and lies to subtract the populations' possible well-being attainments.

Since the 1990s, the UNDP has been measuring individual well-being attainments with the human development index (HDI) assigning scores to population in countries by taking factors such as life expectancy, literacy and individual income's purchasing power parity (PPP) levels, and physical quality of life index (PQLI) to measure the well-being of a population by combining infant mortality, life expectancy and literacy. This move by the UNDP coincided with the time when globalization was in a rapid expansion. The concept of social well-being, which we use here, takes a step further by including the coherence of a society's social arrangements and conducive space for individual actors. Capabilities and freedoms are the independent variable, whereas individual functionings, capabilities and freedoms are the outcome or dependent variable.

Thus, what is pertinent for analyses is the strength and weakness of the institutional arrangement for well-being attainment, the degree of coherence of the actors and agencies in promoting such well-being and the capacity of the culture, values, morals, tradition and prevailing commonsense habituated over historical time to resist internal and external policy reversals and retreats in relation to well-being development. We have thus inverted the parameters to be measured from the individual to the societal and social.

Social well-being should thus be understood as system-wide societal achievement not just as aggregate individual well-being measured by discrete factors such as life expectancy, morbidity and per capita income adjusted to PPP (purchase power parity). It is within the systemic social process rather than merely counting the discrete attainments of education, health and nutrition by the individual, which distinguishes social well-being from other well-being. It is also the quality of well-being and living as much as any measures of longevity, knowledge and health that matter. That is, social well-being affirms that the well-being of a given society cannot be exhausted merely by reckoning mathematically the levels of discrete well- being functionings of the individuals constituting it. That is, it cannot be established merely by individual well-being aggregation. Social well-being focuses on how society's functionings work to make the individuals in it function well as the organizing principle. Social well- being is thus more than the sum of the aggregates exhibiting an emergent novel property of system-wide scope.

Measuring social well-being attainment does not exclusively rely on these data because: a) GNP and per capita as an indicator is limited; b) human development index (and/or associated measures) fails far short of capturing the habituated commonsense the society has built up for social well-being measures; and c) physical quality of life index is not enough. Though the UNDP improvement on measures of per capita income is a progressive step, intellectual thought and policy ought to concentrate in developing the conceptual framework on social well-being attainment as the core of social development to progress further society's moral, intellectual, cultural and political performance and success.

ALTERNATIVE WELL-BEING MEASUREMENT IN THE ERA OF GLOBALIZATION

When relating our proposed well-being thinking and measurement to globalization's impact on economic growth, inequalities of incomes, poverty reduction and human ill-being destruction and the creation of human well-being. The objective is to clarify how the on-going globalization is dealing with the diversity of social issues. Since Sen has opened a door to philosophical approach to economics and development, we intend to come up with a concrete thinking on alternative well-being measurements.

The impact of globalization on well-being attainment

We shall elaborate the central thesis of globalization by extracting it from the available voluminous literature and correlating the impact of globalization on the determinants or means of well-being achievement (basic, additive, multiplicative well-being, and including freedom from subtractive, fracturing and divisive impacts on well-being), with the threshold of social well-being actually attained from the countries selected for comparative evaluation. By this new conceptual device of social well- being attainment, it is possible that the materially richest country such as the USA may come low in overall social well-being attainment rating, while some poorer countries' social well-being can be higher than expected.

What is perhaps most significant about the globalization thesis is, for better or worse, the re-fashioning of some of the key political and economic determinants of well-being development. It is therefore important to extract the way in which globalization has re- worked the means of social well-being attainment. In brief, since the 1980s, there has been a remarkable convergence of economic change with social transformation affecting virtually all regions of the world. Common features, which express these changes, have been the following: over-emphasis on market liberalization, privatization, de-regulation, reduction in government expenditure on social services, and state retreat from economic activities. The state's role in economic and social engineering is being questioned contrary to the Keynesian celebration of the state as the chief determinant of welfare provision and the architect of the post- war social- democratic consensus. With globalization, liberal ideas penetrate into the restructuring of state, economy and society. The market has been selected as the chief mechanism to make adjustments and restructuring of society, economy and the state. Globalization became the sort of code-name chosen to describe and express the processes and changes in economy, state and society as spearheaded by liberalization, privatization, de-regulation and cutbacks on public spending and service provisions.

Taken together, the above can be seen as the drivers for globalization. While these are easy to identify, globalization itself is very difficult to theorize either in the field of international relations and/or development studies. It is a highly contested concept. Conceptual difference in defining globalization is partly to do with the differing normative assumption and the polarization of views on the potential and likely consequence from the process itself. Some have argued globalization increases global welfare. Others emphasize the mal-distribution aspect of this welfare. There is thus no agreed consensus as to the meaning of globalization.

In what way is the on-going globalization different from interdependence and transnationalism which have been used to capture the tendency of the global political-economic dynamic? Both interdependence and transnationalism made the nation-state and the transnational economic interest groups as leading actors in international relations. The former describes "the reciprocal effects among countries or actors in different countries" (Keohane and Nye, 1997: 8), while the latter refers to the decrease of influence of state and the increase of primarily economic actors across boundaries. As the UNRISD points out,

> Global restructuring continues to accelerate, driven by and lockstep with global financial flows – over 90 per cent of which are speculative.... These new forces of globalization have already undermined national sovereignty – not only in domestic macro economic management of fiscal and monetary policy, but also in loss of social policy options in health, education, safety nets, employment, environment and even the values and culture of citizens. (UNRISD, 1995: 27)

Globalization can be conceptualized in many ways. In practice it has taken the form of global restructuring in the industrialized countries, shock therapy in Russia and Eastern and Central Europe, and structural adjustment in the less developed countries of Africa, Asia and Latin America. That is to say, globalization has manifested itself in different forms in various regions of the world: in the mature industrialized world globalization has brought about economic restructuring, de-regulation, privatization, weakening of labour unions and cut backs on welfare provisions and public expenditure. The main feature has been to weaken the state provision and protection of welfare rights and entitlements thus directly impacting on the quality of life of the population.

In the developing world globalization takes the form of structural adjustment to discipline the state and de- centralization through market and social liberalization in civil society. "... the major beneficiaries of adjustment have tended to be small groups of individuals with access to foreign exchange... we are witnessing peculiar types of social polarization and fragmentation, both of which are detrimental to the social and political order..." (UNRISD, 1995: 4) In the former Soviet-bloc countries and what are now known as transitional economies, globalization has imposed them a "shock therapy" excision of their economics and social system. According to a commentator "the ex-socialist countries have exchanged security for freedom and totalitarianism for crime" (UNRISD, 1995: 5).

It is important to ask what implications the empirical existence of globalization as an idea, practice, rhetoric/discourse and policy has on the quality of life of the populations of the countries where globalization inspired policy measures have been carried out either in the form of restructuring, shock therapy and structural adjustment. What does globalization imply for the quality of life improvement and achievement of the population from countries which have undergone some globalization inspired policy measure? How does it frame policy approaches or styles towards quality of life gains and more generally social well-being achievement?

Neoliberal globalization has been associated with the retreat of state from economy, the sharp polarization between the winners and losers and the dwindling interest in solidarity, as well as the privatization of the development project in the South itself. There seems to be a yearning for a strong state that admits its involvement in the economy, the return of solidarity to regulate the supposed disparity between the losers and gainers from globalization, and the de-privatization of the development project in the South by a credible return of state partnership with non-state actors and even its steering of the free market. The latter approach may reverse the on-going globalization towards well-being achievement.

Alternatives such as sustainable globalization have been offered to harmonize globalization with social well-being attainment and solidarity (Muchie, 2000).

Measures of well-being attainment

Reviewing existing literatures, an empirical analysis of data since the 1990s from varied sources reflects the interests, desire for influence and aspirations of the various stakeholders by paying due attention to how the data is generated and who generated it and for what specific audience and purposes. Though the "new globalization" began around the early 1980s, the true test of the "liberalization, privatization and stabilization" policies associated with the "new globalization" can best be evaluated a decade after the policies have been put in place.

An alternative approach to well-being attainment, as we suggest, is to introduce a new structural variable related to systemic performance as an independent variable. That variable is what we have proposed *social well-being* indictors. Social well-being, as we have previously explained, covers aspects over time in a broad range of social phenomena and social arrangements relating to individual, family, community and society. Social well-being indicators should include community capacity, self-determination, cultural sustainability, societal and human relations, social mobility, participation and belonging, fair distribution of wealth and resources, crisis-bearing capacity, etc.

This variable will measure the attainment or lack of it related to globalization's impact in undermining or bolstering systemic structures that provide services to alleviate poverty, reduce inequalities and remove the conditions of ill-being production. Social well-being is the base for individual well-being. They are not mutually exclusive. A weak social structure incrementally may show numbers of people whose individual well-being becomes improved, but such improvement is reversible and may not be sustainable. For example, the challenge facing China today is that its integration with global capitalism is simultaneously creating a dual processes: on the one hand, its economic data in the last two decades are impressive regarding market growth, GDP and GNP per capital income, global export share and the rise of import; on the other hand, inequalities and marginalization among the population and between regions are becoming alarming. This will test China's capacity in being able to maintain a certain degree of political coherence, family and social relations as well as basic cultural heritages. This is what we refer to the "capacity" in attaining or sustaining social well-being.

A strong social structure may have a reduced number of people whose individual well-being may not improve, but the overall trend is likely to have an irreversible and sustainable well-being improvement curve. This makes it necessary to formulate: The necessary condition for an irreversible well-being attainment is reached when:

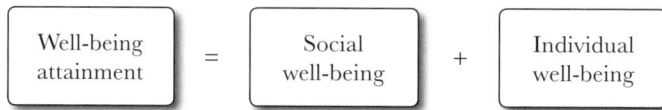

$$
\boxed{\begin{array}{c}\text{Well-being}\\\text{attainment}\end{array}} = \boxed{\begin{array}{c}\text{Social}\\\text{well-being}\end{array}} + \boxed{\begin{array}{c}\text{Individual}\\\text{well-being}\end{array}}
$$

We intend to open the black box of social structure in the evaluation of well-being, inequalities and poverty in relation to globalization. The relocation of the research focus for the individual well-being to social well-being is to open a new perspective to include the amenability of social structure to well-being production and achievements. Furthermore, such research can create knowledge and ideas for changing institutional arrangements and policy directions to assist irreversible and sustainable well-being attainments.

CONCLUSION

The goal of development is to offer people more options and freedoms. One of their options is access to income and wealth – not as an *end* in itself but as a means to acquiring quality of life. But there are other options and freedoms as well, including long life, knowledge, political freedom, social-cultural sustainability, personal security, community participation and guaranteed human rights. People cannot be reduced to a single dimension as economic creatures, they are also social beings. To link Sen's development thinking with our debates and for a better understanding of well-being attainment and measurement, we argue that some developing countries around the world struggling with the process of development have made varying degrees of success while others are much deeper into crises, depending the criteria of indicators. Many measures cannot simply be assessed by professional economic data. Our motivation is to extend the analysis on well-being understanding as well as to challenge the application of economic science to social issues so as to set a link between economic development and an ethically justice society.

Globalization is re-shaping individuals and institutions in most economies of the world. Liberalization, de-regulation, privatization, denationalization and cutback on public spending and services and the roll back of the state in economy are some of the salient policies that have been used by governments. Here we intend to emphasize not so such the economic impact of globalization in terms of observable phenomenon (e.g. poverty and income distribution, economic growth, trade, welfare) but more the destructive impact on human society in terms of invisible social-cultural-psychological holocaust (deep insecurity, marginalization, concentration of power, erosion of social capital and despair). This non-monetary impact has strong implications for the rise of potential contending social forces often in their violent forms and with their diverse names and labels to challenge the dominant ideological, political, economic and social order.

NOTES

1   The US president Truman was among the first who used the word "underdeveloped" in his speech on January 22, 1949 when he took office: "We must embark on a bold new program for making the benefits of our scientific advances and industrial progress available for the improvement and growth of *underdeveloped* area...."(Berthoud, 1992:6, italic added).

2   According to the Food and Agricultural Organization (FAO), the hungry within developing countries outside the Eastern Bloc and China rose by approximately 15 million during the 1970s and by 37 million during the first few years of the 1980s (FAO, 1991:30). In over 70 countries, per capita income is lower today than it was 20 years ago (Ramonet, 1998). However, the only exception is China: by 2004 it has lifted 500 million out of poverty in a generation – one of the greatest achievements in human history.

3   This report, written by leading researchers and activists like Jerry Mander, John Cavanagh, Sarah Anderson, Debi Barker, Maude Barlow, Walden Bello, Robin Broad, Tony Clarke, Teddy Goldsmith, Randy Hayes, Colin Hines, Andy Kimbrell, David Korten, Sarah Larrain, Helena Norberg-Hodge, Simon Retallack, Vandana Shiva, Vicky Tauli-Corpuz and Lori Wallach, examines the impact of globalization on poverty alleviation and other indicators of human well-being. The report refutes repeated claims on the part of the leaders of the Bretton Woods institutions – World Bank, IMF, and the World Trade Organization (WTO), as well as various government officials – that globalization is the best way to help the world's poor (source from www.ifg.org).

4   Subjective well-being (it can also be called emotional well-being) refers to an individual's evaluation of his/her physical and spiritual well-being. Such an evaluation is often expressed in affective terms, such as "being happy", "feeling lost", etc.

5   The three-tiered system refers to a well-organized health care system. In urban areas the tiers consisted of street health stations, community health centers, and district hospitals and in rural areas village stations, township health centers, and county hospitals. This three-tiered system was designed to promote an efficient allocation of health care resources at the grassroots level between primary and tertiary care facilities. It was a very innovative delivery system especially for less developed countries that were lack of medical specialists and could not afford modern equipment.

REFERENCES

Anderson, Sarah and Cavanagh, John (2000) *Top 200: The Rise of Corporate Global Power.* Washington: Institute for Policy Studies.

Amin, Ash, et al (1994) "Editorial." *Review of International Political Economy*, 1(1): 1-12.

Berthoud, Gerald (1992) "Market", in Wolfgang Sachs (ed.) *The Development Dictionary: A Guide to Knowledge As Power.* London: Zed Books Ltd.

Castells, Manuel (1999) *The End of The Millennium.* Oxford: Blackwells.

Cerny, Philip G. (1995) "Globalization and the Changing Logic of Collective Action." *International Organization*, 49(4): 595-625.

Cooper, Richard N. (2000) Review Essay "The Road From Serfdom: Amartya Sen Argues that Growth Is Not Enough." *Foreign Affairs*, 79(1): 163-167.

Dickson, Anna (1997) *Development and International Relations: A Critical Introduction.* Cambridge: Polity Press.

Food and Agriculture Organization (1991) *The State of Food and Agriculture 1990*. Rome: The UN Food and Agricultural Organisation.

Frank, Andre G. (1990) "A theoretical Introduction to 5000 Years of World Systems History." *Review*, 13(2): 155-248.

Ramonet, Ignacio (1998) "The Politics of Hunger." *Le Monde diplomatique*, November.

Keohane, Robert O. and Nye, Joseph S. (1997) *Power and Interdependence: World Politics in Transition*. Boston: Little, Brown.

Li, Xing (1999) "The Transformation of Ideology from Mao to Deng: Impact on China's Social Welfare Outcome." *International Journal of Social Welfare*, 8(2): 86-96.

Li, Xing (2002) "Shifting the 'burden': commodification of China's health care." *Global Social Policy*, 2(3): 248-252.

Muchie, Muchie (2000) "Searching for opportunities for Sub- Saharan Revival under Globalisation." *Futures*, 32(2): 131-147.

Muldoon, Matthew F. et al. (1998) "What are quality of life measurements measuring?" *British Medical Journal*, 316(7130): 542-545.

Nussbaum, Martha and Sen, Amartya (eds.) (1992) *The Quality of Life*. Oxford: Oxford University Press.

Rawls, John (1971) *A Theory of Justice*. Oxford: Oxford University Press.

Ree, William E. (1999) "Achieving sustainability: reform or transformation", in David Satterhwaite (ed.) *The Earthscan Reader in Sustainable Cities*. London: Earthscan.

Rist, Gilbert (1997) *The History of Development: from Western Origins to Global Faith*. London: Zed Books.

Sachs, Wolfgang (ed.) (1992) *The Development Dictionary*. London: Zed Books.

Sen, Amartya (1999a) *Commodities and Capabilities*. Oxford: Oxford University Press.

Sen, Amartya (1999b) *Development as Freedom*. Oxford: Oxford University Press.

Sen, Amartya (1999c) "Democracy as a Universal Value." *Journal of Democracy*, 10(3): 3-17.

Scott, Joanne (1995) *Development Dilemmas in the European Community*. Buckingham: Open University Press.

Stewart-Brown, Sarah (1998) "Emotional wellbeing and its relation to health." *British Medical Journal*, 317(7173): 1608-1609.

UNDP (1990&1991&1998) *Human Development Report*. New York: Oxford University Press.

UNRISD (United Nations Research Institute for Social development) (1995) *Report of the UNRISD/UNDP* International Seminar on Economic restructuring and Social Policy. New York: UNRISD.

Wilkinson, Richard (1996) *Unhealthy societies: the afflictions of inequality*. London: Routledge.

Watkins, Kevin (1995) *The Oxfam Poverty Report*. UK: Oxfam.

World Bank (1981) *World Development Report*. New York: Oxford University Press.

CHAPTER NINE

Towards an Alternative Globalization

Johan Galtung

PART I: GLOBAL STUDIES: WHAT NEEDS TO BE DONE?

Nothing is as global as the globe itself, and the processes to overcome its divisions, including inter-state borders: so-called globalization. However, the discourses usually found in politics, political science and journalism focus on economic globalization only, and under that heading on the spread of US-UK--Reagan-Thatcher style--capitalism into all corners of the world, for a border-free global market economy. And under that heading the initial focus was on the finance economy and access to stock exchanges. This special process was dignified in 1993 with the term "globalization." The term stuck, and one victim of that narrow focus was the anti-globalization movement.

There are very good reasons indeed to be against US-UK style capitalism in general, its financial aspect in particular and hence against its spread to all corners of the world. Capitalism generates growth in cycles, also for the bottom of the economy, and inequality all the time, being a system for the transportation of wealth upwards. With increasing liquidity available at the top the finance economy also grows in cycles, with occasional declines, crises and crashes in the value of financial goods; goods for buying-and-selling, not consumption. If these financial goods also serve basic needs, like houses (as opposed to, for instance, gold), the result can be catastrophic, like the foreclosures for millions of US families at present.

However, as will be argued, the issue is complex. There are bad and good globalizations. Better be against the bad, like world epidemics and tsunamis, but also better be in favor of the good, like inoculation and global warning. Judgment is needed. Forty years ago[1] (Galtung, 1980 (1967) 617-644) I gave a public lecture, "On the Future of the International System", based on stages of socio-economic development. I used four stages, primitive P, traditional T, modern M, and neo-modern, but switched to the more common post-modern PM. Thus, P-T-M-PM was the dependent variable. It was an ordinal scale in time, obviously discontinuous, separated by (quantum) jumps often called revolutions, like the "Neolithic revolution" from P to T, the "industrial revolution" from T to M and the "automation/information revolution" from M to PM.

What were the independent variables? The focus being socio-economic I used *agricultural productivity*--how many people can be fed by one person extracting food from nature--and *speed of transportation (of goods and persons) and communication (of information)*. Both of them are continuous, linear, and generally seen as parts of progress. Difficult to argue against.

With this discourse, history becomes a dialectic between productivity and speed as the *forces motrices* of history on the one hand, and social formation on the other. The dialectical principle used by Marx for means and modes of production, transition from quantitative changes to a qualitative jump, holds. Social formations being holistic, maintained by deep structural and cultural forces, they will resist change. But in the end the change will also be precisely that, holistic.

To the primary extraction sector comes tertiary services, a secondary sector processing and a quaternary information sector. Groups-clans-tribes engaged in subsistence turn into villages-city-states engaged in barter turn into states engaged in money turn into regions and world-states engaged in credit economies.

That last step is today called "globalization."

A humanity engaged in hunting-gathering would use walking-swimming-rowing for transportation and eye-ear-mouth for communication; a humanity living on the land would use animals- wheels-wind for transportation and dispatches for communication; an industrializing humanity would use steam-combustion engines for transportation and PTT for communication; and a humanity in the information age would use jet-engines for transportation and satellites for communication. And the magnitude of humans covered by transportation-communication would grow from 10^{0-2} via 10^{2-5} and 10^{5-8} to 10^{8-10} [2]. All according to that paper.

Roughly speaking this is human macro-history. Obviously, the stages can co-exist side by side in space--like the present author living in villages in France and Spain with traditional characteristics yet parts of modern and post-modern formations.

In short, all of this was highly foreseeable. So why all the hue and cry? I would argue basically because of inadequate analysis, including the one presented. The two <u>forces motrices</u> are real enough and will survive most attacks even when other factors are added. They seem unstoppable, are technical and in that sense "material", like the Marxist means of production.

But before an innovation a spirit senses a potential and tries to make it an empirical part of the world of facts. That spirit of a changeable world is partly collective and partly individual on top of that. Daniel Lerner, in his important *The Passing of Traditional Society* (Lerner, 1958), used "psychic mobility", the capacity to image oneself elsewhere, like in a city while the body is languishing on the land. Or in another social stage where the potential is empirical. There is Aristotelian causa finalis and formalis, not only causa materialis and efficiens.

There are cultural factors at work underlying the techno-socio-economic, and under "socio" there are of course political and military factors. Higher agricultural productivity liberates some for symbols, decisions and force, services: in short *power*. Brahmins, kshatriyahs and vaisyas on top of sudras and parias. As transportation-communication improves their effective control covers ever longer distances for idiom-meaning, decision-making and invasion-occupation and exchange-trade. Did they globalize?

Of course they did. Like nature always did. The cosmosphere embraces the globe and more, and both atmo- and hydro-sphere globalize by winds and currents. The lithosphere is more static with sometimes highly global seismic and volcanic articulations. Biosphere birds and fishes in atmo- and hydrosphere globalize all the time. So do animals, down to micro-organisms--maybe riding as parasites on others and they globalize in epidemics, whether bacteria or virus-based. Plants/trees are rooted but their seeds are blowing in the wind and carried by the waters.

How about humans? Strange animals. They were actually globalizing all the time. *Völkerwanderungen* - giant, global nomadism - started long before the neolithic revolution. They are usually seen in terms of pushes away from where they were, the Resources/Population ratio being too low and unable to multiply Resources by Technology to increase agricultural productivity from 1:<1 to 1:1.1 to 1.25 to 1.33 and so on.

But maybe there was also a pull, maybe they wandered because they wondered what was on that other side? From a point of origin in East Africa they covered the world. DNA analysis seems to indicate that the Thor Heyerdahl rafting approach rather than wandering must have played a rather minor role.

So, if almost everything, except maybe mountains, trees and flowers, are moving all over, where is the problem? In a human work accident called *the state system*, with territorial borders. Humanity was always divided by fault-lines--gender, generation, race, class, included/excluded, nation and territorial borders. But the state system was driven by a maniac desire to draw jealously guarded borders between ours and yours, informed by the Roman Law *dominion* principle: what can be owned should be owned, by one and only one owner. The outcome is the world multi-colored modernity map challenged by *forces motrices*.

The four dimensions open for more holistic global studies:

Globalization as development along four power dimensions

	Economic	Cultural	Political	Military
Primitive	Hunter-gatherer	Countless	Countless	Ritual
Traditional	Villages Towns Cities	(Christianity in Europe)	(500 polities in Europe)	Caste Duel Battles
Modern	Towns Cities States	*2000 nations* defines by TIME idiom SPACE	(50 polities in Europe) *200 states* defined by borders	Wars between states, justified by nation ideology
Post-modern	States Regions World	Civilizations Humanity	(European Union) Regions World State	State-terrorism Terrorism ?

Clearly, any analysis of globalization in terms of "economic- postmodern" only is intellectually deficient, and not only because the Silk Road connected traditional and primitive formations millennia ago, as argued forcefully by Andre Gunder Frank. There are also the other three columns in the Table. And there are leads and lags, (a) synchronies and (dis)equilibria, within and among the social units. History and development cover not only traditional to modern economically but all stages along at least four columns.

Thus, the two world religions, Christianity and Islam, were giant early efforts at globalization, spreading their singularist- universalist messages about the only valid truth for everybody. The military/economic/political follow-up was invasion-conquest, colonialism and imperialism, the difference being whether it was seen as an extension of the mother country with flag, idiom etc, or as a power structure. But globalizing it was, particularly in the modern form of UK colonialism and post-modern US imperialism.

In the logic of this Table the bottom line is exactly that, the End of History, with *one world economy-market, one world nation-humanity, and one world polity-the world state*. And then what? In a giant world formation with giant unsolved structural and actor conflicts: increasingly giant violence. So, what do globalized transformation and violence prevention look like?

No answer is heard, and that prompts an obvious question. Those who talk most loudly about globalization and its benefits recently lost their colonies covering 25% of the world and are now parts of the decline of an empire with 700 bases in 135 countries. Is globalization with USA/UK on top their substitute? The anti-globalization movement sees this very clearly (Seattle, Genova, Gothenburg, Berlin, Heiligendam etc.), but have not come up with a counter-image of a good globalization. Like for the peace movement in general the reasoning is, we agree on what we are against, we are divided in what we would favor, united we stand but divided we fall, politics is about numbers.

That, of course, is not necessarily so. New ideas that even quickly became dominant often came out of small minorities, even a minority of one. Quality may easily overrule quantity when the going is rough; democracy/consensus is more for smooth sailing.

Flying at high altitudes over the intellectual landscape provided by the Table sensitizes us beyond holism to a dialectic that never ends. Contradictions come and go, new contradictions come and go, and endlessly so. There is no end of history, except in some self-limiting Western minds, including Hegel and Marx. To see that take a look at the Table's non-economic columns.

USA-UK seems to entertain the illusion of a self-regulating world market. But the contradiction between rich and poor, with growing gaps among and within states, makes a mockery of that illusion. The poor will not resign to their plight forever. And neither the Ten Commandments nor the Sermon on the Mount mention distribution, only the evil of envy, and that the poor in spirit (meaning who?) are blessed for theirs is the kingdom of heaven. Christianity is the religion UK tried and USA tries to globalize, with some Good Samaritans striving to alleviate the pain. Not strange it comes up against Islam with its strong emphasis on *zakat*, sharing, and caring. Neither religion runs the ground alone. Nor does Hinduism, still with its caste fatalism, up against Buddhism with its neither too little, nor too much. In short, there is no one humanity on this rather crucial issue.

Nor any one polity that might mitigate giant contradictions, however imperfectly, like a world democracy in the shape of a United Nations Second, Peoples', Assembly. First in line opposing any such attempt are precisely the USA with 5% of humanity and the UK with 1%. They use their Security Council, and if that does not work to their liking, they use NATO also for economic penetration against Serbia and in Afghanistan, or the EU for the "recognition" of Kosova, and the non-recognition of Palestine. Do they really believe they can prevent democracy from entering globalization?

A market--village, state, and region-world--is participatory even when manipulated. The World Bank, the International Monetary Fund and the World Trade Organization are not and consequently attract the major demonstrations. And the "strongest military power ever" is beaten by the dialectic of countervailing power, the peoples' wars against the state's wars. The more ingenuity in one, the more ingenuity in the other, in an endless dialectic.

Unless, that is, the contradictions are solved, or at least blunted by being transformed. The question mark at the bottom right may have conflict transformation, *conflict hygiene like hygiene for health*, as a possible answer; too important to be left to states and diplomats-generals-politicians alone. People of all kinds would have their say. Neither primitive, nor traditional, nor modern formations were adequate at transforming contradictions and became victims of their inadequacy. Of course, the strong in what once was may have sensed the writing on the wall and entered the new formation at some adequate point, like those who were lords over villages and city-states left the sinking traditional ship to enter vigorous modernity as marshals and foreign secretaries. Like some might board a space ship for Moon, Mars, Venus etc.

Good globalization, not the US-UK visions, includes a world culture of sharing and caring, a world polity with no veto power and genuine democratic participation, and provision for empathic, nonviolent and creative conflict transformation. The alternative is endless postmodern warfare and suffering like today.

Would that be the End of History? No. New contradictions enter, like between material and spiritual growth, or in universes beyond Terra. Some can be sensed today; others not. History never ends, only tables. As long as there is Humanity there is History.

PART II: THE INSTITUTIONALIZATION OF GLOBAL DEMOCRACY

What does it take to democratize this historical process?

[1] *Abolition of permanent Security Council members' veto*
Highly recommended here is reading about how that veto power was used: to postpone, some years, the inevitable (decolonization, China's entry into the UN, etc.). There are exceptions, but by and large the veto has only served as a brake on history. The argument heard is that this is the condition for Big Powers to be in the UN. However, if special privileges are the condition then they do not belong in the key organization of a world heading for global democracy.[3] They would of course be most welcome back when they are ready to accept democracy. And the Security Council, like the ECOSOC, should be made more representatives of all states. In addition to the incompatibility with democracy, "one state one vote", their track record does not justify any privilege. An expanded Security Council to 54 members like the ECOSOC (Economic and Social Council), reporting to the UNGA (General Assembly) which itself would be in a position to pass resolutions in security matters, have special sessions, would be a great step forward.[4]

[2] *Abolition of rich member states' implicit economic veto*
The membership fees cannot be equal in a very unequal world, but they should not be so unequal that some countries can exercise power by threat-

ening to cripple the institution economically if they withdraw. The right to withdraw belongs to any democratic order,[5] as does the right to join when conditions are fulfilled. But withdrawal of one or a few members should be decoupled from crippling the organization. An upper limit of 10% of the budget might be reasonable. And a member not paying dues for X years will of course have its membership suspended.[6]

[3] *The UN has to balance efficiency with general participation*
In a democratic organization not only decisions but also tasks are shared so as to ensure the participation of all - in the case of the UN the participation of governments, delegates and experts from all countries. No doubt technically more competent experts can often be found in some countries more than others. But this misses the point: the outcome should be owned by as many member states as possible to ensure their participation in *all* stages of the process. But efficiency and adequacy should also be safeguarded. Not all members have to participate at all levels; but across issues and over time they should all be given a chance.

[4] *The regional state organizations: "one voice", one vote.*
It is not unreasonable to give them only one membership if they have as a rule to "talk with one voice" (the Soviet Union, the European Union). But some flexibility can be exercised.

[5] *The world state organizations: A need for consultation and coordination.*
One important coordinating organ, ACC,[7] fulfills some of this function for the UN family of organizations. It is a good idea to have a forum for all IGOs to bear on UN decisions. But this is not what democracy is about. Democracy is not about IGOs influencing IGOs; at that level consultation and coordination are called for. Democracy is about "lower level" actors, less powerful in terms of coercive and remunerative power - sticks and carrots, military and economic power - but high on moral power. The ultimate "lower level" actor is the individual, all over the world, however humble - however *shudra*, perhaps even a *pariah*, equipped with "one per-

son, one vote", not equipped with the additional power for the *brahmin* (academics), *kshatriyah* (statesmen) or *vaishyah* (merchants).

[6] *The transnational corporations: A need for consultation.*

Given the high correlation in the world between military and economic power decision-making power within the UN for a body of transnational corporations means additional power to those with "big bangs and big bucks." On the other hand it is desirable to give the TNCs the opportunity to articulate their concerns, and to enter into a permanent dialogue about how to work for the major UN goals of peace, development, a clean environment and human rights. This consultative role can be implemented under the provision given by the UN Charter, Art. 22,[8] as a United Nations Corporate Assembly, UNCA, a permanent consultative body.[9] In that dialogue the fine balance between receiving and giving advice, and mutual accountability, can be drawn. The UN has a right to demand of TNCs a plan for basic needs satisfaction, high employment and a clean environment; misery, unemployment and pollution being major "side-effects" along the TNC economic cycles. And the TNCs on their side have the right to demand compensation for losses incurred by economic sanctions for political reasons.

[7] *International People's Organizations: A need for consultation*

The UN has achieved one of the most brilliant strikes for democracy by giving NGOs not only consultative status, but a major role to play in the NGO for a parallel to UN conferences. This is democracy by articulation, not by representation, and could well be imitated by the UN General Assembly, and by many national parliaments around the world when in session. But there are also NGOs that are more powerful than any state, and in the total NGO system the West is over-represented. To give them decision-making power is to double the power of the already powerful. Better build on the CONGO[10] system that already exists, given a higher profile.

[8] *Local Authorities: A need for consultation*

Practicing the principle of subsidiarity, giving the actor at the "lower level" more weight to compensate for top-down decision-making, should open the doors for local authorities. They are below state governments even if the megalopolis and metropolis of the world rank far above many states in significance. As mentioned earlier, they have great potentials as peace actors. The Council of Europe has been a pioneer in the field of state-local governments' cooperation. There is much for the UN to learn. A *United Nations Local Authorities Assembly*, UNLAA, could relate to the UN the same way as a UN Corporations Assembly.

[9] *People: A need for direct decision-making in the world as in the states.*

Being the ultimate sovereign, there is no substitute for fair and free direct elections to a *United Nations People's Assembly*, UNPA, and not only in a consultative capacity. In the longer run world referenda and initiatives will emerge. The UNPA would function like any other parliament, making laws, budgets and appointments. The UNGA would head the executive organ. A parliament should be grafted onto the infant global governance that has accumulated experience in two incarnations in this century, the United Nations building on the League of Nations.

This means adding to the UNGA for governments a *Second Assembly*, an UNPA, for People; a *Third Assembly*, an UNCA, for corporations; and a *Fourth Assembly*, an UNLAA for local authorities. *But only the Second Assembly would have ultimate decision-making power.* The Third and the Fourth Assemblies would be there in consultative capacity, like the *Fifth Assembly*, CONGO, of NGOs with consultative status. The *First Assembly*, UNGA would only be first in a chronological sense.

This raises questions of conditions for membership in these assemblies, and of the interrelationship in decision-making. Applicant states have to be recognized by the current Member States to become members of the UN. It is the government of a state that applies, not the people, since governments generally do not ask their people whether they want to join[11]. The applicant government is then assessed by other governments.

A list of possible criteria for a non-territorial world citizen wanting to be admitted to a UN Assembly might include[12]:

> [1] *Is the organization internationally representative?* Does it have members in sufficiently many countries distributed over a sufficient number of continents, preferably also across cultural and political, not only geographical divides?

> [2] *Is the organization sufficiently democratic?* Is the leadership of the organization accountable to the members, can it be changed through a process of election?

> [3] *Is the organization concerned with basic human needs and rights?*[13] Or, is the focus on rather narrow interests of rather special groups?

> [4] *Is the organization capable of reflecting world perspectives?* Or, is the perspective only regional, even national? And if so, is this reflected in the power distribution inside the organization (presidents, executive committees, councils, locations of headquarters, funding)?

> [5] *Does the organization have certain permanence?* Or, is it rather ephemeral, something that easily withers away?

Imagine we apply such reasonable criteria to states. Point [1] would favor multi-national states provided the rulers are capable of reflecting that kind of diversity. Point [2] would favor democracies. Point [3] implies general human solidarity, as opposed to solidarity with own gender, generation, race, class and nation only. Point [4] focuses on world interests, not only on promoting limited state (national) interests. And point [5] favors states with proven permanence, which unfortunately may also mean proven repression of people and peoples.

Of these five tests many states would pass only the last, "permanence" being interpreted as territorial control. Neither secession, nor revolution, is around the corner - and if they are, recognition might be withheld. But that criterion is possibly the least meaningful for non-territorial actors, so easily undergoing fission and fusion, coming in and out of existence all the time, operating as they are in an unlimited functional and value space, not constrained by the finiteness of the world territorial.

In choosing criteria such as the five mentioned, we would in fact be judging non-territorial actors more severely than we judge states. But then, why not? Why should the criteria remain constant? To demand of an NGO president or secretary general that he has the members fully "under control", with no minorities seceding or revolting, would certainly undermine the marvelous flexibility of non-territorial actors.

Would these criteria also apply to the transnational corporations? A TNC is often internationally representative and relatively permanent, but far from democratic. Maybe it should become democratic? And maybe production for basic human needs, and for world perspectives beyond size of assets and turnover, should be given priority? Including employing as many people, not as few people, as possible?

Delegates to the UNGA will continue to be selected by the governments, but to the UNPA, the UNCA, the UNLAA and CONGO should, ideally, be democratically elected[14]. Imagine, then, that we have all assemblies well constituted, how would they relate to each other? To answer that, a comparison with another inter-state organization at a higher level of integration, the European Union, may be appropriate.

Using the modern society as a model, with the usual division of state power into executive, legislature and judiciary, then the UNGA (corresponding to the European Union Council of Ministers) is one executive, exercising (soft) governance, and the ACC of Specialized Agencies (corresponding to the European Commission) another, albeit in very embryonic form. The legislature, in even less than embryonic form, would be the UNPA; with both the UNGA and the Specialized Agencies being accountable to the United Nations Peoples Assembly. The International Court of Justice would play the role of the judiciary. This is what parliamentary democracy as we know it is about, and something like that is bound to come about, sooner or later. We had better start preparing.

The European Union has two executive heads: the rotating presidency of the Council of Ministers, and the Chairperson of the European Commission, corresponding to the territorial and functional tracks, of the EU. Should this inspire a similar construction at the world level, with one Secretary General for the Member States and one (Deputy) Secretary General for the Specialized Agencies? Or would it be better to continue as today, with one executive head for both, even if the task is superhuman?

The totality would not be that complicated. There would be the UNPA gradually rising in power relative to the UNGA, taking on more and more functions and decisions; and in addition there would be the three consultative organs, for the corporations, the local authorities and the nongovernmental organizations (UNCA, UNLAA and CONGO). In return for consultative status they offer accountability: if you are given tasks under a contract, then you also have to make yourself accountable and transparent.

More problematic is how the People's Assembly should be constituted. As mentioned before, some people are more territorially rooted than others, but it seems fair to have the same kind of constituencies, vote catchment areas, for all. Practically speaking everybody is a citizen somewhere, and very many people are even registered somewhere as voters. Voting for a UN representative could be as easily attached to a state-wide vote as could a local vote. The general formula might be that each state should have the right to one representative per million inhabitants, the minimum number of representatives being one. An interesting problem would be whether states that are not members should nevertheless have a right to send representatives to the UNPA, making it a true World Assembly.

At present this would give us about 6,000 representatives; somewhat unwieldy, but not impossible. The condition for sending an elected delegation would be that the delegation had been truly elected, not selected, by free, fair and secret ballot. Ideally any election should be preceded by a debate on key global issues, and the choice would be between candidates, or between global parties as they emerge. They will.

The representatives will also be put to work in committees working between the sessions, which might be at summer time before the UNGA is convened (the third Tuesday in September); following the UNGA agenda and any item they might like to add.[15]

It stands to reason that there will be a limit to what a majority can decide, just as for domestic democracy. Sovereignty shields will blunt the impact of majority decision-making; no doubt shields that will gradually be pierced, but never break down completely. Like human rights protecting individuals. A process.

In conclusion only some words about the obvious: the UN will not be the only organization to carry the burden of global democratization, but today by far the most important one. The project known as state democratization has been going on for some centuries now. Many states have probably been overtaken by such non-states as international people's organizations in level of democratization. Some NGOs have, like some states, been the products of innovative risk-taking by strong personalities; but even if their role should be recognized their hold on an organization must be time-limited. Local government is probably neither more, nor less, democratic than state government.

Lagging behind are the corporations, organized as private fiefs of strong CEOs hiring and firing, accountable only to the bottom line of money, not the bottom level of people. Corporate democracy, and consultative dialogues with consumer organizations might, at first look like tying the hands of the CEO; but a second glance may reveal new business opportunities. People might simply have good ideas. The world cannot in the longer run tolerate major pockets of authoritarian rule in its midst. Where people are affected by decisions they have a right to co-decide.

States beware: as other key actors (NGOs, TNCs, LAs) see the linkage between globalization and democracy, states fail to do so and state-systems overdo Westphalia sovereignty (350 years are enough!), these other systems may overtake and pass the state-system as carriers of the popular will. Being expressions of an ethos of non-territoriality and fluidity one of them may one day even overtake and pass the UNGA and relate better to the UNPA than the old state-system articulated in the UNGA. If so, then early UN democratization becomes even more significant.

NOTES

1   16 August 1967, at the Makerere University College. Kampala, Uganda, to be precise.

2   Obviously, I did not predict that China and India would pass the 1 billion, 1 000 000 000, mark.

3   They may then start their own organization and veto each other as much as they want.

4   Concretely this means that Article 12 of the UN Charter will have to be changed since it is designed to protect the big powers by making it impossible for the UNGA to pass resolutions on matters considered by the UNSC.

5   Like the right not to vote. When that right is used by a sufficient number it constitutes an important, nonviolent protest, and becomes an important part of the democratic repertory. The same applies to any organization, including of states. The USA, the UK and Singapore probably hoped to have that effect when they withdrew from the UNESCO, but they were too few and their arguments too obviously self-centered.

6   Obviously, the United States cannot both struggle to reduce the UN budget, keep the high assessment of 25% and on top of that not even pay. To be able to survive as a member with that record much informal power is needed, and much submission to that power.

7   Administrative Committee on Coordination.

8   Art. 22: "The General Assembly may establish such subsidiary organs as it deems necessary for the performance of its functions."

9   Another possibility, hinted at by Boutros-Ghali above, is to build on the tripartite structure of ILO, the International Labor Organization built on governments, employers' organizations and employees' organizations. At any rate, the ways and means must be found whereby the most dynamic sector of our global reality is brought into the most representative decision-making organization.

10 Conference of Non-Governmental Organizations in Consultative Status with the Economic and Social Council, under Article 71 (Chapter VIII) of the UN Charter, covering some 1,600 NGOs in addition to the many affiliated with other organs of the UN, including the specialized agencies.

11 Switzerland did so for UN membership in March 1986, and the answer at that time was no. And so far (fall 1994) only three governments of the 12 presumably democratic Member States of the European Union have had a referendum over something as fundamental as the

Maastricht Treaty (Denmark, France and Ireland). See also the story of putting the EU Draft Constitution to the democratic test.

12 From the author's *United Nations, United Peoples*, forthcoming.

13 This would certainly include the third generation of human rights, adding the collective rights to peace, development and a clean environment to the right to self-determination. See the last chapter of Johan Galtung, *Human Rights in Another Key*, Cambridge: Polity Press, 1994.

14 In practice a transition period of 10 or even 20 years may be in order, with a governmental pledge to work on a system of election rather than selection, appointment, of delegates.

15 The proposal by Boutros-Ghali, "urging the Inter-Parliamentary Union to convene every three years at a United Nations location in order to foster international dialogue and debate on the United Nations and issues before the United Nations and its Member states" would be an excellent beginning. It is worth remembering that the European Parliament had an initial stage based on state parliamentarians before direct elections were introduced.

REFERENCES

Galtung, Johan (1980) *Peace and World Structure -Essays in Peace Research, Vol. IV*. Copenhagen: Christian Ejlers Forlag,

Lerner, Daniel (1958) *The Passing of Traditional Society*. New York: The Free Press.

NOTES ON CONTRIBUTORS

Christian Ydesen is Doctoral student, The Danish school of Education, University of Aarhus, Denmark.

David P. Ellerman is currently a visiting scholar at University of California/Riverside having retired from 10 years at the World Bank where he was Economic Advisor to the Chief Economist, Joseph Stiglitz, the United States.

Gorm Winther is Professor, Department of Development and Planning, The Faculty of Engineering Science and Medicine, Aalborg University, Denmark.

Johan Galtung is Dr. Hc Mult, currently co-director of "Transcend a Peace and Development Network", and a former Professor of Peace Studies at the University of Hawaii and Oslo. He has been visiting professor at Princeton University and has been an advisor to several UN institutions.

Li Jizhen is Associate Professor, Department of Innovation and Entrepreneurship, School of Economics & Management, Tsinghua University, China. He is visiting associate professor affiliated with the Department of Business Studies, Aalborg University, Denmark.

Li Xing is Associate Professor, Department of History, International and Social Studies, The Faculty of Social Sciences, Aalborg University, Denmark.

Mammo Muchie is Professor, Department of History, International and Social Studies, The Faculty of Social Sciences, Aalborg University, Denmark.

Michael K. Sørensen is Doctoral student, Department of History and Civilization, European University Institute, Florence, Italy.

Steen F. Christensen is Associate Professor, Department of Language and Culture, The Faculty of Humanities, Aalborg University, Denmark

Woodrow W. Clark is currently a Lecturer at University of California (UCR) Riverside and Los Angeles in Sustainable Development, the United States.